S0-BSR-648

Turns of Event

Turns of Event

Nineteenth-Century American Literary Studies in Motion

EDITED BY

Hester Blum

PENN

UNIVERSITY OF PENNSYLVANIA PRESS

PHILADELPHIA

Copyright © 2016 University of Pennsylvania Press

All rights reserved. Except for brief quotations used for
purposes of review or scholarly citation, none of this book may
be reproduced in any form by any means without written
permission from the publisher.

Published by
University of Pennsylvania Press
Philadelphia, Pennsylvania 19104–4112

www.upenn.edu/pennpress

Printed in the United States of America on acid-free paper
1 3 5 7 9 10 8 6 4 2

Library of Congress Cataloging-in-Publication Data
ISBN 978-0-8122-4798-5

Publication of this book has been aided by a grant from the
Center for American Literary Studies at the Pennsylvania State
University.

Contents

᮫

Introduction

⌐⌐

Academic Positioning Systems

HESTER BLUM

The history of the Americas in relation to the West begins with a turn: a wrong turn, as the story is commonly told. Christopher Columbus, the Genoan sailing in search of Cathay on behalf of Spain, encountered unexpected islands that he mistook for the Indies. This landfall came after he decided against returning to Europe when the voyage had proceeded farther than his frightened sailors had thought navigationally possible. In the parlance of quips about his "failure to ask for directions" (as Michelle Burnham glosses it in her contribution to this volume), Columbus took an errant turn, mistaking the Americas for Asia. This is a witticism that can serve as a distraction from the scale of his conceptual and ideological errors—the effects, that is, of half a millennium of the subsequent histories of settler colonialism, slavery, displacement, land seizure, and resource depletion attendant on Columbus's (and Europe's) turn to the Americas. The monumental consequences of the Columbian encounter and its aftermath have been extensively covered in Americanist scholarship; still, I invoke the navigator's deviation briefly here, in launching this volume on the critical "turns" made in recent years in pre-1900 American literary studies, in order to underscore that *turns* in literary history have been at once ideological, conceptual, and material. Columbus's "wrong" turn becomes shorthand, in this respect, for the far more consequential actions that were in turn inaugurated by the maneuver.

Making light of his misapprehension does not erase the route by which we came to an excess of 500 years of New World colonialism, but it diverts attention, perhaps, from the contours and transit of that voyage itself.

Whereas Columbus's error proceeded from misdirection, the intellectual and historical resonance of critical turns emerges instead from corrective or constitutive mobilizations of resources. In recent years literary studies has undergone a series of field redefinitions that have been characterized as "turns," including (but far from limited to) the linguistic, transnational, hemispheric, postnational, spatial, temporal, religious or postsecular, aesthetic, and affective turns. The critic and student alike can find propulsive momentum in such movement—or else might be rendered dizzy. These shifts in the field, at once ideological, methodological, and dedicated to canon reformation, are in part invested in recognizing the artificiality and intellectual limitations of certain kinds of boundaries (whether national, political, linguistic, physiological, or temporal) in studying forms of literary and cultural influence and circulation. Geopolitically oriented turns have gained particular visibility in pre-1900 American literary studies, as Monique Allewaert discusses, and have produced at once new critical methodologies and expanded literary possibilities for classroom instruction.[1] The essays collected here seek both to understand the reasons for the critical mobility within the field of Americanist scholarship, and to argue for its propensity to turn as its constitutive strength. *Turns of Event* meditates on the stakes and motivations of those moments when American literary studies of the long nineteenth century—an exceptionally kinetic scholarly field—self-consciously claims to gather up its constituents and venture in new directions.

Turns of Event considers what is at stake in the category of the turn itself as a meta-disciplinary reflection. Its chapters seek to understand the conditions that produce shifts in momentum, when an approach practiced by a few becomes a movement, when change becomes collective. Rehearsing the specific contours and trajectories of the various turns the field has made in recent years is not our primary aim, however. This volume offers a view of the state of the field of pre-1900 American literary studies that locates the field's strength in its constant, mobile re-invention, its drive to regenerate and extend without fracture or dissolution. These turns are not fads or fashions or weather vanes. Nor are they negations, nor revolutions, nor wheels on fire. The turns that continue to sustain Americanist scholarship reflect instead the field's flexible qualities of reinvention, its comfort with critique and discovery and hope. It is this aspect of the critical turn that signals the *event* of this volume's title: the formative interventions that recur throughout the field's history and its critical self-consciousness. Like Columbus's errant voyage, such events are manifold, and bear high stakes, in their own way. The consequences and opportunities range from citational and evidentiary practices to canon expansion, resource allocation, and institutional futurity.

The notion of a turn marks a differentiation between what came before and what is to come, indicating routes plotted if not yet explored, imagined if not yet surveyed. The fact that intellectual reorientations have been predicated on the use of this particular term suggests an orienteering impulse, one that presumes transits that have continuity, linearity, and cartography. To turn is to have followed a path, a line of demarcation that has subsequently been altered; while the terminus of that turn might be unknown or imagined, it bears an established trajectory, a traceable origin. Turns are observable when there has been a change. Although the early definitions of turn, according to the *OED*, presumed a revolving motion, a coming round full circle, this is not the present academic sense of the word, which instead stipulates that a turn in the nominal form is "an act (or, rarely, the action) of turning aside from one's course; deflection, deviation…a detour…change, alteration, modification." As Judith Surkis reminds us in her contribution to a recent *American Historical Review* forum on "Historiographic 'Turns' in Critical Perspective," even as turns have "directional movement," they are also "formative: they shape and reshape by cutting away."[2] Turns change, transform, convert. Scholarly turns are extrapolations or deviations, not revolutions; they use the language of revolution (as the founding of the United States itself did) without the event's permanent state of crisis, and without its dangers of reactionary return.

We speak of critical "movements," "fields" of study, "areas" of interest or expertise, "shifts" in approaches. Scholars write of "circulation," of "exchange," of "mobility" and "fluidity." These figures of motion and tropes of space require navigational language. While there are many such terms at play in academic discourse, arguably none is presently more pervasive in its attempts to capture broad intellectual momentum than the turn. The chapters that follow are less interested in the particularity of turns themselves than they are in the propensity of C19 literary studies to desire revolutionary movement, to join broader critical interests in turning as a way to reject stasis, to signal newness. It is not clear, however, how long critical turns can sustain themselves. If a scholar takes the directional figure too far, does she end up back at the start, or in vertiginous disorientation? At what point is a turn understood to have straightened out, as it were, and assumed the primacy of the main route? *Turns of Event* aims to provide a conceptual and methodological frame for thinking about how literary critical studies conceives of its own movements. It presents, at the same time, provocative new work by leading scholars in pre-1900 American literary studies. The contributors offer both critical reflections on why—and to what effects—*turning* has become characteristic of the self-characterization of intellectual and literary critical movements, as well as focused investigations of the geopolitical turns that have arguably had the most visibility in Americanist study in recent years. The first half of the volume, "Provocations," contains a series of conceptual essays that engage with specific turns in order to reflect on the theoretical underpinnings, effects, and potentialities of the new directions at stake in their critical trajectories. The second half of the volume, "Turn-by-Turn Directions: Transnational, Hemispheric, Oceanic," features four scholarly essays that model the related geopolitical turns that have been so prominent in American literary studies in recent years.

The contributors to this volume are mindful of the broader range of scholarly turns unfolding throughout critical studies, particularly those that have had an effect within C19 literary scholarship. Let me here provide a quick breakdown of some of the leading turns, at the risk of leading the reader through excessive switchbacks (or subjecting her to too many figures for turning). Perhaps the first recognizable use of the word "turn" to describe a critical movement reconfiguring humanistic studies in recent years was the *linguistic turn* of the early twentieth century, which Richard Rorty identified in the 1960s; this came when philosophy turned from a focus on historical objectivity to an interest in the use and structure of language.[3] In Americanist scholarship of the long nineteenth century, the most prominent turns of the past decade or so have been the *transnational* and *hemispheric turns*.[4] These are turns away from the nation-state as a unit of analysis by scholars who find it neither historically accurate nor intellectually and ideologically productive to think of literary creations as strictly state-bound. U.S. cultural and political exchanges and formulations have ever had transnational and hemispheric dimensions, participants in this influential turn argue; its significance has been such that *Turns of Event* devotes its second half to a series of case histories on the transnational, hemispheric, and oceanic turns (see the chapters in this volume by Ralph Baucr, Monique Allewaert, Sean X. Goudie, and Michelle Burnham). Bearing some conceptual affinities with transnationalism, the *spatial turn* in social and cultural theory in the late 1970s and early 1980s gave rise in literary studies more recently to the *cartographic turn* Martin Brückner discusses in his contribution, in which metaphors of "mapping"—a common modifier in academic titles—evoke a geographical imagination.[5] Resisting a sense of magisterial command, the *temporal turn* has found ways to envision time that are nonlinear and nonhegemonic; whether deep time or queer time, transhistorical time or transnational time, the new temporality resists unified notions of time, as recent work by Wai Chee Dimock, Dana Luciano, and Lloyd Pratt has been demonstrating.[6] The *religious* and *postsecular turns* have some temporal dimensions in their intellectual investigations of the place of and methodologies for the study of religion in American culture.[7] In some ways aesthetics has been seen as its own practice of the divine, but it had receded with the rise of ideological criticism and historicist work. The *aesthetic turn* (or return) in literary studies in the past

few years seeks to bring such analysis back into conversation with political and historicist criticism.[8] On the other hand, calling into question
the automatic presumption of political readings (or paranoid readings,
or other symptomatic reading practices) has been the impetus for the
reparative turn emerging from Eve Kosovsky Sedgwick's work, as well as
for the related turn to *surface* rather than symptomatic reading (issues
Christopher Castiglia alludes to in his discussion of recent calls to move
"post-critique").[9] Reading practices are the subject of much discussion
lately, in fact, as digital media has amplified the possibilities for (and
cautions about) the transmission, digestion, and analysis of textual
media, such as in the *descriptive turn* to distant reading practices in big
data analysis.[10] Meredith McGill's contribution describes the institutional history of these textual studies. And while there are other turns I
could invoke here, I will rest on the *affective turn*, which explores those
structures of feeling that allow individuals to experience social processes
as if emanating from inside (see Geoffrey Sanborn's chapter, which opens
this volume in the spirit of both aesthetic and affective turns).[11]

   Turns of Event provides what we might call academic positioning systems—or, variously, signposts, or checkered flags, or explanatory keys,
or eject buttons—for these proliferating turns. The suggestive chapters in
our volume's first half, "Provocations," trace the theoretical and methodological development and institutional emergence of certain turns, as
well as issuing calls to arms. As the geopolitically oriented turns known
as transnational and hemispheric studies (and associated oceanic forms,
Atlantic, Caribbean, Pacific, archipelagic, and so forth) have held a certain prevalence in American studies in recent years, the second half of
this volume, "Turn-by-Turn Directions," proceeds to a series of scholarly
essays that exemplify these subfields.

   Geoffrey Sanborn opens the collection with a proposal that the
molecular-level jostlings we might imagine variously as dancing or cellular formation or classroom teaching produce an "affective amplification" (in Silvan Tomkins's term) that becomes increasingly vital to the
defense of post-secondary face-to-face education in an age of MOOCs

and other forms of online, faceless learning. But this is not a dirge or a reactionary move; in "Turn It Up: Affects, Structures of Feeling, and Face-to-Face Education," Sanborn argues instead, movingly, that "academics who are capable of speaking of intellectual transformations as turns are academics who are capable of thinking of their work not as a war of positions but as a sequence of positionings, who are capable of modeling a relation to their work that is expansive and light." The very digital transformations that endanger the traditional classroom Sanborn evokes are central to Meredith McGill's chapter, "Literary History, Book History, and Media Studies." Considering the academic embrace of digital tools within the context of the institutional history of book history, McGill observes that while the digital turn has in many respects advanced the study of material texts, it also raises questions about book history's possible place in the larger field of comparative media studies. "The erosion of the book as the norm or gold standard for the transmission of culture has made us more acutely aware of print's long, uneasy history of jostling with a multitude of other media forms," McGill writes, in an essay that provides crucial answers to ongoing questions about print, publishing, and literary and media circulation.

In orienting material textual and scholarly discourse, academic jargon recurs frequently to metaphors of "mapping." "Today, at the height of the 'cartographic turn,'" Martin Brückner writes, "we are increasingly in the habit of . . . using the term 'map' with such elasticity that maps have become applicable to any and all phenomena and practices, from simple metaphoric assertions . . . to the more complex but equally flawed assumption that mapping is applicable to everything that has a real or imaginary surface through which we can establish links for tracking affinities or differences." Brückner's chapter, "The Cartographic Turn and American Literary Studies: Of Maps, Mappings, and the Limits of Metaphor," confronts such orienteering metaphors with the materiality of maps themselves, providing a prescription for best literary mapping practices. We might say that the orientation of academic style in recent decades has been directed toward certain argumentative fashions. Christopher Castiglia closes the first half of the volume by turning upside down the expectation that scholarship should be founded solely on critique, instead calling for hopefulness as a critical mode. In his bold, visionary "Twists and Turns," Castiglia rejects the hermeneutics of Cold War suspicion. The "imaginative idealism of hope is not critique's opposite, as is often alleged," Castiglia writes; rather, "they are deeply and productively imbricated."

The volume's second half, which provides a sequence of chapters focused on the turns in transnational and hemispheric studies and other geopolitical-related areas of inquiry, opens with Ralph Bauer's investigation of the frequent use of the phrase "paradigm shift" in recent metacritical reflections about the transnational turn in American Studies. In "Of Turns and Paradigm Shifts: Humanities, Science, and Transnational American Studies," Bauer invokes a fascinating archive drawn from the histories of science and of the Spanish conquest in the New World to "focus our attention on the *colonial history* of the 'paradigm' in the empirical sciences, as it originated from the breakup of Renaissance humanism, the emergent gulf between the humanities and the natural sciences, as well as the subsequent hegemony of the empirical method in modern Western culture." If I have been noting the geopolitical tendency of the most visible turns in C19 American studies, the credit is due to Monique Allewaert's formidable theorization of the figure of the turn in "The Geopolitics and Tropologies of the American Turn," the iconography of which suggests that one of the notable features of the trope of the turn is its emphasis on "a partiality that does not promise a trajectory or telos." Allewaert provides a reading of an anonymous short story, "Theresa—A Haytien Tale" (1828), that models a reorientation of Americanist scholarship from a global perspective presuming the existing totality of one world, to an archipelagic orientation presuming an emerging totality produced by the relation between many islands.

Allewaert's archipelagic focus is in conversation with the Caribbean studies on display in Sean X. Goudie's chapter. In "The Caribbean Turn in C19 American Literary Studies," Goudie demonstrates how the relatively recent fascination with the Caribbean—which he traces to the 500th anniversary of the Columbian encounter, among other significant historical moments—is more accurately a return to a long nineteenth century of still largely unexamined Caribbean-North American literary and cultural relations. Goudie exemplifies such examinations in his discussion of the work of Maine-based painter Winslow Homer, Jamaican-born author Louis S. Meikle, and Harlem Renaissance writer Eric Walrond. The final chapter in the second part of the volume takes on an Asian and Pacific prospect that broadens to become oceanic in scope. Michelle Burnham's "Oceanic Turns and American Literary History in Global Context" proposes a turn toward oceans as a way to challenge the terrestriality of the continent and the temporality of the Revolution—orientations that have long grounded the fundamentally linear national narrative that shapes American literary and cultural history. In her readings of a selection of Pacific narratives, Burnham illustrates "a different dimensionality of movement altogether, one in which the islands stay in place while the globe repeatedly turns around them, situating each story within a new body of water."

Burnham's striking closing vision of Copernican reorientation might stand in for Americanist criticism's perspectival ambitions, as well as for its capacity for conceptual acquisitiveness. *Turns of Event* aims to show the scope and limitations of such global turnings in pre-1900 American literary studies. Its chapters provide analytical anchors in a widening gyre of critical turns, while simultaneously demonstrating the capaciousness of Americanist scholarship in its evidentiary diversity and its motile critical imagination.

PART I

Provocations

Chapter 1

↬

Turn It Up: Affects, Structures of Feeling, and Face-to-Face Education

GEOFFREY SANBORN

I will begin with two accounts of beginnings. The first is from Elizabeth Grosz's *The Nick of Time: Politics, Evolution, and the Untimely*:

> In the beginning, if it makes any sense to talk of a beginning, there were differences, in all likelihood chemical differences, variations in compounds, in different geographical and climatological contexts. These chemical differences, under some unknown and perhaps unknowable conditions, were transformed or transformed themselves into simple organic proteins, whose structure provided some means of reproduction. Life "began."[1]

The second is from *The Great Gatsby*:

> The lights grow brighter as the earth lurches away from the sun and now the orchestra is playing yellow cocktail music and the opera of voices pitches a key higher. Laughter is easier minute by minute, spilled with prodigality, tipped out at a cheerful

word. The groups change more swiftly, swell with new arrivals, dissolve and form in the same breath—already there are wanderers, confident girls who weave here and there among the stouter and more stable, become for a sharp, joyous moment the center of a group and then excited with triumph glide on through the sea-change of faces and voices and color under the constantly changing light.

Suddenly one of these gypsies in trembling opal seizes a cocktail out of the air, dumps it down for courage and moving her hands like Frisco dances out alone on the canvas platform. A momentary hush; the orchestra leader varies his rhythm obligingly for her and there is a burst of chatter as the erroneous news goes around that she is Gilda Gray's understudy from the "Follies." The party has begun.[2]

Each of these passages highlights, in ways I find useful, the moment at which elements coalesce into a temporary but reproducible structure. The value of the first passage is that it emphasizes how absolutely fundamental to existence this process of coalescence is. From the first protein on, without any ultimate purpose, life has been taking shape—or, as Grosz puts it elsewhere, "elaborat[ing] an interior." "It is this process of elaboration," she writes, "that differentiates a cell from a chemical, or the simplest form of life from a stone. [Life] produce[s] a barrier, a cell, an outline, a minimal space or interval that divides it from its world, at least provisionally, but through which it nevertheless accesses those parts of the preindividual, the real, or matter that it requires to continue and develop itself."[3]

The value of the second passage is its emphasis on the affective component of the change. The coalescence of a set of people into a party is driven by a series of intensifications: the "lights grow brighter," the "opera of voices pitches a key higher," laughter increases, groups "swell with new arrivals." The weaving, gliding motion of the "wanderers," rich with confidence, around whom small groups form, climaxes in the solo dance of the "gypsy in trembling opal," which, by introducing an interval of uncertainty—a "momentary hush"—followed by a burst of commentary, turns the gathering into a party: a partitioned-off and subtly cohesive event. By means of the process that Sianne Ngai, drawing on the work of Silvan Tomkins, calls "affective amplification," a simultaneously new and familiar social entity has been formed, one that will enable the partygoers to draw on an ambient reservoir of animation that no one of them could have independently supplied.[4]

I would like to use these passages as a way into a series of thoughts about the recent proliferation of so-called "turns" in literary studies. Rather than focusing on any one of those turns in particular, I would like to step back—way, way back, in the case of the passage from Grosz—and think comparatively about turns in general. By "turns" I mean, in the broadest sense, extemporized reconfigurations—on-the-fly adjustments that produce new cellular structures, perceptual fields, relational systems, or intellectual frameworks. In a more specialized sense, I mean transformations that are, like Raymond Williams's "structures of feeling," fundamentally social in their origin and development, drawing from and feeding back into a changeable network of relationships. If we locate the recent turns in literary studies in each of these contexts—the large-scale context of nonteleological evolutionary changes and the small-scale context of pre-emergent social formations—we can begin to think of them as something more than market-driven fashion statements. More to the point, perhaps, we can stop caring—if we ever did—about *whether* they are market-driven fashion statements. Instead of valuing turns only insofar as they can be distinguished from various kinds of opportunism, or only insofar as they can be shown to be strictly intellectual developments, we can value them as affective amplifications, ways of turning up the volume on our collective interest in a field. Is there a relationship between, say, putting together a literary studies symposium and getting a party started on the dance floor? Yes. Is there anything wrong with that relationship? No.

What, after all, would literary studies be like without the kind of energies that go into and come out of those methodological turns? I can still remember the jolt it gave me in 1993 to read Homi Bhabha's *The Location of Culture*, a book that so completely inverted my thoughts on Melville and cannibalism that I threw away my finished dissertation on that subject and wrote from scratch the manuscript that became *The Sign of the Cannibal*. It is even easier to remember, because it is closer in time, the excitement I felt at a 2005 conference when I found that Sam Otter, who had, like me, originally self-identified as a historicist, had recently been thinking, like me, about aesthetics. That encounter led to an MLA panel called "The Aesthetic Turn," which led, in turn, to a coedited collection of essays on Melville and aesthetics. In each of these cases, my work was both initiated and sustained by the feeling of being in the vicinity of something new, something other people were just beginning to think and say. It was not just that I was abstractly concerned with a certain set of ideas or that I was cravenly concerned with my professional fate, although I suppose it is possible to say that each of those things is true. The crucial feature of those experiences was the pleasurable surge of what Ngai calls the "basic affect of 'interest' underwriting all acts of intellectual inquiry."[5] By "intensif[ying] the effects of operations associated with other biological subsystems," that surge of interest induced the heightened, intermingled state Williams associates with structures of feeling: "thought as felt and feeling as thought, practical consciousness of a present kind, in a living and interrelating continuity."[6]

Those energies would not have been mobilized, or at least not mobilized to that degree, by a culturally dominant methodology or a purely private thought experiment. It was because postcolonial theory and posthistoricist aesthetics were incipiently social phenomena—visible, to a certain extent, but still blurry around the edges—that they attracted me with such force. That is to say that they were, and are, not so much turns as *turnings*, with all the presentness and ongoingness the present participle implies.[7] The reason Williams chooses to call preemergent social formations "structures of feeling" rather than "structures of experience" is that "experience" is, for him, a "past tense" concept, evoking "formed wholes," and thus orienting us away from "meanings and values as they are actively lived and felt."[8] What interests him about this phenomenon, and what has interested so many of his readers in it, is that it is neither formal nor formless; it is indeed a structure, an interlocking set of "specific internal relations," yet it is also "still in *process*."[9] This is the characteristic he hopes to capture by means of the word "feeling," and, I would suggest, the characteristic at least partly evoked by the word "turn."

Especially if one puts an exclamation point after the word, as Pete Seeger did, three times, in the title of a song that the Byrds would subsequently make famous.[10] Even though the lyrics of the song suggest, and are usually taken to imply, an endless cycling through calendrical stages, the triple interjection of its title—"Turn! Turn! Turn!"—like the protesteth-too-much moral of *The Scarlet Letter*—"Be true! Be true! Be true!"—or the *really* protesteth-too-much conclusion of *Absalom, Absalom!*—"*I dont I dont! I dont hate it! I dont hate it!*"—evokes an implicitly interminable restarting from the same implicitly virtual point.[11] To rise swiftly to a fresh statement, and then to rise and state again, and again, is to call attention to the groundlessness and arbitrariness of the act of stating, the act of taking semantic shape. It is to gesture toward the turnability of existence, the permanent possibility of fresh forms, and to do so not through an evocation of perpetual motion, but through a series of breaks. It is, finally, to associate structure with feeling, to associate the taking of shape with a surge of affective intensity.

It is hard to overestimate the significance of these kinds of unsettling, exclamatory bursts. "Life," Samuel Weber writes in *Benjamin's -abilities*, "is only rendered 'present' by expending itself, that is, by opening itself to a movement of iteration in which it is constantly being altered."[12] Nevertheless, even though that process of opening, becoming present, and surrendering to the movement of iteration is going on everywhere all the time, it is generally hidden from our view by a screen of habit-memory. It is possible, however, not only to perceive that process, but to actively, consciously participate in it, in the same way that a surfer may be said to participate in the rising, cresting, and collapsing of a wave.[13] The more we are aware of our affective involvement in our intellectual activities, the more aware we will be of the continuity of our intellectual activities with all the cultural and extracultural ways in which life is rendered present. And the more we allow our affective involvement to be amplified, the more we will be able to feel, and communicate, that such things matter. This is why our current habit of designating various shifts in literary studies as turns is, for me, so promising. Academics who are capable of speaking of intellectual transformations as turns are academics who are capable of thinking of their work not as a war of positions but as a sequence of positionings, who are capable of modeling a relation to their work that is expansive and light, and who know, maybe all too well, that "the rock of the world [is] founded securely on a fairy's wing."[14]

We can take this a step farther. What I have suggested so far is that the metaphor of turning *can* have an effect not only on the way we think about our work, but also on the way we do our work. I now want to suggest that this formulation is, under the present circumstances, not strong enough, that the stunningly rapid development of MOOCs (massive open online courses) has made it necessary to articulate the value of traditional college courses, and that the metaphor of turning should, even must, contribute to that articulation. If we do not pursue the implications of that metaphor all the way into the work that we do in the classroom, the discipline of literary studies, in spite of all of its potential for growth, could very easily end up turning and turning in a weakening gyre, increasingly remote from what Grosz calls "those parts of the preindividual, the real, or matter that it requires to continue and develop itself."[15] Only by taking seriously the continuity of intellectual processes with other life and nonlife processes, only by conceiving of teaching and learning as intensifications of living that are fundamentally relational and involve leaps into unpredictable forms, can we preserve and extend the vitality of the work that we do.

Here it may be helpful to turn to yet another account of beginnings, drawn from Gilles Deleuze's and Felix Guattari's *What Is Philosophy?*, where it is used to illustrate the claim that "the other person is the existence of a possible world":

There is, at some moment, a calm and restful world. Suddenly a frightened face looms up that looks at something out of the field. The other person appears here neither as subject nor object but as something very different: a possible world, the possibility of a frightening world. This possible world is not real, or not yet, but exists nonetheless: it is an expressed that exists only in its expression—the face, or the equivalent of the face.[16]

The model of face-to-face experience that Deleuze and Guattari offer here is significantly different than the model to which we are accustomed, in which togetherness is associated with reality and community, nostalgically understood. For Deleuze and Guattari, the face of the other is, as Richard Rushton puts it, "a circumscribing that gives the world its shape"; by reducing "the infinite to the finite," the face "energizes the world as a place where things happen."[17] Far from restoring us to a communal world, that is, the face initiates a radically uncertain communication, not by communicating anything in particular, but by establishing "the prior level of communicability, the 'is it possible?' that precedes the *what* of thinking, saying, feeling."[18] The face tells us that we have something to learn, that there are other worlds than the ones we are used to, and it does so in a way that both energizes us and holds out the prospect of a continuing energization.

Or at least it can. Most of the time, the faces we encounter have little in common with the face in the example above, not only because under normal conditions we rarely see fear-flooded faces, but because we tend to see faces as expressions or non-expressions of subjectivity, rather than as indices of possibilities. In the classroom, for instance, successfully socialized students tend not to betray much on their faces, and what a teacher tends to look for in their faces—with hopefulness and/or anticipatory frustration—is a subjectivity that confirms the teacher's own subjectivity: an affirmation that the assignment has indeed been followed and the lesson has indeed been grasped. Most teachers no doubt imagine that in their classrooms, face-to-face experience is at least occasionally more significant than this. But significant in what way? To what degree? For whom? For how long? What, at the end of the day, does face-to-face education offer that online education does not? Is it really nothing more than a more effective—in theory—delivery-system for knowledge, a kind of enhancement, via "personalization," of what one's less fortunate peers receive online? If so, then face-to-face education boils down to luxury treatment and a leg up on the competition—or, more exactly, the unevenly realized possibility of each of those things—and it is hard to see why we should fight for it.

If, however, we identify as the crucial feature of face-to-face education its capacity to reveal faces as possible worlds, the case is very different. In this conceptual model, what differentiates face-to-face education from online education is not a more personal touch, but a greater receptiveness to the micro-bursting of the evolutionary process, understood, in properly Darwinian terms, as a non-teleological becoming. That process is triggered, Grosz writes, by a "moment of impersonal consciousness, when the subject diverts momentarily into singularity, when the personal gives way to the impersonal and the living connects with and is driven by events beyond it."[19] This is, as Emerson puts it, the "way of life," and the more one abandons oneself to it—the more one draws, by "do[ing] something without knowing how or why," a "new circle"—the more it is capable of penetrating one's own restrictively individual way of life.[20] The problem with online education, from this perspective, is not that it is too impersonal, but that it is not impersonal enough. It may give me, as a student, things that are useful to me, but it is unlikely to take me out of myself, to make something deeper and wider than my personality stir in me. A digitized, task-subordinated, and implicitly ornamental face is never going to be as absorbing, as conducive to what Emerson calls "the shooting of the gulf," as the face of someone right in front of me.[21]

Bound up with the question whether teachers and students should face one another, in other words, is the question of *how* they should face one another. The best answer to the latter question, it seems to me, is that they should do so in ways that maximize the possibility of turns. A classroom turn is obviously smaller in scale than a disciplinary turn, but it is no less driven by affective amplification, no less responsive to the incipience of formations, and no less grounded in the virtuality, the turnability, that inheres in all things. A classroom turn is an opening to power, in Emerson's sense, a power that "resides in the moment of transition from a past to a new state" and "ceases in the instant of repose."[22] Although certain turns may feel especially climactic, no one of them—no one insight, argument, question, synthesis, shock, or leap—is as significant as the turnability each of them exposes. If the profoundest aim of education is to provide access to the existential capacity to think and feel otherwise, then the best place for education is the face-to-face classroom, where what is impersonal or pre-individual in oneself is most likely to be amplified to the point of structuration by what is impersonal or pre-individual in another.

I am not arguing that the goal of education is a generalized depersonalization, any more than I am arguing that intellectual life should consist of flitting for flitting's sake. I *am* arguing that the metaphor of turning suggests something important about the biological and social dimensions of academic experience. In academic life, as in every other form of life, there is, potentially, "a small space of excess that functions outside of natural selection, where life does not simply fulfill itself in surviving in its given milieu successfully enough to reproduce, but where it actively seeks to transform itself."[23] Seeking that transformation—seeking to know more exactly, perceive more clearly, express more precisely—makes it possible for something new to take shape, to leap at an odd angle into the unknowability of its reception. This, the minimal form of a potential turn, emerges from a social experience "*in solution*"—a structure of feeling—and is precipitated in turn into a social milieu.[24] It is not, as Emerson frequently suggests, an orphic event, proceeding from "the Supreme Cause."[25] It is, instead, as Pete Seeger insists, the product of an occasion, proceeding from and toward its own "time," a time that both initiates and awaits the forms that will make it recognizable. We cannot know, at any given moment, if it is a time for a party, or a time for a disciplinary breakthrough, or a time for a shift in the thinking and feeling of the people in a classroom—or, in the Ecclesiastes-derived lyrics of Seeger's song, "a time to gain, a time to lose, a time to rend, a time to sew, a time for love, a time for hate." Part of the strange joy of the experience I am describing here, however, is that we do not have to know. All we have to do, all we can do, is turn toward the immaterial prospect of that time, whatever it is, rerouted toward it by energies we cannot entirely claim as our own, hoping—or swearing, as Seeger does—that we are right, that something will follow from our actions, that we are not only of but for our moment, that it is not, after all, too late.[26]

Chapter 2

⤳

Literary History, Book History, and Media Studies

MEREDITH L. MCGILL

My title places in apposition three fields of study that possess rich areas of overlap, but that have carved out separate domains for themselves, often defining their object of study by contrast with one another. Some of the differences between and among Literary History, Book History, and Media Studies can be clarified by considering these disciplines' mid-twentieth-century precursors. If this essay were written fifty years ago, my title might refer to Literary Criticism, Bibliography, and Communications, and we would, I think, rest assured that these were very different areas of study, requiring sharply different kinds of training. In the contemporary division of academic labor, however, the overwhelmingly historically minded discipline of literary studies has forged a loose alliance with the interdisciplinary field of book history, in part by splitting the object of study into "text" and "book." While this distinction might seem untenable from the perspective of book history (where exactly does the text end and the book begin?) it is underwritten on the literary side by a capacious definition of textuality that permits all aspects of signification to be drawn into the critic's sights.[1]

Until recently, literary history has maintained a careful distance from media studies—a discipline that is often located outside the bounds of the liberal arts, in professional schools with some responsibility for practical training or conferring degrees in journalism. Indeed, literary studies and media studies might be said to have formed a kind of mutual non-aggression pact across the high/low distinction. Of course, literature departments now make regular forays into the territory of media studies, offering courses in popular culture, cultural studies, and particularly film, but they tend to leave the study of most twentieth- and twenty-first-century media to departments and schools of communication. Media studies programs examine the politics, economics, technology, infrastructure, history, and culture of mass media, but they retain a curious blind spot when it comes to print, rarely attending to the era before the advent of film, radio, and television, and largely ignoring the transformation of modern books and periodicals by these competing media. If literary history and media studies have managed, mostly, to stay out of each other's way, it has in part been by subordinating the common ground staked out by book historians, the history of the mediation of culture by print—territory that properly belongs to neither literary nor media studies.[2]

This rough and ready division of intellectual labor has recently been undermined by a turn to digital media, the study of which has been embraced by media studies programs and has put pressure on book history to define its relationship with a host of new interdisciplinary formations, from media archaeology to the digital humanities.[3] The pressure for a closer alliance between book history and media studies comes from a number of sources: the digitization of huge swaths of the print record, so that it is suddenly possible to study book history with little or no access to rare books (shifting the material grounds of the discipline from books, periodicals, broadsides, and manuscripts to pdf images of texts, and the locus of study from libraries and rare book rooms to searchable, if often cumbersome and error-ridden, databases); the refinement of methods for the study of large corpora, so that large-scale shifts in publishing patterns and textual reception suddenly seem perceptible and documentable; the significant investment by the federal government in the digital humanities; and our everyday experience of what Jacques Derrida has called the "withdrawal" of paper and the printed book within our multimedia landscape.[4] The erosion of the book as the norm or gold standard for the transmission of culture has made us more acutely aware of print's long, uneasy history of jostling with a multitude of other media forms. As book history seems on the verge of being taken up, albeit as a junior partner, into the larger field of comparative media studies, it seems worth asking: what has been the return on book history for literary critics—that is, how well has it served their interests?[5] Should literary critics invested in book history welcome or resist such a merger? And how will literary studies be affected by the recasting of an interdisciplinary field that has deep roots in the discipline but has developed an institutional identity outside its borders?

Disciplinary Interdisciplinary in the Study of the Book

What was at stake for *historians* in the development of the field of book history is quickly visible from Robert Darnton's now famous (if much disputed) depiction of "the communications circuit" in his 1982 essay "What Is the History of Books?"[6] (Figure 2.1) Critics of this model usually call attention to its problematic linearity, moving as it does (without switchbacks, interference, or interruption) from authorial origination through the various stages of production, circulation, and reception. But what is most striking from a *disciplinary* perspective is the number of important areas of historical study that Darnton represents as contained within the circle: intellectual, economic, social, political, and legal history. Darnton's model of book history does not so much displace these subfields as minimize their importance, making them tributaries to the main current of a cultural history reimagined in socioeconomic terms. Darnton draws on their authority to link what he called "esoteric specializations" such as analytical bibliography, printing history, sociology of knowledge, and transportation history, "cut off from each other by arcane techniques and mutual misunderstanding" (11).

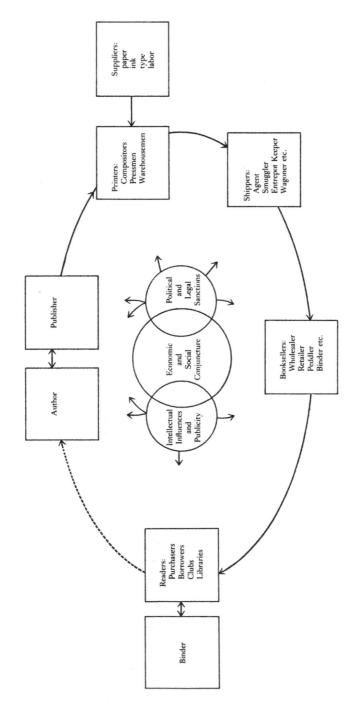

Figure 2.1. The communications circuit. Robert Darnton, "What Is the History of Books?" *Daedalus* 111, 3 (1982): 70.

In an essay published the same year, Roger Chartier describes intellectual and cultural history's struggle with the legacy of the interpretive methods of the *Annales* school historians; his account helps to explain why Darnton's model might have been particularly welcome.[7] The *Annales* school privileged collective "mentalities" over individual thinkers; the unconscious, the automatic, and the impersonal over conscious thought; ordinariness over representativeness; massive documentary collections over particularly influential texts; and the explanatory power of the repetitive and quantifiable over individual agency or the transformative power of events. Book history arrived just in time to rescue cultural and intellectual history from its *annaliste* diminishment, demonstrating how social relations are mediated by culture. Book history's emphasis on the transmission of culture permitted a problematically elite and abstract history of ideas to, in Chartier's phrase, "[annex] the terrain of popular thought" (296). Classic studies such as Darnton's *The Business of Enlightenment* (1979) brought lofty, revolutionary ideas into contact with the strategic decisions of ordinary businessmen, introduced common actors such as typesetters, booksellers, and smugglers into the story of the Enlightenment alongside eminent philosophers, and shifted historians' attention from the origins of radical thought to the diffusion of ideas on a massive scale.

Book history helped change the balance of power between and among subfields within the discipline of history; it has, however, played a different role in literary studies, which reacted in different ways to the mid-twentieth-century pressure to place the humanities on a more rational, scientific foundation. When book history arrived in literature departments in the mid- to late 1980s, it drew interest and attention from literary critics trained in (or at the very least exposed to) the microscopic forms of material textual analysis pioneered by bibliographers. Originating in the attempt to establish definitive texts of early modern drama—in particular, the works of William Shakespeare—the discipline of bibliography developed a remarkable set of practices for recording and managing the kinds of differences that are introduced through the production of multiple editions of a work, often inferring processes of production from the physical objects themselves.[8] In G. Thomas Tanselle's suspiciously elegant formulation, bibliographers attend to the material aspects of printed books that readers are *not supposed* to attend to, while book history attends to those design elements that authors and publishers expect to influence readers.[9]

In order to establish authoritative texts of literary classics, bibliographers and textual critics developed rigorous methods for weighing historical evidence about texts. They also aimed in their definitive editions to produce a material embodiment of the kind of text demanded by the reading practices of New Criticism. Textual editors, who used the idea of the "author's intention" to stabilize a variable textual field, maintained a complex, symbiotic relationship with the New Critics, who relied on stable texts to cut interpretation free from authorial determination. At the heyday of the discipline in the mid-twentieth-century bibliographers were, like digital humanities scholars today, the recipients of major government grants to produce authoritative editions of national classics that we still rely on for our teaching and scholarship.[10]

Bibliography is the subdiscipline of literary studies tasked with managing the difference between the ideality of the literary text and the material history of its production, the difference between the text-in-general and the text-in-particular, the one you refer to and the one you can hold in your hand or display on a screen. At a fundamental level, the development of bibliographic principles was made necessary by the centrality of the practice of reprinting to the regional, national, and international circulation of print. For most of the history of print, extending the reach of a literary work required reprinting it, and the consequent resetting of type ran the risk of introducing differences between and among texts that were nominally the same, advertised as the same, or otherwise acknowledged to be versions of the same. The existence of multiple copies of a work provides the justification for the construction of critical editions and remains the principle of intelligibility of textual editing; an edition (as opposed to an "issue" or "state") is defined by the resetting of type. "Mere reprints," however—increasingly present in our world as digital facsimiles of printed texts—also represent the form of textual reproduction from which scholarly editors would most like to distance themselves; they signify the abandonment of critical standards, the eclipse of the need for textual criticism.

In his influential 1949 essay "The Rationale of Copy-Text," bibliographer W. W. Greg set out to craft a policy that would allow editors to evaluate the different kinds of authority represented by the first printing and later reprintings of a literary text. While the first edition of a work is presumably set from, and therefore closest to, the author's manuscript, it often contains errata that are corrected in later editions of the work. Later editions, however, inevitably introduce new errors through the resetting of type, raising the often unresolvable question as to which changes can be considered revisions to the text, and which must be treated as printers' errors. In developing his "rationale" for choosing and weighing the authority of the "copy-text"—the particular copy of a literary work that an editor uses as a baseline for a critical edition—Greg charts a course between mechanistic obedience to the chosen edition, which he associates with the German tradition of classical editing, and the belles-lettristic practice of "eclectic" editing, which allowed an editor, in choosing between and among variants, to use his or her aesthetic judgment to "improve" the text. In order to liberate editorial judgment within the confines of scientific practice, Greg drew his now famous distinction between "substantives" and "accidentals," those aspects of a text that "affect the author's meaning or the essence of his expression" (the substantives) and those "such as spelling, punctuation, word-division and the like, affecting mainly its formal presentation . . . the accidents of the text."[11] Counterintuitively, Greg insisted that editors were *bound* to preserve the "accidentals" of the edition they chose as copy-text, while they were obliged to exercise—and defend—their judgment in cases of "substantive" readings. Greg argued that preserving the accidentals of the copy-text (most often an early edition of a work) would help control for degeneration across the sequence of copies, while insisting on editorial intervention in the matter of substantives would keep printers' errors from being mechanically passed along from copy-text to critical edition as if they were the work of the author. The ideal result, in Fredson Bowers's succinct formulation, would be a scholarly edition that combined "the superior authority of most of the words in the revised edition with the superior authority of the forms of words in the first edition."[12]

If Bowers's confidence in this distinction between words and their forms seems impossible to sustain, bear in mind that in editorial practice, the distinction between substantives and accidentals functions as a hypothesis to be tested by astonishingly close, even microscopic reading practices. Textual editors make thousands of minute discriminations—reading letter by letter, and comma by comma—as they assemble texts, collate different editions (and different issues and states of the same edition) in order to establish norms, reveal variants, evaluate their findings, and construct a text for a new edition by choosing among the options they have uncovered. Greg's "Rationale of Copy-Text" gave textual editors license to distrust the authority of any single edition of a work. It encouraged them to seek out and test their hypotheses against multiple copies, and provided a theoretical tool for distinguishing between significant and insignificant variations across a sequence of editions.

There are many reasons for the gradual marginalization of bibliography within departments of literature: the internal critique of bibliographic method; theoretical debate over the recuperability and pertinence of the author's intention; the embrace of textual variation; the appeal of literary and cultural theory; and the compelling distraction of the canon wars, about which bibliography had little to say. But literary critics currently find ourselves with a disciplinary predicament: we have a vastly expanded canon of literary works (and writing to which we are interested in paying attention), compounded by a confusing and seemingly ungovernable outpouring of digital facsimiles and remediated, web-based texts. And yet, our disciplinary investment in thinking about the physical aspects of literary works hasn't kept pace with this radical expansion of texts and potential objects of our attention. While the continued importance of Shakespeare has meant that specialists in early modern literature have remained in strong dialogue with bibliographical theory and method, students of American literature are most likely to encounter methods for understanding texts in the context of their production and reception through the interdisciplinary field of book history.

This is in many ways an excellent thing. Ambitious collaborative projects such as the five-volume *A History of the Book in America* (2000–2010) have produced a remarkable consolidation of knowledge about authors and publishers, books, periodicals, and ephemera; manufacturing and labor practices; the regional, national, and transnational book trade; institutions of literacy, readers, and reading practices. Literary critics working in this interdisciplinary field have been successful in challenging assumptions that have long guided Americanist literary study. To name just three: Leon Jackson's *The Business of Letters: Authorial Economies in Antebellum America* (2008) questions literary historians' strong emphasis on professional authorship, providing a nuanced account of the multiple informal economies in which authors participated; Trish Loughran's *The Republic in Print: Print Culture in the Age of U.S. Nation Building, 1770–1870* (2007) challenges the link between print culture and nation-formation by arguing for the dominance of regional print networks well into the nineteenth century; and Thomas Augst's *The Clerk's Tale: Young Men and Moral Life in Nineteenth-Century America* (2003) shows how institutions of reading, such as mercantile libraries, grafted character-building rhetoric onto practices of literacy, defining market culture as a primary arena for the extension of American ideals of independence and self-reliance. And yet the shift from bibliography to book history has placed such training outside our discipline and under the leadership of historians, many of whom have surprisingly little regard for texts or the text-as-object. As Tanselle has noted about book history, "the social study of book design hardly seems to be bibliography at all" (29).

I have argued elsewhere that book historians' interest in the social locations of culture frequently renders the material and rhetorical analysis of texts of negligible importance.[13] Much of book history turns to texts to illustrate the ways in which they are subject to determining forces imagined as wholly exterior to them. In many studies, the physical form of the book is invoked as a principle of constraint, the details of its embodiment delimiting the range of possible meanings of particular texts. In other studies, the history of a text's publication and reception is used to bring into focus the material (but often invisible) social networks across which books travel as they are solicited, published, bought and sold, borrowed and exchanged. For all their demystifying, anti-idealist rhetoric, book historians are often looking through and not at the book. In these modes of analysis, a text's structure, its negotiations with genre, its thematic preoccupations and figures of address are invoked only insofar as they are impinged on from without. Either a text's field of signification is limited and disciplined by history, or the text is used to illuminate a set of social structures that are imagined to surround and contain it.

Book history as practiced by historians retains a strongly humanist bent; it is primarily interested in persons and social relations between and among persons, and not texts, discourse, or rhetoric. Bibliographer D. F. McKenzie may have set the tone for book historians' dismissal of bibliography in his brilliant 1969 essay "Printers of the Mind,"[14] in which he rejected a number of assumptions about early modern publishing that had been derived from bibliographic analysis in favor of evidence of labor practices detailed in publishers' archives. McKenzie argued that bibliographers engaged in textual analysis had projected imaginary social relations, and that history provided a remedy for bibliographical uncertainty through accounts of the lives of real laborers. You will recall that all the way stations in Darnton's "communications circuit" are occupied by persons. Book historians are often surprisingly confident of the difference between what lies inside and what lies outside texts, favoring solid "external" over speculative "internal" evidence. To choose but one example: Jonathan Rose's *The Intellectual Life of the Working Classes* (2001) assembles an extraordinary archive of workers' autobiographies and examines them for evidence of reading practices, promising to return the history of reading to the solid terrain of real readers. But the structure of the memoir itself—its generic conventions, its strategies for hailing its reader and for hailing the reader as a potential writer, have no place in his analysis. "Literary theorists have speculated about hypothetical readers," Rose acknowledges, "Wolfgang Iser's 'implied reader,' Stanley Fish's 'informed reader,' Jonathan Culler's 'qualified reader,' Michael Riffaterre's 'superreader'—but they are not relevant here."[15] Many historians working in the field of book history are indifferent to or openly contemptuous of the evidence that can be derived from close reading of a literary *or* bibliographical kind.

Much of this is ordinary, productive interdisciplinary skirmishing, but literary critics working in book history can often feel like franchisees of a business owned and operated by historians. Literary critics are by training exposed to a broader or different range of material phenomena clamoring for their attention than those that ordinarily underwrite scholarship in book history: on the one hand, the materialities of language, form, and genre, which *require* close attention to the text; and, on the other, literary texts' often powerful engagement with material social and economic forces that are invisible, occluded—even fetishized—at the level of the book-as-object. It seems possible to identify the lineaments of a "book history" style of literary criticism, shaped by its struggle to reconcile these competing disciplinary and interdisciplinary imperatives. Some of the hallmarks of this style, at least within Americanist literary scholarship, would include: a gravitational pull toward literary sociology; the avoidance of or delayed encounter with major canonical works (as if the fragile methodological bargain that enables literary-critical book history can't withstand contact with major texts and their critical traditions);[16] and an emphasis on the close reading of paratextual material, those parts of the printed book that hover with delicious indeterminacy between text and book, opening out to the agency of book history's broader cast of characters while retaining their status as essential to the text "itself," whatever that is. The paratext splits the difference between text and book—the sign, I think, of a disciplinary refusal to leave the text behind.[17]

Literary critics have labored to create a version of book history that can countenance textual evidence, not ignore it or explain it away. Eager to populate our histories with the many agents, in addition to authors, who are responsible for producing and sustaining literary culture (from publishers and reprinters to booksellers, distributors, government censors, reviewers, advertisers, librarians, and reading club leaders), critics seem perpetually in danger of imagining literary texts as curiously inert objects of external processes—of disregarding the interventions into the literary marketplace made by texts themselves.

Book History and Media Studies

Will the uptake of book history into comparative media studies or a capaciously imagined turn to digital humanities accentuate or help reverse this tendency? While the rise of quantitative methods for literary study is disturbing to many, I think we have reason to hope—and to press—for a reintegration of literary history, book history, and media studies on terms that are perhaps more favorable to those trained in literary study. For one thing, the comparative nature of much recent work in media studies—the shift from writing medium-specific histories to understanding how media establish and compete for position in a broader, multimedia environment—places a premium not on technology but on discourse. Recent studies of early film, photography, and computing by Geoffrey Batchen and Lisa Gitelman, for example, have demonstrated the rich uncertainty of moments of origin, the cross-fertilization of media forms, and the long reach of the imaginary projection of their capacities.[18] If book history has been moving in the direction of a simplistic materialism, media studies has been shifting in the direction of discourse. Scholars working in comparative media studies are in many cases in better rapport with literary critics' engagement of an expanded range of materialities than book historians have been.

Moreover, the field of comparative media studies—one that seeks to understand dynamic relations between and among print and the mass media of the long twentieth century—might well discover not only that literature falls within its purview, but also that literary texts can offer crucial insights into the politics, economics, technology, infrastructure, history, and culture of media writ large. Indeed, literature's long history of negotiating its relations with other arts makes it a privileged site for thinking about media shifts.[19] Poetry, for example, has a long claimed multimedia status—threatening to overwhelm sense with sound, offering a different way of seeing, and toying with our consciousness of page (or screen). Poetry's claim to be an aural and a visual *as well as* a verbal art challenges the sequential narratives of media history, narratives that tend to proceed as if there were only one medium per epoch, each separate from its predecessors and successors: handwriting, print, photography, film, radio, TV, internet. Rather than assuming that poetry is what remains the same despite its transit across different media, can we imagine a book history or media history fine-grained and supple enough to recognize the interventions in these histories made by particular poems and poetic genres? Kevis Goodman's *Georgic Modernity and British Romanticism* (2004) offers one model for thinking about literary texts as integral to the history of media.[20] In this study, Goodman treats the georgic as a medium on par with the visual medium of the microscope, arguing not only that the genre was revived in response to scientific innovation, but that the two are rivals, both using magnification to raise questions about the plurality of worlds. This is a pioneering critical work that helps to define common ground between literary studies and media studies, one that takes genre as seriously as technology. Can we imagine a revitalized book history that would entertain the idea that hexameters may have had as much to do with the successful circulation of Longfellow's *Evangeline* as the marketing genius of Ticknor and Fields? Or that the history of *ekphrasis* may have influenced the relations between text and image in illustrated books as much as changes in print technology?

Finally, the proliferation of texts made newly available by digital databases, Google Books, and the Internet Archive raises with renewed urgency many of the questions that bibliographers had been tasked to solve: what are the principles of order governing the world of digitally remedi-

ated texts? How might we organize, weigh, and navigate the range of editions that are now available to us for research and teaching? In an article
in *Digital Humanities Quarterly* surveying print-on-demand editions of
Milton's *Areopagitica*, Whitney Trettien argues that the emphasis on
plain-text searching in digital scholarly editions has newly hardened the
distinction between the text and the book, that impossible division across
which literary history and book history have warily transacted their business.[21] For instance, the two kinds of display offered on a top-notch scholarly site such as the *Walt Whitman Archive* (http://www.whitmanarchive
.org) demonstrate how digital remediation drives a wedge between what
in the world of print might be considered two kinds of attention or modes
of reading. The web site invites us to toggle between searchable xml and
high resolution page images, offering us a choice between two kinds of
editorial fidelity: to the words in the order in which they appear, and to
the visual characteristics of the printed page. The fact that these two
modes of display can be viewed at the same time—on a single screen—
may distract readers from their very different material properties and capabilities. Moreover, as Trettien argues, scholarly web sites' emphasis on
searchable xml promotes the idea that digitization frees a text's semantic
content from its material supports, leaving the facsimile page images as a
monument to or placeholder for what has been left behind.

This double vision is in many ways an improvement on the technology of the critical edition or the variorum edition, both of which must
find a way to account for material differences within the single medium
of print. Like the critical edition, variorum editions seek to produce a
uniform text for purposes of reproduction and citation. However, in
doing so, variorum editions rewrite the history of circulation as a matter
of choice between and among textual variants. This history is both highly
selective in the physical differences it encodes, and difficult to rearrange
so as to testify to the multiplicity rather than the singularity of a literary
text. For example, in Thomas Ollive Mabbott's definitive *Collected Works
of Edgar Allan Poe* (1969–78) (Figure 2.2), the editor works hard to make
a sequence out of an extensive and overlapping history of reprinting in

THE RAVEN

"Be that word our sign of parting, bird or fiend!" I shrieked, upstarting —
"Get thee back into the tempest and the Night's Plutonian shore!
Leave no black plume as a token of that lie thy soul hath spoken!
100 Leave my loneliness unbroken! — quit the bust above my door!
Take thy beak from out my heart, and take thy form from off my door!"
       Quoth the Raven "Nevermore."

And the Raven, never flitting, still is sitting, *still* is sitting
On the pallid bust of Pallas just above my chamber door;
105 And his eyes have all the seeming of a demon's that is dreaming,
And the lamp-light o'er him streaming throws his shadow on the floor;
And my soul from out that shadow that lies floating on the floor
      Shall be lifted — nevermore!

          [1844–1849]

VARIANTS

1 while/as (*U*)
3 nodded/pondered (*G*); tapping/rapping (*G*)
4 rapping, rapping/tapping, tapping, (*G*)
9 sought/tried (*A, B, C, E, F, H, L, P*)
11 name/named (*Q, U*)
18 This is is/That it is (*C, L, N, U*); Only this (*Q*)
26 mortal/mortals (*W*)
27 stillness/darkness (*A, B, C, E, F, H, J, L, N, P, U*)
28 Lenore?/Lenore! (*A, B, C, E, F, H, J, L, N, P, U*)
31 Back/Then (*A, B, C, E, F, H, L, P*)
32 again I heard/I heard again (*A, B, C, E, F, H, J, L, N, P, U*); somewhat/something (*W*)

39 a minute/an instant (*A, B, C, E, F, H, J, L, N, P, Q, U*); a moment (*M*)
43 ebony/ebon (*Q*)
51 living human/sublunary (*A, C, E*)
55 the placid/that placid (*R*)
60 Then the bird said/Quoth the raven (*A, B, C*)
61 Startled/Wondering (*A, C*)
64 till his songs one burden bore/so, when Hope he would adjure (*A, B, C*); songs/song (*H*)
65 that melancholy/the melancholy (*D, E, F, H, L, F*; melancholy changed in *S*, but the change erased; only sa[d] can be read*)
65 Stern Despair returned, instead of the sweet Hope he dared adjure — (*A, B, C*)
66 Of 'Never — nevermore.'/That sad

TEXTS

(*A*) *American Review*, February 1845 (1:143–145); (*B*) New York *Evening Mirror*, January 29, 1845, reprinted from same types in the weekly *New-York Mirror* for February 8; (*C*) *Southern Literary Messenger*, March 1845 (11:186–188); (*D*) letter to J. Augustus Shea, February 3, 1845, now in the Pierpont Morgan Library (lines 60–66); (*E*) *New-York Tribune*, February 4, 1845; (*F*) *Broadway Journal*, February 8, 1845 (1:90); (*G*) *Broadway Journal*, May 24, 1845 (1:330; lines 3–4 in a review); (*H*) London *Critic*, June 14, 1845; (*J*) *The Raven and Other Poems* (New York, 1845; copyright September 12), pp. 1–5; (*K*) manuscript written as an autograph, late 1845 (lines 103–108); (*L*) New York *Literary Emporium*, December 1845 (2:376–378); (*M*) *Graham's Magazine* for April 1846 (28:165–167; many lines quoted in "The Philosophy of Composition"); (*N*) Philadelphia *Saturday Courier*, July 25, 1846; (*P*) Rufus W. Griswold's *Poets and Poetry of America* (8th edition, published May 29, 1847) pp. 432–433; (*Q*) *Southern Literary Messenger*, January 1848 (14:34–35; lines 1–6, 9–18, 37–108, in Philip Pendleton Cooke's "Edgar A. Poe"); (*R*) manuscript "Inscribed to Dr. S. A. Whittaker of Phoenixville [Pennsylvania]," September 1848; (*S*) J. Lorimer Graham copy of *The Raven* (1845) with manuscript revisions, 1846–1849; (*T*) Richmond *Semi-Weekly Examiner*, September 25, 1849; (*U*) Philadelphia *Saturday Courier*, November 3, 1849; (*W*) *Works* (1850), II, 7–11.

Figure 2.2. List of variants and alphabetic key to sequence of texts, Edgar Allan Poe, *Collected Works of Edgar Allan Poe*, ed. Thomas Ollive Mabbott, vol. 1 (Cambridge, Mass.: Belknap Press of Harvard University Press, 1969), 369, 363.

periodicals of radically different formats, localities, and fields of circulation.[22] Variorum editions encourage us to accept the essential "same-
ness" of the literary text as what publication history has to tell us, rather
than as what a theory of literariness tells us about texts.

Digital Bibliography

The task of accounting for a text's materiality and for various versions'
difference from one another has gotten considerably more difficult now
that, with the (relatively rare) exception of letterpress printing, all printed
texts are thoroughly digital objects: beginning life mediated by word
processing software, translated into a markup language for digital printing, and often circulated as an e-text or printed book only after a request
has been delivered through a web-based portal. If the history of the
twenty-first-century book is unquestionably a multimedia affair, so is
contemporary scholarship in literature and book history, but we make
our way through the thickets of digital facsimiles without the scrupulous
attention to material differences that bibliographers bestowed on multiple printed versions of canonical literary texts. Even our most-highly
regarded digital databases such as Early English Books Online (EEBO),
Eighteenth-Century Collections Online (ECCO), and the Early American Imprint Series tend to erase or suppress their layers of mediation and
the principles of selection and historical contingencies that have shaped
their contours.[23] Trading on the thrill of access to rare printed works,
these collections of high-quality digital facsimiles do not disclose the
editorial exclusions and technical limitations produced in the process of
digitizing extant microfilm collections and running the scans through
optical character recognition programs (software that translates letter
forms into machine-coded text). There are to my knowledge no standards of disclosure of the nature and complex materiality of digital facsimiles and web-based texts, and no standards for advertising the editorial and technical limitations of digital archives. We are always in danger

of taking large collections to be comprehensive simply by virtue of their size, and of assuming that digital editions, which for highly contingent reasons have been made readily available to us, are historically representative. Who, if not literary critics, working with bibliographers and digital humanists, will give meaningful shape and depth to the flattened world of digital texts made instantly available as a list of search results?

Digital media appear to have provided literary criticism with its own *Annales*-moment, in which the business-as-usual of literary interpretation threatens to be swamped by the ready availability of once rare sources. The survival of both the critical edition and the representative or exemplary text is also threatened, diminished in importance by massive databases of digitized print that make it difficult to ignore the ordinary, the unremarkable, the repetitive, the quantifiable. My hope is that a return to traditions of thought internal to literary studies and not a retreat or an abandonment of our subject will help us navigate the rapidly shifting terrain of this new world.

Chapter 3

↜

The Cartographic Turn and American Literary Studies: Of Maps, Mappings, and the Limits of Metaphor

MARTIN BRÜCKNER

A survey of literary studies reveals a relatively sudden and now wide-spread fascination with all things cartographic. According to the *MLA International Bibliography*, published essay and book titles using the word "map" and its variants increased exponentially over the past forty years. Before 1990, a total of 503 titles used the terms "map" or "mapping." After 1990, the enthusiasm for using "map" as the defining label grew by a factor of three (Figure 3.1). Between 2001 and 2010 the search term "map*" identified over 1,400 titles in books, essays, collections, and dissertations. A fifth of these titles—281 to be specific—were published in the subject area of "American literature." Literary studies were hardly alone in this pattern. Their numbers track those of other databases: after 1990, the *Arts and Humanities Citation Index* records a dramatic increase in titles using the keywords "map" and "mapping," and so does (on a slightly smaller scale) the historian's go-to source *America: History & Life*.[1]

To give more descriptive examples of how published materials use the "map" label, consider the following samples in literary studies. Recent essay titles posted by the MLA bibliography include phrases such as

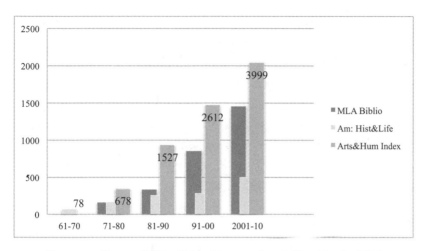

Figure 3.1. Keyword "Map*" by titles-per-decade listed in the *MLA International Bibliography* (black), *America: History & Life* (light gray), and the *Arts & Humanities Citation Index* (gray). Absolute numbers reflect the combined total of the three databases per decade.

"Mapping Critical Femininities," "Mapping Reconciliation Travel," and "Maps in Children's Literature." The current critical impulse is to map or offer a map of everything from "Subjectivities" and "the Literary and Critical Terrain" to "the Body's Movement," "the Contemporary Gay Novel," and "Desire." If we turn to the world of book publishing, acquisition editors seem to prefer the label "cartography" over "map," with the former hailing topics that range from time, networks, black women, and travel to disease, grace, architecture, or danger. Race, class, feelings, faith, sexuality—literary studies currently seem to map it all. And this mapping effort represents merely the tip of an academic iceberg; the vast bulk of "mappings" happen in research areas including linguistics and anthropology, psychology and neuroscience.

When looking at numbers and titles, the literary studies focus on maps and mappings resembles a cog in an academic wheel that is best described as the "cartographic turn." To do justice to the bibliographic records, the cartographic turn is not an ordinary turn fulfilling basic connotations such as a fickle "changeabout," a slight "curve," or a subversive "deviation."

Rather, it suggests a programmatic "shift," a major "trend," a new "direction."[2] On the one hand, the hard numbers beg us to examine the critical deployment of map terminologies as if it were a Kuhnian paradigm shift (a category of critical movement examined by Ralph Bauer in Chapter 6 of this volume). The exponential growth of map language in literary analysis has all the markings of an episodic moment that may well end up revolutionizing the conceptual continuity of literary studies because it offers idioms and methodologies that promise renewal and innovation or supersession and foreclosure of current forms of literary criticism. On the other hand, the sudden turn toward mappings bears the markings of yet another "fashionable fascination" haunting all tropes that promise a change in the course and connotation of language and its study; by the same token that maps have provided literary critics with a new and helpful analytical tool, some voices already worry that the figure of the map has become too pliable, stripped of any particular meaning or purpose in critical practice.[3]

Addressing hard numbers and soft language, this chapter explores the cartographic turn with a special emphasis on American literary studies by asking the following questions. Why do maps guide our analytical thinking and critical inquiry? What can maps do for us that, say, other conceptual terms like "image," "structure," or "text" cannot? And perhaps more important, what do we mean when we use the term "map" and "mapping"? We are living in the historical moment when our media culture privileges electronic maps over conventional paper ones. Old-fashioned "mappery"—the planning and designing of maps—no longer signifies school projects involving crayons and carefully crafted outline maps. Nor does it mean using an unwieldy road atlas or barely legible directions on paper napkins. Most of our map encounters involve digitally mastered images and application of Geographical Information System (GIS) software, not to mention the fact that with every online purchase or interaction we are generating geographically tagged information. In short, as we embed ourselves daily in both physical and virtual spaces, what are we to make of the pervasiveness and prominence of the language of maps and mapping in literary studies?

To provide some answers, this chapter approaches the cartographic turn in three steps. First, to better situate the cartographic turn in the present, a brief history of its intellectual home will help us ground the current penchant toward using the map lexicon as both critical language and practice. Second, a brief summary of literary studies explores how theory was put into practice in critical approaches to American literature, in particular examining changing attitudes toward the map and mappings at the fault line of literary production and reception. The final section offers a critique and reevaluation of the cartographic turn by debating the pros and cons of making maps and the act of mapping the basis of literary studies and critical analysis.

〜

A genealogy of the cartographic turn has to begin by acknowledging its profound debt to the "spatial turn" of the late 1970s and early 1980s. Also called the "topological" or "topographical" turn, the spatial turn came about when space was rediscovered as a conceptual category in social and cultural theory.[4] The emphasis on space came as a response to, or rather critique of, analytical practices and a mode of historicism in which, to quote Michel Foucault, "Space was treated as the dead, the fixed, the undialectical, the immobile. Time, on the contrary was richness, fecundity, life, dialectic."[5] In the course of the 1980s, the critical focus on *zeitgeist* expanded into a new and exciting emphasis on what could be called a new *raumgeist*; or rather, and this is in view of the linguistic home of many of the more influential spatial theories, academia became thoroughly enthralled by a *l'esprit de l'espace*, a spirit of space. With "space" coming to life as a new epistemological framework, its professors provided us with an attractive lexicon for feminist, postmodernist, and postcolonial inquiries, including the focus on public art and the grammar of cultural discourse. Henri Lefebvre and David Harvey provoked our interest in spatial politics, calling out the capitalist nature of the modern production of space. While Foucault described a multiform world structured by institutional spaces and heterotopias, Michel de Certeau introduced the notion of spatial practice as a function of everyday life. Gilles Deleuze and Félix Guattari postulated a rhizomatic lifeworld whose mappings resemble at once representations of early modern portolan charts, the Möbius strip, and the roots of a sod of grass. Fredric Jameson claimed the spatial aesthetic of cognitive mapping as a means for documenting histories of class struggle, and so forth.[6]

Inquiries into the nature of society, politics, and the arts came to rest on spatial terminologies that included place and region, location and displacement, positionality and territory, travels and itineraries, landscapes and architecture, city views and oceanic worlds. Material, metaphorical, and theoretical spaces were "emplaced," "traveled," and "explored"; they were "colonized," "decolonized," "territorialized," "regionalized," and "globalized." As this spatial idiom began to inform critical approaches, it injected new meaning into academic conversations about the relationship of power and politics, the arts and social life. Within a decade, it had at once produced contested conceptions of space, and, as noted by Neil Smith and Cindi Katz, become a force demanding a new "critical awareness of the translations connecting material and metaphorical space."[7]

While the spatial turn promised "boom years for cartographic metaphors," the "cartographic turn" was truly set into motion by the radical revision of the historiography of maps and the conceptual understanding of mapping.[8] Cultural geographers such as Edward Soja, Derek Gregory, Denis Cosgrove, and Doreen Massey (to name only a few) re-accredited mapped spaces as a new subject of inquiry. At the same time, historical cartographers Brian Harley, David Woodward, Denis Wood, and Christian Jacob changed the way we think about maps: they exposed the ideological authority of maps; how maps had played an active role in the nexus of power-knowledge while framing the geographies of the modern world; in particular, how the map emerged as a critical tool for the modern state and its agencies where it was shown to have shaped both moral and social spaces for nationalistic, imperial, and bureaucratic purposes that frequently resulted in physical or intellectual colonization.[9]

Central to the reassessment of the history of maps, map-making, and mapping habits was the general demystification of the map as a media and communication platform. Instead of insisting that maps were universally accepted scientific tools offering empirical and objective information, historians and theorists demonstrated (after a decade-long argument) how maps were representations that operated like a written text and were thus beholden to rules informed by semiotics, grammar, and rhetoric rather than mathematical proofs, quantitative reasoning, and geographical accuracy.[10] While for many students of cartography it was difficult to accept that maps operated similar to linguistic signifiers, critical attitudes today will side with Denis Cosgrove, who reminds us that "colours and symbolization, for example, are chosen and applied to maps according to widely accepted design principles, but their relationship to the appearance of landscapes represented on topographic maps, or the bands within the infrared spectrum on a remote sensed images, are necessarily arbitrary."[11] By the end of the 1990s, it had become routine to address the framing, selection, and composition of mapped spaces and information as the result of imaginative choice or artistic design practice, not as the product of physical reality or scientific law.

The "cartographic turn" not only was here to stay but increased its appeal from the moment when mappings were recognized as a discourse. While maps were now considered a textual construct producing variable meanings, mapping itself was increasingly recognized to represent merely one stage in the cultural production of space and practices surrounding expressions of spatial imaginings. When we approach the spatial turn in hindsight, it is today apparent that in the often politically charged spatial discourse, "maps" and "mappings" quickly emerged as one of the most evocative and productive spatial terminologies. Whether we studied novels or paintings, dance or political theory, academic disciplines treated both their subjects and their own field as mappable constructs by adding the terms of cartographic representation to our analytical lexicon. As we interrogate data, ideas, and arguments, we frequently couch our findings using the cartographer's dictionary: we "survey," "en-

close," "plot," "map," "chart," "coordinate," "grid," and "navigate"; more
recently, we have begun to "carto-code" and "geo-reference."

Also in hindsight, we can now observe that with the rise of a new
map consciousness, the academic community at once expanded and
shifted its attention from mappable spaces and maps as finished objects
to the processes of map-making and mapping, that is, the "acts of visual-
izing, conceptualizing, recording, representing, and creating spaces
graphically."[12] Indeed, at the beginning of the twenty-first century we
could say, along with Wood, that the cartographic turn had come to re-
volve around a "map discourse function."[13] Regardless of the goals or
outcomes of our critical inquiries, inherent to each and every application
of maps and mappings is one particular function: to connect and to establish links (albeit selective ones) between physical, social, and imaginary places and other kinds of things, such as taxes and voting rights,
rainfall and endangered species, drone strikes and epidemics, fictional
plots and imagined worlds. As the bibliographic records demonstrate
today, scholarly work has embraced maps as a critical methodology in
great part because the discourse of mapping not only offered novel means
of investigation—from framing arguments to rethinking concepts to
representing evidence—but provided an interdisciplinary tool allowing
the comparative study of the cognitive, performative, semantic, and
symbolic aspects of everything from human expression, social actions,
and environmental phenomena.

⌐⌐

In American literary studies, the cartographic turn triggered an at once
highly productive and diversified response, with scholarship applying
maps and mappings across a broad spectrum defined by investigative
methodologies ranging from the literal and metaphoric, to the bibliographic and digital. The extreme ends of the critical spectrum are represented by two kinds of work: on the one hand, Mary Ellen Snodgrass's
Literary Maps for Young Adult Literature (1995), a handbook for second-

ary and college education using the graphic image of rudimentary maps for reconstructing the settings, character movements, and plots in select canonical texts; on the other hand, Matthew Wilkens's "The Geographic Imagination of Civil War Era American Fiction" (2013), an innovative meta-study using advanced computing techniques, including GIS generated digital maps, to track the distribution of named places in nearly three thousand titles of American fiction published between 1851 and 1875 in order to revaluate core assumptions about spatial imaginings in American literary history.[14] In between, I suggest that the cartographic turn has divided the spectrum of critical approaches into three categories: maps and authorial production, mappings and reader reception, and map discourse as analytical technique.[15]

First, maps and authorial production. The perhaps most pervasive strand of research has examined how American authors use cartographic representations in their writings. In this line of research, literary scholarship frequently refers to the way actual maps have been integral to the writing process and spatial representation in novels, poems, and plays. For example, the assessment of how the textuality of maps shaped narrative structures and descriptive strategies in early histories and travelogues from John Smith's *General History of Virginia* to William Byrd's *History of the Dividing Line* to the multi-authored journals of the Lewis and Clark expedition.[16] Or, the relationship between Charles Brockden Brown's childhood fascination with maps and his later fictional construction of the American wilderness or "America's first city," Philadelphia, as a topographical warren and psychological maze.[17] Or, investigations that show how nineteenth-century cartography informed, for example, Harriet Beecher Stowe's abolitionist novel, *Uncle Tom's Cabin*, and the fascinating genre of "holy land" literature popular during the nineteenth century.[18] Parallel work in textual scholarship, especially research into the authors' manuscripts and personal letters, has offered crucial insights showing how the cartographic archive affected the very writing process and thus the relationship between text and space, for example, in Melville's stories "The Encantadas" or his epic novel, *Moby-Dick*.[19]

Authors introduced another facet of authorial mapping themselves
when they applied or experimented with the paratextual function of cartographic texts. Map inserts were staples of travel writing, advice literature (in particular when addressing immigrants), and news novels such
as *Nellie Bly's Book: Around the World in 72 Days* (1890).[20] By comparison, American fiction incorporated actual maps rather sparingly, and
then mostly when addressing children. Offering geographical authenti-
cation and lectoral guidance, map inserts were commonly found in
young adult fiction, like Hezekiah Butterworth's "Zigzag" series (*Zigzag
Journeys in the Western States of America; the Atlantic to the Pacific*
[1884]) or in Elizabeth W. Champney's "Vassar girls" adventures (*Three
Vassar girls in South America: a holiday trip of three college girls through
the southern continent, up the Amazon, down the Madeira, across the
Andes, and up the Pacific coast to Panama* [1885]). One subset of authorial mapping, usually of a collaborative and transhistorical nature, in-
volves authors, publishers, and scholars who turn to map inserts when
producing special editions (James Fenimore Cooper's French imprint of
The Pioneers; see Figure 3.2) or posthumous critical editions (Edgar
Allan Poe's *Narrative of Arthur Gordon Pym*).[21] The perhaps rarest subset
of authorial mappings—and this is the one that attracts critical attention
the most—consists of works in which authors engage with maps self-
consciously, either by inventing fictional maps to go with their fictional
world (here I think of Frank Baum's Land of Oz or Faulkner's Yoknapa-
tawpha County) or by letting language, literary form, and map mesh to
the point where mapping becomes a form of poetics in itself: for example, Henry David Thoreau's authorial construction of Walden Pond as
verbal description, surveyor's map, and ontological metaphor of nationhood and identity, or William Least Heat-Moon's thick description of
Kansas in *PrairyErth: A Deep Map*.

    Second, mappings and reader response. Over the decades, reader-
centered approaches to maps and mappings have outpaced critical attention to authorial mappings. On the most basic level, reader responses
tend to focus on references *to* maps before launching into readings *of*

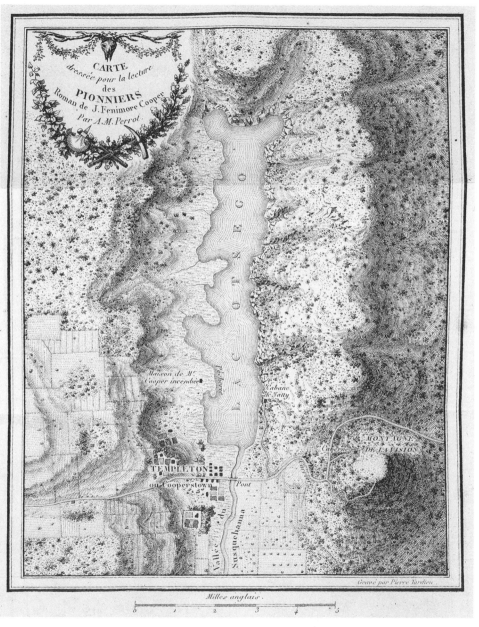

Figure 3.2. Pierre Tardieu, *Carte dressee pour la lecture des Pionniers: Romain de J. Fenimore Cooper. Par A. M. Perrot* (Paris, 1828). Courtesy American Antiquarian Society.

maps, literary texts containing maps, mapping activities, or mappable constructs. Since the early 1970s, basic "readerly mapping" tends to identify the literary use of maps according to two modes of reception defined by "unimaginative" (literal) and "imaginative" (metaphorical) map reading.[22] Unimaginative map reading, according to Phillip and Juliana Muehrcke, separates the reader from the map, keeping actual maps or map imagery at arms length because maps and all interactions with maps are considered exclusively in abstract terms, as nothing more and nothing less than a composite of graphic ciphers (the example given is Norman Mailer's novel *The Naked and the Dead*, in which, battling a war and fighting the soldier's emotions, the character of Major General Cummings imagines a reality in which men can be reduced to mere "figures on the map"). Conversely, imaginative map reading infuses the map with a life of its own, comparing it to a quasi-organic construct, a separate but parallel lifeworld proffering an evocative place for the imagination to experience new feelings and explore the fictive world's narrative potential (for example, we find this depicted early in James Dickey's novel, *Deliverance*, when the narrator, by looking at a map, begins to construct not only an invisible world parallel to the physical, but one he can enter and leave at will).

In general, reader responses involve approaches in which the individual reader is invited to move between the cartographical and the textual within the space of the codex of the book. This can involve macro-readings exploring everything from map-like language to the literary distribution of aesthetic or political concepts. Or it takes the form of micro-studies examining the relational meaning of graphic map inserts framed by the word "map" and the literary cartography underlying lyrical passages describing architectural or social of psychological formations, and so forth.[23] In view of recent studies fusing book history and the history of reading, critical work applying a reader-centered approach to mapping now examines both historical and contemporary patterns of quotation, intertextuality, and consumption, identifying reading habits that refer to other map experiences, for example, to maps situated outside the textual space of the codex and a reading process that can involve the critics' very first map encounters at home or school, personal habits of navigating roads or floor plans, or computer-generated choice of online map servers. While readerly mapping is being constructively explored through different models predicated on reader response theories and reading histories, it appears that many map-reading activities—from cursory to analytical—presuppose or culminate in an experiential relationship in which readers (implied or critical) engage with the text through acts of mapping to the point where we begin to create our own maps, be they ad hoc chalk maps on blackboards, carefully designed maps supplementing textbook editions, or digital maps data-mining literary texts.

Third, map discourse as analytical technique. Many of the authorial and the readerly approaches to maps tend to be informed by theoretical models and critical methodologies whose discussion of maps and mapping has provided new perspective and energy to literary criticism. Studies invested in "literary cartography" frequently call on terms and protocols developed by critics working on the margins of literary criticism, for example, by de Certeau (maps are "a memorandum prescribing actions"), Deleuze and Guattari ("the map does not reproduce an unconscious closed in upon itself; it constructs the unconscious"), or Jean Baudrillard ("the map precedes the territory").[24] As map discourse pervaded discussions of literary form and the tools of literary analysis, it was only a short leap to imbue established critical terms with a mapping function, from the classical rhetorical "topos" to the early modern neologism of "plot" to poststructural uses of "survey" and "metonymy." Moreover, it was the logic of the map discourse that encouraged us to speculate about how maps affected literary culture collectively. If we consider Benedict Anderson's critique of nationalism in relation to the history of the novel and Edward Said's exploration of culture and imperialism, not to mention more recent discussions of transnational literature and identity, maps and the language of maps continue to offer both a corrective lens and constructive idiom for reviewing and addressing American literatures across time and space.[25]

That map discourse holds a unique kind of sway over American literary studies can perhaps be seen best in debates over the configuration of

American literary history in which mappings have continually shaped our perspective on authors, genres, and the canon. Between the 1920s and 1950s (thus during the founding decades of American literary history as a scholarly field), wall posters entitled the "Booklovers Map of America: A Chart of Certain Landmarks of Literary Geography" (1926) or "A Pictorial Map Depicting the Literary Development of the United States" (1952) offered snapshots of a place-based conception that plotted out book titles, iconic images, and author names across the surface of the national map (Figure 3.3).[26] Recent editions of *The Norton Anthology of*

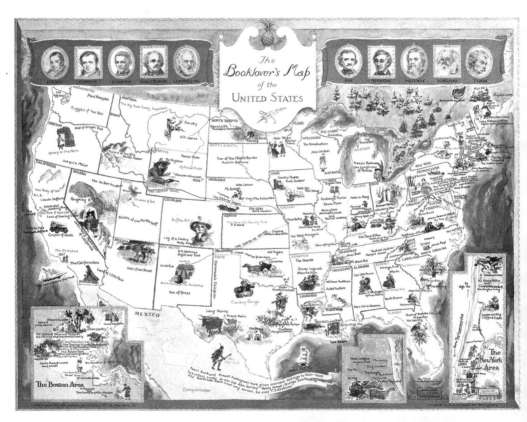

Figure 3.3. Amy Jones, *The Booklover's Map of the United States* (1949).
Courtesy Library of Congress. © 1949 R.R. Bowker, a ProQuest LLC affiliate.
Amy Jones, Designer and Illustrator.

American Literature still include maps in the endpapers—"North America to 1700" in front and "The United States: A Literary View" in the back—suggestively making the representation of the map become the graphic and material container of literary history.[27] Indeed, if we accept Franco Moretti's approach to the European novel, "literary geography" emerges as an alternative to literary history because only by mapping the text (and he really wants us to use graphic maps) will we "bring . . . to light relations that would otherwise remain hidden."[28] The computational powers of "literary GIS" applications now offer methodological models that take Moretti's map-based and map-producing readings of fiction a step farther. Through digitization, texts are now transformed into mappable metadata, so that any given text becomes a map capable of bridging the gap separating textual and cartographic representations of spaces that we consider real, imaginary, or critical.[29]

⤿

In seeking out the map as the basis for developing a methodology for an American literary cartography, critical approaches seem to be attracted to maps and mapping strategies for reasons that help to address one of my opening questions, especially the question of what the cartographic turn can do for us that other conceptual turns cannot. As I surveyed critical approaches, one answer and reason for embracing maps has to do with the way we engage with maps visually. To discuss the core subjects of literary studies—for example, imagery, action, plot, or characters—in terms of maps or mappings is to call on the "synoptic power" of the map as a specific kind of visual experience and mode of seeing. Not to get too technical, but according to the most rudimentary definitions, the map is a flat image of the earth or its regions; as such it spreads out the world before the eyes for those who know how to read the world "at one glance." But at the same time, we have to realize that this is a fiction; our eyes themselves do not see the earth or region—rather, our mental vision constructs it, and helps us imagine space. To reference the map, then, is to reference a mode of seeing the world from two perspectives: the visual perspective of the cartographic eye, the kind of gaze often associated with the "god-trick," and at the same time the demiurgic projection of the mental eye, the mind's eye or the imagination.[30] The application of maps and mappings makes available a unique double vision through which to view the mechanics of creative writing, while at the same time to review its multi-faceted and variably scaled epistemological and ideological underpinnings.

A second reason the cartographic turn may have appealed to us so much has to do with the graphic nature of maps: in the world of discourse-making—from signification to narration to textual production and transmission—the map provides a graphic referent of great ontological effect. On the one hand, like written or spoken language, a map in its everyday use hardly draws attention to itself. Maps appeal to both conceptual and social users because they promise transparency without interference, blocking out the noise and clutter of mediation.[31] Neatly framed and mostly shown right-side up, maps depict lines connecting mapped points in a fashion that creates at once a clinical setting and a forensic rhetorical tool. The graphic representation of mapped information looks more like a neat geometrical proof or exercise in logic than like a potentially messy translation of mapped spaces to the space of the map. On the other hand, the map's material style of representation offers a unique mode of cognitive organization: by the same token that its representation of lines, toponyms, and the grid help project and organize spaces, it is the map's hard copy that in producing connections between words, narration, or fields of inquiry makes these connections seem physically "detachable, connectable, reversible, modifiable, and ha[ving] multiple entryways and exits."[32] As a material sign and text, the graphic map is a paratextual element that, because it can be inserted and removed, manually expanded and collapsed, at once provides and contains, as Jacob writes, "an implicit commentary on the text whereby [mapping] defines not only its subject but also its position in a hierarchy of representative genres, appealing to generic conventions, defining the conditions as well as the authors of the drawing, pointing out who its receivers and what its concrete uses should be."[33]

The deictic function underlying the visual and graphic modalities of the map discourse may explain that third reason driving the cartographic turn in American literary studies, the map's discursive work as metaphor. Because in cartography "space is used to represent space," as Neil Smith and Cindi Katz observed early in the turn, "mapping not only assumes a particular space as given" but posits that the function of maps and mapping "is to produce a scale representation of this space, a one-to-one correspondence between representation and represented."[34] Variously called a schema, a matrix, or an analog by scholars working in areas ranging from cartography and linguistics to philosophy and art history,[35] maps performed the unusual cultural work of a metaphor whose meaning is inadvertently and almost by default considered to be more "real" or "accurate" than that of other metaphors used for representing a specified purpose— say, the representation of the female body and the nation-state, romance and sexuality, movements inside empires and the diaspora, or the paths taken by the Lewis and Clark expedition or the escape route taken by runaway slaves in Harriet Beecher Stowe's *Uncle Tom's Cabin* or the *Narrative of the Life of Frederick Douglass*.

Because of the map's association with the supposedly infallible empirical sciences, as Smith and Katz predicted sagaciously two decades ago, the map emerged as a useful metaphor for "defining new areas of inquiry or giving new form to a particular problem or set of problems."[36] On the upside, the widespread use of map metaphors suggests that maps belong to those useful tropes, as Kenneth Burke reminds us, that through invoking a "perspective process" assist us in reducing the unfamiliar to the familiar, providing a dialectic metaphor whose aim it is to serve at once experimental and heuristic purposes, seeing something in terms of something else.[37] Or—and here we can follow Ernst Curtius's treatment of metaphor—while the concept of metaphor implies movement and a change of place (in short, something very much akin to a "turn"), it entails above all a translation process: first, the transfer not only of information but of meaning from the mapped to the map; and second, in the process of translation map metaphors invariably come to signify a natural correspondence between fictional form/content and reality.[38]

And that brings me to the downside. As with all good metaphors, map metaphors tend not to leave many traces. And that is precisely the problem with the critical application of map and mapping terminologies, especially in literary studies where both the literary accounts of spaces and the criticism of such accounts all too often "pass without any gap from the space on the map to the real space outside the map."[39] Today, at the height of the "cartographic turn," we are increasingly in the habit of ignoring this gap by using the term "map" with such elasticity that maps have become applicable to any and all phenomena and practices, from simple metaphoric assertions such as "My head is a map" to the more complex but equally flawed assumption that mapping is applicable to everything that has a real or imaginary surface through which we can establish links for tracking affinities or differences, be they manifest in pictures or diagrams, written passages or physical artifacts, sense perceptions or political theory.[40] It seems to be the function of a good "turn" that from the moment that its operational trope—such as the map—becomes one of the "Metaphors We Live By," the discourse's metaphoric dimension diffuses the ontological and epistemological value of maps, rendering its critical capabilities weak if not meaningless.[41]

This is not to say that we are there yet, or that we ought to curb the multitude of map-inspired discourse. But for those of us who find maps and mapping to be an elegant, efficient, and constructive method for doing investigative and critical work, we need to remember the gap and what happens inside the gap, that is, during the process in which our quick invocation of "map" and allusion to mapped spaces appears to seamlessly connect the textual insides to imagined or real outsides (be it a place, a database, a movement). As easy as the cartographic turn has made it for me to invoke the language of the map when discussing travelogues and slave narratives, sentimental fiction and epic poetry, I now find myself reaching for the emergency brakes in order to slow down the turn and consider how in the very process of translation the internal logic of cartography structures everything from the vaguest reference to a map to the most sophisticated cognitive mapping.

1. The map is not the territory. We often confuse the map model with the territories or reality the map is supposed to represent; in short, we confuse models of reality with reality itself.[42]

2. The territory cannot look back. Reading a map requires visual and intellectual appropriations that refer to a represented space through an analogical linkage that is socially sanctioned.[43] As a two-dimensional and nonfigural image, the map defies the interpretive mechanisms of classical mimesis. A map in itself represents nothing, and unlike a portrait or painting, mapped spaces preclude visual reciprocity. The "mapped," that is, the map's "gazees," "objects," and "territories," cannot look back at either the map or the map gazer because they are caught in perpetuity in a two-dimensional "Flatland," to borrow from Edwin Abbott Abbott's novella, in which geometrically measured characters are incapable of shifting their subject position because they cannot imagine the world as "Spaceland," a world constructed of three or more dimensions.

3. Maps imply absolute space: as much as the map allows us to redefine the field of visual perception (even to the point where ocular and mental vision coincide), from the moment we invoke maps we are predisposed to invoke abstract conceptions of space. For many of us, references to maps and mapping practices invariably apply spatial definitions formulated during the seventeenth and eighteenth centuries. Following the work of Isaac Newton, René Descartes, and Immanuel Kant, our dominant representation of space tends to be measured in absolute terms: space is infinite and a priori; empty and geometrically divisible; and, in the case of Newton, empirical evidence of an omnipresent god.[44]

4. Maps are nomothetic instruments. Similar to the biblical tale of God giving Adam the ability to name things, maps give us the ability to name and inscribe the world in terms that are deemed unassailably authoritative, like natural laws, not propositions but facts of lasting meaning. This has the effect that like the microscope, the telescope, or the

scanner, mappings resemble prosthetic devices that extend and refine the field of sensorial perception. At the same time, the map's prosthetic function turns into a prophetic one—the map's nomothetic capability of positing the lasting existence of named locales or spatial relations enables us (or seduces us) to invent assertive rules addressing everything from planning flood controls to predicting a good meal in the city to assessing narrative structure and the individual's state of mind.

5. Maps are material/s. The problem lies in the naturalization of maps. Because of the rapid translation of "map" from graphic image to pervasive abstraction, the cartographic turn is poised to imbue maps and mappings with too much metaphor and thus empty them of meaning. In order to be mindful of the gap between the space on the map and the space outside it, between model and reality, we need to consider that maps and mappings are defined by production and reception, by their presence as artifact, and by their participation in the processes of communication. To fill the gap, for example, we should consider mapping at the junction of medium and graphic technique: for all their visual and graphic qualities, maps are surface structures embedded in hard material objects.[45] Even if the map's generic form promises a bijective (one-to-one) experience, the applied practice of mapping tends to be an objective experience (the sense of maps is related to the object): mapping matters involve murals, stone carvings, ceramic tile, mosaics, tattoos, clay tablets, glass, papyrus, paper, textile, wood, leather, metal, and today the computer screen. To invoke the map as metaphor thus is to invoke a specific mode of signification inseparable from the materiality of social life.

6. Finally, maps are ideological. Inherent to the map discourse function with its double vision and unique mode of seeing is a perspective resembling, as W. J. T. Mitchell writes, "a figure for what we could call ideology—a historical, cultural formation that masquerades as a universal, natural code."[46] This perspective is in general dialectical. To apply mapping as part of our methodology is to invoke a writing system that assumes the selectivity of its graphic contents, that acknowledges, on the one hand, the distancing between population and territory, while, on the

other hand, rendering visible those relationships that other forms of mediation have kept invisible. In both selections, the map's visual and
graphic function objectifies spaces that not only include static settings
and the bodily, but ephemeral spaces ranging from the affective to the
mobile to the aesthetic. More specifically, and here we might find it useful to borrow from Mitchell's nine "Theses of Landscape": just as maps
and mapping are found in all cultures, they are a particular historical
formation associated with a certain set of politics and ideologies more
closely related to organized imperialism than, say, tribal nomadism.[47]

Looking forward and being mindful of the gap, one way of maintain-
ing the cartographic turn and keeping it real, is for us to comprehend the
interconnection between the metaphorical and the material map. More
specifically, we need to examine the material sources of the map's metaphorical groundings. As we pick our paths through a field of literary
scholarship freshly defined by maps and mappings, the study of American literature seems to reflect more than Henri Lefebvre's somewhat sar-
castic assertion "that any search for space in literary texts will find it everywhere and in every guise." Rather, it offers an answer to Lefebvre's
question "how many maps, in the descriptive or geographical sense,
might be needed to deal exhaustively with a given space, to code and
decode all its meanings and contents?"[48] The answer should be clear. As
the bibliographic records of our work show, we are far from being done
using maps and the discourse of mapping because there seem to be not
enough maps available to give expression to the panoply of spaces created in American literature and the fields examining it. In fact, if anything, the records suggest that we suffer from a lack of maps, a lack that
I argue is disguised by the widespread metaphoric use of maps.

To pursue the material sources that inform and shape the map metaphor is *the* story to be told more fully in the future. For now, I look forward to seeing the cartographic turn keep on turning in directions that
keep on historicizing the authority of its concepts; that deploy maps and
mapping practices in all our critical endeavors while realizing the map's
constructedness; and, perhaps most importantly, I hope we recognize

that by entering the cartographic turn we are entering into a complicated agreement in which the map inescapably determines some of the rules and outcomes. And last but not least, we must be mindful that mapping is a process, for we have to remember that "to understand the contents, meaning, significance of any map (as thing or image or metaphor) requires that it be reinserted into social, historical, and technical contexts and practices from which it emerges and upon which it acts."[49]

Chapter 4

༄

Twists and Turns

CHRISTOPHER CASTIGLIA

It is possible that the reason so many "turns" can be claiming to change the field is, ironically, because they are not really changing much at all, but instead shifting the same methodologies and attitudes from one object (or "ideology") to another. One sign that this might be the case is the increasing number of critics wondering about the contemporary viability of "critique," shorthand for the righteous digging around in a text for hidden displacements of the social struggles that evade all but the politically savvy and serious critic. Critiques of critique might lead us to wonder whether what we call turns are actually twists, moving the same gaze to other horizons without shifting one's footing. This might seem facetious, given the political and archival *gravitas* claimed by most "turns," but the choreography of "turns" needs serious reconsideration at a moment when growing calls to reconsider how—and not just what—we read now suggest a desire for something more than another twist to the predictable orientations of contemporary literary and cultural criticism. What might turn us away from what Eve Kosofsky Sedgwick describes as "binarized, highly moralistic allegories of the subversive versus the hegemonic, resistance versus power," the "moralistic hygiene by which any reader of today is unchallengeably entitled to condescend to the thought of any moment in the past (maybe especially the recent past) is globally available to anyone who masters the application of two or three discrediting questions."[1] Heeding Sedgwick's warning that the near past is the easiest to dismiss, how can we move not "post" critique in the sense of opposing what has come before us—not a turning away, that is, but a turning *toward* that will take us somewhere more "pre-" (the *pre-scient* turn)? This will require methodological changes, to be sure, but just as important *dispositional* changes that might, I will argue here, lead us to value the imaginative idealism, the *hope*, at the heart of criticism, where it belongs and where, I contend, it has always been.

Hopefulness, I argue, has always been the defining characteristic of literary and cultural criticism, spanning a century from the socialism of the 1920s to the ideology critique of the 1980s and beyond. It might seem odd to attribute hopefulness to a contemporary criticism apparently motivated by what Paul Ricoeur called "the hermeneutics of suspicion."[2] But I would argue that *true* (as opposed to rote) critique is deeply hopeful. Without an ideal of how the world *could* look, what social visions are possible, an imaginative speculation that shows the current state of affairs to be sadly lacking, we would not be motivated to suspect what postures as the real and the inevitable. Theodor Adorno insists that every utopian statement is a "determined negation," a critique of the present in the act of articulating a more desirable future.[3] But the opposite is also true: through critique, we imply ideals as the metric by which we measure the present and the past. Every critique, in other words, is a determined idealism. Too often, however, those ideals remain closeted, visible only in their negative reflection. As a result, all we see on the surface are the ways that we, like the Cold Warriors described by literary critic Richard Chase, sever, reject, fetishize alienated emotions, dismiss previous generations, and "puff our inner righteousness into an image of the universe and annihilate every other image."[4] But if we stated our ideals—and not just as content but as a way of seeing—we might generate what F. O. Matthiessen called "imaginative vitality" or an appreciation of what Chase called "the moral imagination."[5] Critique and idealism are two sides of the same coin although, like a con game, the coin is currently weighted to display only one side. A critical practice of hope might be thought of, in part, as a continual flipping of that coin, one that never lets the coin land.

Right now, however, and for the last couple decades, the suspiciousness of critique looks very different from hopefulness, an unfortunate separation that I suggest has to do with the historical moment in which the latter disappeared behind the former. During the Cold War, the federal government and its agents whipped citizens into a constant state of anxiety (of nuclear annihilation, subversion of the young, loss of the capitalist "way of life") that found its only outlet (because it was one that ultimately refueled anxiety) in suspicion, a vigilant peering below apparently innocent surfaces for the phantasmatic communist threat that lurked, hidden but powerful, in our midst. Despite the government's encouragement of anxious suspicion (many will remember "duck and cover" exercises), however, even a cursory survey of Cold War U.S. society shows that other dispositional forces existed as well, manifested in the hopeful idealism of the civil rights, feminist, antiwar, worker, student, and sexual liberation movements, among others. For the children of the 1960s who became the cultural critics of the 1980s and 1990s, such hopeful activism motivated their scholarship, although increasingly as a retrospection rather than an ongoing extra-institutional activism. Memories are powerful fantasies, however, and as in all fantasies the mise en scène represents different aspects of the same unconscious. An odd conflation of what were originally distinct social forces gave rise, therefore, to the characteristically paradoxical nature of much late twentieth-century criticism, which evinces both the suspiciousness of the Cold War state and the imaginative idealism of counter-state struggles. The combination produces the schizophrenic self-divisions characteristic of Cold War America itself, schisms between commitments to the political resistance possible in the midst of discursive hegemony and a concept of the totalizing and nefarious discourses that brook no opposition. As critique, with its affective tensions, became graduate school *doxa*, however, the contradiction at least appeared to be resolved, as suspicion—more easily assimilated to most institutional structures than hopeful activism—became the currency of professional advancement, as charges of naïveté, complicity, or complacency drove hopefulness so far into the background it was almost invisible. But hope persists as a powerful motivator for critique, although the latter's often cynical predictability gives the impression that critique has run out of steam, a charge I take to mean that it has lost a comprehension and bold demonstration of the hope at its core. Moving "post" does not mean that we have to give up critique, then, although it does require that we recognize and acknowledge that the imaginative idealism of hope is not critique's opposite, as is often alleged, but rather, they are deeply and productively imbricated.

The persistence of hope into a critical age that would seem, on the surface, devoid of it becomes clear in a particularly telling—and honest— exchange between two critics from different generations. In 2005, Amy Kaplan published "A Call for a Truce" in *American Literary History*, responding to an essay in the same issue by Leo Marx, author of the 1964 "myth and symbol" study *The Machine in the Garden*.[6] Kaplan writes, "Marx eloquently attests to the political origins of the field [of American studies] in multiple, complex, and radical roots that preceded what would later be characterized as a hegemonic Cold War consensus" ("Truce," 141). Kaplan generously acknowledges that, on hearing an earlier lecture version of Marx's article, "it was thrilling to imagine the political and intellectual turmoil, debates, and excitement of the era he describes so well" and to recognize in the criticism written by Marx's generation "the doubleness of critique and affirmation" (141).

At the same time, Kaplan reports her sadness that, in discussing critics of her generation, Marx "sees decline instead of recognizing that there are parallels between these generations or that the production of new and exciting scholarship that emerged from the social movements of the 1960s and '70s might have analogies to the work that grew out of the political ferment of his generation" ("Truce," 142). While Marx "attributes a sense of nobility and idealism to his generation," Kaplan observes, he "makes the political commitments of later generations seem

merely angry and divisive, even when he agrees with their critiques"
(142). Countering Marx's insistence on what he refers to as a generational "Great Divide," Kaplan asserts, "Like it or not (and I like it), we are
very much the heirs of Marx and his generation, even in our rejections
and critiques of the original project and the different, but equally passionate, personal beliefs and political commitments that inspire our
scholarship" (146).

At this point in the essay, Kaplan and Marx part ways over the predictable topic of nationalism. Admitting the presence of nationalism in
his peers' criticism, Marx denies the charge that such rhetoric translates
into a celebratory patriotism. His contemporaries, Marx asserts, "were
more committed—and, oddly enough, more *hopefully* committed—to
the tradition of radical egalitarianism than Americans have been at any
other time of my life" ("Recovering," 127). Popular Front critics, he
claims, were primarily "internationalist," adding that when the American nation *did* appear, it was to mobilize opposition to "egregious forms
of capitalist exploitation and injustice, or to unjust wars." Critics like Marx,
in other words, expressed a "provisional belief in the idea of America"
that was "a compelling means of exposing the discrepancy between a real
and an ideal America" (128–29), setting actual practices in sharp contrast
to "the universal, egalitarian values of the Enlightenment represented by
Thomas Jefferson, Thomas Paine, and Lincoln" (127). In so doing, Marx
concludes, critics of his generation "combined harsh criticism with anxious affection for the world's first and largest experiment in multicultural
democracy" (129).

Although Kaplan gladly acknowledges a joint political mission that
connects the generations, once Marx names ideals as the basis of his critique, however, Kaplan backs away. While Marx "believes that we need
all the more to criticize the United States as measured by the nation's
own profession of values and purposes,'" Kaplan knows "that such pro-
fessions have contributed to an exceptionalism that justifies imperialism
and injustice and that keeps the United States insulated from developing—in dialogue with others—ethical values that go beyond the nation

as a standard of measurement" ("Truce," 146). What Marx identifies as the idealism of his generation, Kaplan sees as an object of suspicion. What both seem to miss is ironically what Marx so well articulates: suspicion of ideological systems and hopeful commitment to ideals are not opposed but mutually constitutive. Marx's commitment to idealism prevents him from seeing the potential negative effects of his rhetoric while Kaplan's adherence to ideology critique prevents her from imagining other uses of nationalism than as a force of conquest and injustice. It is not the necessary opposition between hope and suspicion that causes this generational divide, that is, but the *belief* in that opposition.

Yet Kaplan and Marx, astute and honest critics that they are, refuse to burn the bridge they have built across the generational divide. Although critics of Kaplan's generation lost their faith in America because of the Vietnam War and Watergate, leading them to decry "as fraudulent the presumed commitment of the American republic to the principles—or (as they said) the 'master narrative'—of the Enlightenment," nevertheless, Marx insists, they "reaffirmed their own commitment to the egalitarian principle at its core" ("Recovering," 120). Instead of renouncing that vital principle, they relocated it. They disconnected it from the idea of America as a whole and reattached it to the aspirations of those subordinate groups of Americans—women, African Americans, the working class—victimized by an irremediably discriminatory social system. This redirected application of egalitarian political ideals was a conspicuous—and highly revealing—exception to their all-but-total repudiation of the original American studies project (130). The younger generation of critics, in short, "represents the quotient of persistent if disappointed idealism" (130) shared by both sides of the divide.

For her part, Kaplan agrees with Marx that "disillusionment presupposes the loss of belief." Wondering "whether I do believe enough in the idea of America to want to protect democracy, civil liberties, racial equality, the Bill of Rights, checks and balances, and international obligations from the dismantling of these institutions by the Bush administration," Kaplan admits she "may believe enough in the Enlightenment to think that truth and knowledge, which this administration completely dismisses, should matter to politics" ("Truce," 146).

That Kaplan and Marx can agree about an idealism that motivates the scholarly critiques offered by their generations is noteworthy. Equally significant is the fact that while Marx sees idealism clearly in the work of his generation, Kaplan's idealism is so submerged as to require speculation (wondering "if I do believe") in order to make it visible. The difference is not the presence or absence of idealism, then, but its relative visibility, its acknowledged centrality. And that difference, I am arguing, is the result of the Cold War, a historical period overlooked, perhaps purposely, in the leap from the Popular Front to Vietnam that allows Marx and Kaplan to distance themselves from the intervening significance of the Cold War (even though Marx, who was sixteen in 1935, is more a part of the "myth and symbol" school of the 1950s than the Popular Front critics of the 1930s with whom he aligns himself, presumably to strengthen his defense of pre-divide critical politics). The generation of critics occluded by this genealogy remains as a trace only in the primary disagreement between Kaplan and Marx over nationalism.

It is hardly surprising that Marx and Kaplan would distance themselves from Cold War critics, who have became, in Matthew Cordova Frankel's words, "a bit of an embarrassment," their belief in "imaginative vitality" considered "analytically vague and ... politically suspect."[7] What is lost in this displacement is not simply a chapter in the conveyance of and changes to idealism from Marx to Kaplan, but a source for alternative configurations of idealism and critique that existed, paradoxically, during the Cold War, without being completely *of* it. Between Marx and Kaplan is less a divide than a series of translations and reconsiderations of hope. It is not their distance from Cold War criticism that brings Marx and Kaplan together, in other words, but their resemblances to it.

Before turning to the "missing" generation in this critical lineage, however, let me be clear about what I mean by "hope" here. Hopefulness is not optimism. Hope is far from the belief that "everything will work out fine," but rather the belief that no "fine" can be fine enough to bring satisfaction. Hope as I use the term is profoundly *dis*satisfied. An ideal can take singular shape (an ideal of justice, for instance), but the relationship between the particularity of the ideal and the impossibility of achieving such ideals is one of necessary disappointment, and that disappointment is close to what I am calling hope. Another way to put this is to say that when hope can be satisfied with something conceivable in the everyday world, satisfaction brings completion and therefore the end of hope. Hope in that case is better understood as want, the fulfillment of which at least potentially lies in the already existing world; whereas hope, vested in ideals that as such can never be materialized, exists in perpetual and productive incompletion.

This concept of hope owes much to Ernst Bloch, who in his 1960 "Can Hope Be Disappointed?" argues that we know "*well-founded* hope, mediated, guiding hope," because, unlike hopes with pre-packaged satisfactions, it is almost certainly accompanied by disappointment, without which "*it would not be hope.*"[8] Arising from the crises that unsettle the "actual," disappointment marks hope's continued refusal to "make peace with the existing world," frustrating any assertions of finality, predictability, or restriction that define the articulated objects of ill-founded hope. Such articulations, Bloch believed, produce an excess, and that excess, not the "real" that occasions it, is the stuff of hope.[9] Disappointment, for Bloch, is the hopeful denial of the facticity of the real, of the *is*, in favor of what he calls the "not-yet" that is "an enduring indeterminacy."[10] The practice of hope, seen through Bloch, therefore becomes the working over of the conditions of suffering and grief, of exclusion from the "actual" or interpellation within its hierarchical orders, into the indeterminacies that make freedom from and perpetual reformulation of social "actualities" possible.

Rather than trying to save hope from the supposed crisis of disappointment, then, we might welcome it as a form of crisis, which Gayatri Spivak calls "a *site of hope*." At the heart of both crisis and hope is, Spivak notes, "that moment which you cannot plan for," which forces "something inherited" to "jump into something other, and fix onto something that is opposed." Shaken loose from the stranglehold of precedent and convention, an unanticipated moment can rearrange the social landscape, generating possibilities that seem impossible under the regime of fact, nature, or truth. That is why, Spivak claims, "crisis is not the leap of faith, which hope brings *into* crisis, but rather the leap of hope."[11]

Hope, then, is the itch that prevents social possibility from solidifying into the tyranny of unchallengeable truth. For Bloch as for Spivak, power runs like a current through reality claims, and may be discerned and altered by those released from the real into the vigilantly fantastic position of hope. Discerning that "so-called facts are not standing still, but are circulating and developing," Bloch contends that hope attains the right—the obligation—not only to reveal but to judge the tendencies of the real. At the core of hope, then, is critique, which "does not forget about affliction and, even less, about exodus" but rather necessitates "socioeconomic analysis."[12] Through that analysis, hope seeks "the overthrow (as opposed to the hypocritical reinstallment) of all relations in which the human being is a degraded, subjugated, forsaken, and contemptible creature."[13] Out of this realization comes the possibility of hope despite parties, interests, and communities, opening new grounds for contestation, deliberation, and repair.

Put another way, we know what to critique because we also recognize, on some level, the possibility of a differently functioning version of the real. Idealism can be thought of as a voluntary withdrawal from a supposedly inevitable reality into an imaginative realm of potential; the distortion that arises on an ideal's return to the everyday is the basis of critique. To describe critical hope in terms of withdrawal and return gives it a misleading chronology, however, as both exist as a dynamic simultaneity of incommensurable versions of the "real." What counts as real is the version told from positions of power, discrediting competing versions as "naïveté" or "ignorance." But those fantasies represent someone's (often a collective someone's) ideal realness, and when these two accounts of reality rub, hope lies in the friction. Over time, as dissenting ideals take on language and press more confidently against the officially "real," hopefulness enables social engagement (hope is what, often after years of resignation, leads people to challenge conditions that deny the validity of their reality) and, more important, inspires resilience when social engagement proves painful and disappointing.

The practice of hope, seen through Bloch, becomes the unending working over of the conditions of suffering and grief, of exclusion from the "actual" or interpellation within its hierarchical orders. But the denial of the facticity or inevitability of the real is not simply a negative gesture, a repudiation and resistance. Rather, the refusal of the real is tied, like all critiques, to a powerful idealism, what Bloch calls the "not-yet" that is "an enduring indeterminacy."[14] For Bloch, this is why hope becomes most visible in liminal states such as daydreams, reveries, speculations, intuitions, what Michael Taussig calls "the half-awake world" in which "free-floating attention" generates hope.[15] Emerging from such states does not mean, for Taussig, "awakening from a period of inertia to one of action" but, rather, "piggy-backing, *moving* with the dream world," an imaginative "demystification and re-enchantment" of the real that gives hope "an electrifying role to play."[16]

When we deny the simultaneity of critique and hope, phrases like "dream world" and "enchantment" too easily rhyme with "trivial," "frivolous," "naïve," and "escapist." But the fantastic nature of hope—its imminent illuminations, to borrow Bloch's phrase—does not prevent it from being a potent political or cultural strategy within the already existing world. Rather, disappointment becomes the basis of what Ernst Laclau and Chantal Mouffe call radical democracy.[17] Hope, for Mouffe, marks yearnings for alternative presents, mediation between a desire and a demand. Without hope, there can be no passion and hence, for Mouffe, no politics, since a truly imaginative "social imaginary" requires passionate hope as a "kind of place-holder for all those things that cannot be reduced to interest or rationality," among which she includes "fantasies, desire, all those things that a rationalist approach is unable to understand in the very construction of human subjectivity and identity" (124). Because hope cannot and should not be satisfied—because of its perpetual disappointment—political progress, for Mouffe, comes only through hope's unfinished business, what she calls "the *radical impossibility* of democracy" (128). Arguing that democracy "is something that will always need to be a *project* which we are going to fight for, but knowing that we will never be able to reach it," Mouffe concludes that "there is no final goal—*democracy is a process*" (129).

Like Mouffe, Laclau observes that hope registers an unfulfilling present, being "always related to something which is lacking" (127). Laclau goes so far as to claim that "without hope, there is no society, because no society is able to cope with what simply exists." For him, however, hope is less a matter of incompleteness, as it is for Bloch and Mouffe, than of emptiness. Laclau describes how "empty signifiers" (127) allow groups with diverse demands who might otherwise be dispersed by the supplying of those demands to converge under the umbrella of an "empty" ideal, forming what he calls "a political frontier" (146). Such frontiers strengthen hope by allowing those who make demands to feel part of a larger—even a universal—collectivity, while also giving specificity to abstractions that become anchored, through particular demands, to historical contingencies (147–48). The exchange between universals and particularities generates what Laclau calls "a moment of hope" (130).

Laclau, Mouffe, Spivak, Bloch, and Taussig all demonstrate that hope need not be the willfully blind or naïve optimism, the self-interested want, or the deferred futurity it is often taken to be. Rather, where we find democracy failing, struggles disappointed, rhetoric evacuated, or society in crisis, we find hope as a powerful force for social change.

As I have already suggested, the kind of hopeful critique I am calling for here can be found not in our avant-garde future but, ironically, in our Cold War past, when critics used the romances of Nathaniel Hawthorne and Herman Melville to cultivate hopefulness as the explicit mingling of refusal and aspiration. While critics writing after the Cold War developed methodologies indebted to Cold War state strategies, critics who wrote during that period developed remarkably unsuspicious critical practices. Some may argue that this is because they supported rather than opposed the isolating individualism and xenophobic nationalism of the Cold War consensus. Yet midcentury critics produced work that, if exceptionalist, was vehemently critical of the Cold War United States, took up seemingly individualist myths to stimulate greater collective debate, and understood imagination not as a flight from political realities but as an ethical mediation between ideals and a corrupted civilization. In so doing Cold War critics such as Newton Arvin, Richard Chase, R. W. B. Lewis, Lewis Mumford, C. L. R. James, and Richard Poirier offer viable intimations of what a hopeful critique might look like. Without steering clear of political commentary (midcentury thinkers were at least as critical of the Eisenhower and Nixon administrations as Kaplan is of Bush's), the ultimate goal, for them, was the preservation of values, even as their frequent disagreements in private and in print showed that values were to a large extent the "empty signifiers" referred to by Laclau, and therefore the occasion for debate and redefinition.

A compact example of the critiques literary scholars leveled against midcentury America and the unsuspicious idealism that enables them can be found in the preface Mumford wrote in 1956–57 for the thirtieth anniversary reprinting of his *The Golden Day*.[18] As the nuclear arms race escalated and McCarthy's House Un-American Activities Committee wielded tyrannical power, Mumford's was a vision of the imagination as a space of social engagement beyond the totalizing binary logic of the Cold War superpowers. For Mumford, criticism's duty is to inspire ideals that counter the stultifying norms of Eisenhower's America, which he saw as underpinning logics of inevitable annihilation. He makes a claim for "the importance of the poet and the artist and the thinker, as a counterbalance to the over-valuation of . . . a civilization plainly threatened by barbarism from within" (x). That barbarism comprises, for Mumford, the hardheaded practicality and conventionality that made mandatory what he names "every kind of cowed conformity" (xxi).

Mumford set poets and thinkers in opposition particularly to scientists like Robert Oppenheimer who propelled the arms race only to regret their contributions once they realized the implications of the weapons they helped develop. One of his regrets as he evaluates the earlier edition of *The Golden Day*, Mumford admits, is how easily in 1926 he dismissed Henry Adams. Thirty years later, Mumford had come to believe that Adams was one of the first American writers to see the "disintegration of Western Civilization" (xxviii) that would result from scientific and mechanistic innovations if not tempered by artistic vision. "Long before the scientists concerned were sufficiently roused from their sleep-walking routines to realize what they were in fact doing," Mumford writes, Adams "saw, if they did not, that the train of events set in motion by the accidental discovery of the Becquerel rays would, in time, threaten the structure of civilization, making 'morality become police' and creating bombs of 'cosmic violence'" (xxviii–xxix). Making him his ally in opposing nuclear escalation, Mumford attributes to Adams the capacity to attest "to the meaning of the present crisis in world civilization" (xxix) through "the clairvoyance, as well as the scholarly historic insight, of his foreboding mind" (xxix).

Mumford was hardly alone in leveling such critiques. In 1955, during Eisenhower's first term as president, R. W. B. Lewis issued a cultural jeremiad in the form of an aesthetic treatise. For Lewis, the myth of the American Adam opposed a chauvinistic culture that had produced as its ideal the Man in the Gray Flannel Suit, valorizing a pathological social normality, rampant militarism, and the xenophobic self-policing of McCarthyism. "Ours is an age of containment," Lewis lamented; "we huddle together and shore up defenses" rather than "looking forward to new possibilities."[19] In Cold War America, Lewis believed, "a sterile awareness of evil uninvigorated by a sense of loss" had led to "a habit of forgetfulness" and "the expressed belief in achieved hopelessness" (9). To counter this defensive fatalism, Lewis argued for "the moral and artistic possibilities of a century ago" (196). Deprived of such aesthetic possibilities, epitomized by the romanticism of Hawthorne and Melville, "Our culture," Lewis warned, "will at the very least be a great deal drearier" (9).

A notable precursor of Mumford's concern for "world civilization," Lewis's faith in Romantic possibilities, and both men's perception of Cold War America as a culture in crisis, can be found in C. L. R. James. In his 1950 *American Civilization*, James asserts that "the bureaucratization and centralization of social life" had brought about "a state of hopelessness" and poisoned the American spirit that arose only in "mass movements, uprisings of the people, and unofficial individuals."[20] Proving that national exceptionalism and cogent social criticism are no more mutually exclusive than critique and idealism, James observes:

> Liberty, freedom, pursuit of happiness, free individuality had an actuality and a meaning in America which they had nowhere else. The European wrote and theorized about freedom in superb writings. Americans lived it. That tradition is the most vital tradition in the country today. Any idea that it is *merely* a tradition, used by unscrupulous July 4 politicians to deceive the people, destroys any possibility of understanding the crisis in America today. The essential conflict is between these ideals, hopes, aspirations, needs, which are still the essential part of the tradition, and the economic and social realities of present-day America.[21]

James's defense of the ideals of American nationhood marks him as one of the most powerful practitioners of hope at midcentury, a fact made all the more remarkable by his inhumane imprisonment by "unscrupulous July 4 politicians." Like his contemporaries, James used those ideals as the basis of a potent critique, without the necessity of denying idealism's place in the genesis of cultural analysis. And like those contemporaries, James forged his idealism from materials gleaned from Romantic literature—James found Melville in particular possessed of "a clear vision of the future"—from which he learned the value of aestheticizing social resistance, making from the literary imagination a democratic countersociality, represented by Melville's association of mariners, renegades, and castaways.[22]

Mumford's, James's, and Lewis's opposition of romanticism and Cold War culture was taken up in Richard Chase's 1949 study of the works of Melville, in which he condemned "the good and loving mediocre citizen," whose "ineradicable emotional needs" were fulfilled by a "machine-like existence."[23] In contrast to that deadened existence, Chase offered as an ideal the crew of the Melville's *Pequod*, who form "a heroic democracy" where a people "free, frank, and proud" stand "opposed to the modern Diana of ill fame, 'unanimous mediocrity.'"[24] The following year, Newton Arvin claimed Melville as a socialist who learned from "rubbing shoulders with the brutalized, exploited, and mostly illiterate seamen" how to value the "actualities of the human struggle."[25] In his 1957 *The American Novel and Its Tradition*, Chase aligned what he echoed Lewis in calling "aesthetic possibilities" with the "extreme range of experiences" characteristic of those who live "radical forms of alienation, contradiction, and disorder."[26] Within "the borderland of the human mind where the actual and the imaginary intermingle," Chase argued, romantic writers generate and value the "blissful, idyllic, erotic attachment to life and to one's comrades, which is the only promise of happiness."[27] Chase's notion of the romantic imagination as a liminal space built from social alienation and encouraging new possibilities for counter-sociality became, in 1967, Richard Poirier's "world elsewhere." Just as with Chase's "extremes of experience," for Poirier bizarre and exaggerated aesthetics are "an exercise of consciousness momentarily set free," a freedom most visible in the romance and its focus on the "foolish, preposterous, and sexually irregular."[28] Restricted within a boundaried "consciousness" that was the interior equivalent of the defensively bordered nation, the reader of romance, given a momentary "world elsewhere," could become imaginatively transnational, "a law unto himself," ignoring "all outward allegiance, whether to nature or society."[29]

As Poirier's reference to the "sexually irregular," Chase's to the love of comrades, and Mumford's to "relationships and values" that are "somehow illicit" (xix) suggest, the ideal imagination was for these critics related to a particularly idealized same-sex sociality (an ideal that surfaces in much queer theory today). For many midcentury critics, the imagination, in an age that enforced separations between people though fearful suspicion, became a space of queer affiliations made between those Mumford called "outcasts, recluses, exiles" and whom James called "outcasts, renegades, and castaways," who could save what both critics called "world civilization" through their imaginative reformulations of values tried and found wanting in their "real world" context. Although the collective movements imagined by James do not often appear in midcentury criticism, they persist in sociality's queer potential for social transformation. For these critics, sociality marks the emergence of alternative values into a hostile world, and therefore was consistently a means for challenging Cold War constructions of the real and imagining other, more ideal worlds. Arvin, for instance, believed in "the unappeased, perhaps unappeasable, but never quite abandoned reaching out for the perfect mutuality of an ideal friendship."[30] Those friendships brought forth "all that was visionary, enthusiastic, and illusory in the romantic habit of mind."[31]

There are, of course, important differences among these critics. And it would be disingenuous to claim that there are no currents of national exceptionalism in these works. The repeated use of *our* and *us*, the focus on *American* romanticism, and the glib references to "the American mind" show otherwise. If I choose selectively in these works, focusing on similarities rather than differences, purporting to find there what I wish to find here, it is because I want what Van Wyck Brooks called a usable past, as they did in turning to romanticism. That past is a creation, not a discovery, not a destiny ("Discover, invent a usable past we certainly can," Brooks wrote, "and that is what a vital criticism always does"[32]). Making that past requires intellectual risks, even, perhaps, irresponsibility. To admit to selective choice, biased reading, critical desire, or inconclusion (and what criticism does not involve these?) is to acknowledge both collaboration with and the inaccessibility of the past. It is also to make explicit one's critical hopefulness, rather than hiding it behind claims to unimplicated objectivity. But it will almost certainly prove embarrassing,

which is what keeps in place the exhausted practices of critique with which
I began. Nothing is as vulnerable to criticism—if not to say mockery—as
hope, often dismissed as naïve, provincial, or shallow. As Taussig notes,
"a lot of intellectual activity . . . correlates lack of hope with being smart,
or lack of hope with profundity."[33] But embarrassment may be preferable
to the vertigo produced by literary criticism's proliferating "turns," man-
ifestations of a twitchy dissatisfaction with a Cold War critique ill suited
to a post-Cold War world. In that world, the best thing we can do is,
perhaps, to turn back.

⌒

"What was it possible to think or do at a certain moment of the past," Eve
Sedgwick asks, "that no longer is? And how are those possibilities to be
found, unfolded, allowed to move and draw air and seek new voices and
uses in the very different disciplinary ecology of even a few decades' distance?"[34] Good questions, and not ones with easy answers. But in "the
current climate of retrospection," Rita Felski suggests, as we "reassess
methods of reading that have come to seem stale and unsurprising" we
might find our future in our past.[35] It is not that we can recreate the past,
nor should we. But efforts to invent useable and hopeful pasts might help
create what Taussig calls "an incandescent present" that "can dismantle
the institutions of the present and then presumably build them anew."[36]
That may be what Mary Zournazi suggests when she calls hope "a kind
of future nostalgia" to which she attributes "the spark of hope—the idea
of other histories being brought into the present."[37]

In 1955, R. W. B. Lewis wrote, "We stand in need of more stirring
impulses, of greater perspectives and more penetrating controversies,"
disrupting "the sheer dullness of unconscious repetition" and invigorating the sense of "unbounded possibility."[38] Four years later, Newton
Arvin accused his colleagues in literary studies of peddling "the cant of
pessimism."[39] Arvin asserted, "We hug our negations, our doubts, our
disbeliefs to our chests, as if our moral and intellectual dignity depended

on them."[40] The echoes of these exasperated complaints in many contemporary critiques of critique suggest that the Cold War is not over yet, at least not in literary criticism. But it is starting to be.

And as it comes to an end, literary critics are creating desire-lines around what appears to be an epistemological impasse represented by the word "critique." Following their paths, however, it is hard not to get lost in the proliferating "turns" as we orient (and disorient and reorient) ourselves through what has come to seem more a marsh than a field. Without understanding the changing historical circumstances that, to borrow from Raymond Williams, make one form of critique recede and another emerge, it is hard to turn without finding oneself facing the wall one tried to circumvent, or turning too quickly away from what that wall may have supported. Rather than hasty and unself-conscious "new" theories of reading or entrenched defenses of the same old same old, we might need what Chase called "a kind of thought which is bounteous, in the sense that it is open-minded, skeptical, and humanist."[41] We might, in other words, untwist ourselves and give hope its turn.

PART II

Turn-by-Turn Directions:
Transnational, Hemispheric,
Oceanic

Chapter 5

⟋

Of Turns and Paradigm Shifts: Humanities, Science, and Transnational American Studies

RALPH BAUER

When Shelley Fisher Fishkin publicized the phrase "transnational turn" in her 2004 presidential address to the American Studies Association, she noted that her remarks were occasioned by many recent books and articles published during the 1990s and early 2000s that challenged the "national *paradigm* of the United States as a clearly bordered geographical and political space"—books and articles by border theorists such as Gloria Anzaldúa, critics of American Empire such as Amy Kaplan, and Inter-Americanist literary historians such as José David Saldívar.[1] More recently, Paul Jay, in *Global Matters* (2010), has celebrated the "transnational turn" that literary studies have taken in recent years as one of those "paradigm shifts" that periodically invigorate our field.[2] Many more intermittent examples of the proliferating iteration "paradigm shift" in reference to the emergence of transnational approaches in literary and cultural studies could be cited here, but (as far as I am able to tell) the first literary scholar to use the phrase in this sense appears to have been Priscilla Wald, who, in a 1998 issue of *American Literary History*, declared that American Studies was in the middle of a "paradigm shift" from a national to a transnational frame of reference. As she observed, the call for a transnational perspective

> resounds not only in American studies, but throughout the academy and elsewhere in US culture. . . . The abundance of terms invoked to describe it—*critical internationalism, globalism, transnationalism*—illustrates the point: scholars and theorists, aware of the need for a *new paradigm*, are still in the process of trying to understand how to theorize it.[3]

What do these literary and cultural critics mean by referring to the emergence of transnational American studies as a "paradigm shift"? The English word "paradigm" is rooted in the Latin word *paradigma*, which was used primarily in the study of grammar but originally derives from a Greek word that simply meant "pattern" or "example." In *Prior Analytics*, Aristotle distinguishes paradigmatic reasoning from both inductive and deductive reasoning. "It is evident," he writes, that a paradigm "is neither as a part to the whole nor as a whole to a part, but rather as a part to a part, when both are below the same thing but one of them is familiar."[4] As Giorgio Agamben explains this passage, paradigms are singular historical phenomena, but they "obey not the logic of the metaphorical transfer of meaning but the analogical logic of the example. . . . More akin to allegory than to metaphor, the paradigm is a singular case that is isolated from its context only insofar as, by exhibiting its own singularity, it makes intelligible a new ensemble, whose homogeneity it itself constitutes." Where inductive reason proceeds from the particular to the universal and deductive reason from the universal to the particular, the "paradigm is defined by a third and paradoxical type of movement, which goes from the particular to the particular." In fact, it calls into question "the dichotomous opposition between the particular and the universal which we are used to seeing as inseparable from procedures of knowing, and presents instead a singularity irreducible to any of the dichotomy's two terms." But as Agamben also explains, the modern English phrase "paradigm shift" has a more specific connotation, being coined as it was neither in linguistics nor in the humanities but rather in the history and philosophy of science, specifically by Thomas Kuhn's spectacularly influential and now classic *The Structure of Scientific Revolutions* (1962), which has left a lasting mark on poststructuralist historiography of science. Kuhn's notion of a scientific "paradigm" clearly influenced, for example, Michel Foucault's conception of the notion of an "episteme." Although the latter claimed to have read Kuhn's book only *after* having written *The Order of Things* (1966) and often labored to disassociate his archaeological approach to the history of knowledge from Kuhn's, Agamben has demonstrated not only the proximity of the two philosophers' concepts but also the far-reaching methodological influence of the idea of "paradigm" in post-structuralist critiques of knowledge and power (including his own), and in concepts such as panopticon, the great confinement, the confession, the investigation, and examination, or the state of exception.[5]

Given Wald's strong interest in the intersections between literature and science, her choice of terminology to describe the transnational turn in American literary studies may not have been coincidental. Thus, in *Contagious* (2008), she demonstrates how the modern "outbreak narrative" not only "fuses the transformative force of myth with the authority of science" but also "animates the figures and maps the spaces of global modernity" on a transnational scale.[6] However, the transference of the Kuhnian notion of scientific paradigm shifts to describe recent developments in literary and cultural criticism, such as the "transnational turn" in American literary studies, also raises a number of questions. First, to what extent is the Kuhnian notion of a paradigm shift in the history of science applicable to the humanities in general and to the "transnational turn" in American Studies in particular?[7] Second, what is at stake in such "sideways" directional metaphors conceptualizing developments in our historiographic and critical orientations in both science studies and the humanities since the later decades of the twentieth century—"shifts" and "turns," rather than, say, the late Neil Armstrong's famous metaphors of "steps" and "leaps" (uttered seven years after the first publication of

Structure)? Third, what role has the interdisciplinary exchange between the history of science and the humanities played in the transnational turn in American literary studies? And fourth, what can the sciences and the humanities learn from each other as concepts such as paradigm shift travel across disciplinary boundaries?

In this chapter, I would like to explore the implications of the migration of Kuhn's notion of a paradigm shift between the natural sciences and the humanities, especially in regard to an understanding of the transnational turn in American literary studies. In a special issue of *American Literary History* devoted to the transnational turn in literary studies, Geoffrey Harpham has recently pointed out that the humanities have underwritten a nationalist organization of knowledge at least since Wilhelm von Humboldt's and Matthew Arnold's rearticulation of humanism in terms of the academic form of the modern humanities. The study of national literatures as practiced in discrete departments in the modern university "assume[d] the role of the 'spiritual' center not just of the humanities but of the university as a whole." In an era when the truth claims and methodologies of the modern Western natural sciences have transcended national boundaries to the point of attaining an almost global hegemony, "the cultural role played by the humanities," Harpham suggests, "has been to counter the epistemic optimism of the sciences" and to serve as a retainer of distinctly nationalist identities and traditions in the West. Nevertheless, Harpham encourages us to "overcome the longstanding humanist antipathy toward the sciences and begin to imagine a disciplinary reconfiguration that would include, within the larger field of the humanities, those areas of science and technology that address the question of the human."[8] Wai Chee Dimock, in her introduction to the special issue of *American Literary History*, agrees, writing that "our discipline . . . has internalized the form of the nation and reproduced it in the very form of our expertise." She continues:

Humanisitic fields are divided by nations: the contours of our knowledge are never the contours of humanity; they follow the borders of a territorial regime. . . . Nowhere is the adjective *American* more secure than when it is offered as *American Literature*; nowhere is it more naturalized, more reflexively affirmed as inviolate. American literature is a self-evident field, as American physics and American biology are not. The disciplinary form of the humanities is "homeland defense" at its deepest and most unconscious.

In this context, Dimock argues that "interdisciplinary work is urgently needed, for—as evidenced by physics and biology—the reign of *homo nationalis* is less stringent in virtually every other academic field."[9] While Wald's *Contagious* might serve as an apt example to illustrate Dimock's point, the story about the interconnections between globalization and the rise of nationalism ("imagined immunities") that Wald tells does not begin with Typhoid Mary in the twentieth century but reaches back at least to what has been called the Columbian Exchange during the late fifteenth and early sixteenth centuries.[10] Indeed, in *early* American studies, both the reign of the *homo nationalis* and the borderline between the natural sciences and the humanities have long been less securely ensconced, as much of their archive not only predates the historical formation of the modern nation state, the modern sciences, and the modern humanistic disciplines but also defies the modern distinction between the scientific and the literary. Yet, as recent early Americanist scholarship has amply demonstrated, the early modern colonial projects chronicled by the early American archive since the late fifteenth century played a crucial role in these very formations of modernity. Not coincidentally, much of this early Americanist work has focused on the early modern discourse of natural history—a discourse that both antedated and facilitated the modern split between the natural sciences and the humanities.[11]

Below, I reflect on the contributions that early American studies can make (and has made) to the current conversation about the interdisciplinary intersections between the natural sciences and the humanities as well as about the transnational turn. One the one hand, there remains a fundamental difference between what Kuhn called "paradigm shifts" in the natural sciences and critical "turns" in the humanities. Indeed, it is arguably their very resistance to the "paradigmatic" relationships among knowledge traditions implicit in the empirical sciences' "hermeneutic of discovery" that lends the humanities their disciplinary coherence in what Hans Georg Gadamer once called a "hermeneutics of recognition."[12] Unlike the paradigm shift in the natural sciences, critical "turns" in the humanities (such as the transnational turn in American studies) occur in the form of additions of new models that grow out of, overlap, and coexist with established ones, frequently competing with but hardly ever invalidating or replacing one another. Humanistic turns also frequently occur in form of re-turns of older models with a "twist" (the return of "inter-American" and "pan-American" studies of the 1960s as "hemispheric American studies" in the 2000s, for example).[13] The humanistic "turn," in other words, presupposes a continuous and dialogic relationship between tradition and discovery. By contrast, a "revolution" in the modern natural sciences is predicated on an antithetical relationship between tradition and discovery—not a re-volution in the sense of a return to an older stage of purity or perfection, but rather an apocalyptic (or revelatory) *over-turn* of tradition by discovery that supposedly results in a step closer to objective reality. On the other hand, it was precisely Kuhn's concept of the "paradigm," exposing the important role tradition plays also in the history of science—a historicizing impulse he derived from the humanities—that has opened the history of science to the critical practices of the humanities in the wake of New Historicism, postcolonial theory, and especially critical science studies as theorized by disciplinary "hybrids" such as Michel Serres and Bruno Latour. In turn, the opening of archives (such as natural history) not traditionally considered "literary" in (proto-) national literary history has energized various transnational perspectives in (early) American studies, including trans- and circum-Atlantic as well as hemispheric ones, hereby engendering new opportunities for collaboration between science and literary studies. The following two sections of this chapter will reflect on the relationship between a scientific paradigm shift and the humanistic turn with regard to the emergence of transnational American studies. The third section offers suggestions on how critical science studies have informed and might continue to inform transnational perspectives in (early) American literary studies. Finally, I offer some brief reflections on the role early transnational American studies may play in our understanding of the historical relationship between the modern natural sciences and the humanities by considering a seventeenth-century example from present-day Colombia, Juan Rodríguez Freyle's *The Conquest and Discovery of the Kingdom of New Granada*, in light of Bruno Latour's critique of what he calls the "modern constitution" of the scientific object. I will suggest that the dual processes of purification and hybridization Latour sees as foundational in making the epistemic hegemony of the modern natural sciences do not begin with Robert Boyle's air pump in seventeenth-century England but rather with the Spanish conquest of the New World, in the crucible of the sixteenth-century American tropics.

The Kuhnian Paradigm Shift

Before considering the migration of the phrase "paradigm shift" into the humanities, let me briefly recap some of the main ideas of Kuhn's *The Structure of Scientific Revolutions*. Kuhn there challenged an earlier generation of historians, most prominently represented by Karl Popper, according to whom the history of science could be understood in terms of a gradual approximation of knowledge to an ever closer (though never complete) correspondence with a reality objectively "out there" by method of "falsification"—the constant testing of theory against empirical evidence, as well as its refinement or abandonment in the face of any "negative" evidence (i.e., evidence that contradicts the theory). Against this gradualist, progressivist, and positivist model of the history of science as "revolution in permanence,"[14] Kuhn emphasized the essentially conservative nature of what he called "normal science"—the kind of science that most scientists do most of the time during tradition-bound periods of epistemological certainty and stability. Normal science, in Kuhn's terms, is a sort of "puzzle solving" in which knowledge accumulates in research agendas that fill out the blank spaces of the unknown by extending the logic of the prevailing paradigm but that essentially leave its logic intact. Fundamental changes in these practices, or paradigm shifts, occur only occasionally in the history of science and, when they do, disrupt and overturn the older paradigm.[15]

Although Kuhn's definition of a "paradigm" remained notoriously amorphous in the first edition of *Structure*,[16] he (and many subsequent commentators) later explained that it is "what the members of a scientific community share," a certain set of assumptions adjudicating the relevancy, appropriateness, or significance of certain questions, methodologies, or "facts."[17] A paradigm, in other words, is a *tradition* that prevails among certain groups of scientists and is passed down to subsequent generations. As Peter Burke has explained, a paradigm "acts like a cultural grid or filter. . . [and] allows some aspects of reality to be seen more clearly at the expense of hiding others."[18] Shifts in these paradigms occur, according to Kuhn, not so much as the result of a single new discovery that contradicts an existing theory; rather they occur as the result of a gradual accumulation of empirical "anomalies" that cannot be explained in terms of the old paradigm and that eventually overturn the old paradigm only when favored by social, professional, ideological, and cultural contingencies in which scientific practices are always embedded. A paradigm shift, Kuhn wrote, begins with the "recognition that nature has somehow violated the paradigm-induced expectations that govern normal science" and

> then continues with a more or less extended exploration of the area of anomaly. And it closes only when the paradigm theory has been adjusted so that that the anomalous has become the expected. Assimilating a new sort of fact demands a more than

additive adjustment of theory, and until that adjustment is completed—until the scientist has learned to see nature in a different way—the new fact is not quite a scientific fact at all.[19]

Perhaps unsurprisingly, historians of science in the 1960s did not, by and large, give a warm welcome to Kuhn's thesis. They especially objected to his idea of science as an essentially conservative intellectual endeavor, punctuated only sporadically by periods of noncumulative breaks. They also objected to his notion that the history of scientific research agendas, questions, and findings should not only be driven by empirical discovery and objective reason but also *mediated* by social and cultural networks— that scientific truth, in other words, was historically contingent. The most troublesome aspect of Kuhn's account for his contemporary historians of science was an implicit denial that the history of science can be understood in terms of objective progress—that modern physics, for example, is objectively more "correct" than, and therefore superior to, Aristotelian physics and not just a different set of questions and answers that served "equally well" in their time and culture.[20]

Partly due, perhaps, to the largely hostile reception of Kuhn's works by his contemporaries in history of science, his influence has been felt most keenly not in the natural sciences but rather in the social sciences and in the arts and humanities, where it was crowned as *the* book published in the twentieth-century, cited most frequently in the period 1976–83.[21] But there may yet be another explanation for why Kuhn's account should have been most influential in fields outside the history of science: in his "Postscript" to the 1969 edition of *The Structure of Scientific Revolutions*, he revealed that its theses were largely "borrowed from other fields." "Historians of literature, of music, of the arts, of political development, and of many other human activities," he wrote, "have long described their subjects in the same way. Periodization in terms of revolutionary breaks in style, taste, and institutional structure have [sic] been among their standard tools. If I have been original with respect to concepts like these, it has mainly been by applying them to the sciences, fields which had been widely thought to develop in a different way."[22]

It is thus in their opposition to the progressivist understanding of the history of knowledge as "revolution in permanence" (and to Armstrong's linear metaphors of steps and leaps) that the recent metacritical language of the "turn" in the humanities shares certain assumptions with the Kuhnian "paradigm shift" in the history of science. Yet, despite the fact that his notion of "normal science" was admittedly borrowed from the humanities, Kuhn explicitly insisted that the humanities lack "paradigms"— at least in the sense he defined them—and that it is precisely the existence of paradigms that distinguishes the natural sciences from other fields of inquiry. As Kuhn noted, one of the characteristics of "paradigms' in the sciences is their diachronic relationship and the lack (or rarity) of synchronic overlap. This is so because, according to Kuhn, "normally, the members of a mature scientific community work from a single paradigm or from a closely related set." The social sciences and the humanities, by contrast, lack "the unparalleled insulation of mature scientific communities from the demands of the laity and of everyday life. . . . Just because he is working only for an audience of colleagues, an audience that share his own values and beliefs, the scientist can take a single set of standards for granted."[23] Although more recent approaches in critical science studies have unmasked the fiction of scientific detachment from the social and political world,[24] Kuhn's point about the singularity of the natural sciences in this regard still stands: the natural sciences rarely admit of the simultaneous existence of multiple paradigms (the twentieth-century coexistence of quantum mechanics and general relativity in physics being a rare exception in the history of modern science). Their paradigmatic relationship, in other words, is built on the principle of supersession. Changes in the humanities and social sciences ("turns"), by contrast, rarely occur on the principle of paradigmatic supersession, and to the extent that they are occasionally presented as such, they tend to be greeted with skepticism if not outright hostility by the profession.[25]

The Transnational Turn as Paradigm Shift?

To what degrees is Kuhn's analysis about the differences between the natural sciences and the humanities borne out by recent metacritical discourses about the history of the transnational turn in American literary studies? Carolyn Porter, in a seminal statement in her 1994 *American Literary History* article "What We Know That We Don't Know," suggested that the research agendas focused on writers rediscovered by ethnic minority and women recovery projects had begun to

> undermine the fundamental terms by which American literary history must be comprehended and taught. Both the historical and the geographical frames once dictated by the national and nationalist narrative of the US are collapsing, no longer propped up by either the synecdoche of a US read as "America" or the metanarrative by which "American" served to predicate human history's manifest/millennial destiny.[26]

In other words, the transnational turn is the product of a theoretical adjustment to the discovery (or recovery) of "new" literary archives that necessitates not their inclusion into the paradigm but rather a " 're-think[ing]," as Porter put it, of "what we thought we already knew in the context of what we all know that we do not know—how to reconceptualize a field that is clearly no longer mappable by any of the traditional coordinates."[27] In practice, however, the transnational scholarship that has been published since Porter's programmatic essay has led not to a "collapse" of national frameworks but to something that more closely resembles a palimpsest, where transnational geographic frameworks are superimposed on national ones without the latter becoming entirely erased. Thus, Robert Levine and Caroline Levander, in their introduction to *Hemispheric American Studies*, propose the study of a national (American) literature in the context of a "hemispheric paradigm." By this they mean to "avoid some of the pitfalls of those area studies models in which . . . language studies stand in for method, geographical area stands in for disciplinary theory, and indigeneity offers the utopian promise of authenticity." Instead, they mean to "approach the hemisphere and the shifting, evolving nations and regions within it from a spatiotemporal vantage point where comparative approaches bring out the contingency of both the nation and region." From such a perspective, "retaining a national referent . . . of necessity entails an ongoing recognition of the processes through which nations are embedded in and develop gradually out of local and transnational circumstances."[28] Indeed, as Winfried Fluck has observed, there are currently not one but multiple models of transnational scholarship—he identifies two, which he calls "aesthetic transnationalism" and "political transnationalism"—each of which has its own points of origins, institutional and social contexts, and political agendas that ultimately grow out of older American studies models that were focused on the nation-state.[29] None of the forms of transnationalism that are currently dominant in American studies are "a new beginning," he observes; they "have merely extended long-dominant paradigms beyond borders." Fluck continues,

> The transnational can thus not be separated from the national from which it takes its point of departure. In effect, one constitutes the other, and both remain interdependent. Seen from this perspective, transnational American studies, despite their own programmatic claims to go beyond the American nation-state, also imply theories for and about "America."[30]

Although Fluck may be correct in asserting that the various models of transnational American studies he discusses are but an extension of national American studies, one may take issue with his accusation that the practitioners of transnational American studies have "created the false impression . . . that they are doing something new and potentially revolutionary." Most theoreticians and practitioners of transnational American studies, such as Levine and Levander, as well as Jay, have openly acknowledged that their forays into the transnational have grown out of reconceptualizations of (nationalist) American literary history as it grew out of the 1960s, 1970s, and 1980s. Thus, Jay writes that "the roots in political movements outside of the academy and theoretical developments within it that run back to the early 1960s"—developments such as the civil, women's, gay, and lesbian rights movements, as well as the Chicana/o movement. "These demographic changes brought a revolution," he continues, "in both the texts and the issues treated by scholars in literary and cultural studies. Work on women writers and African American, Latina/o, Native American, Asian American, gay, lesbian, and queer literatures transformed the curriculum of literature departments and the research agenda of its faculty in ways that dramatically reconfigured the historical and geographical boundaries of traditional practices." At the same time, Jay attributes the transnational turn to the impact of the postcolonial studies movement, which had "challenge[d] the primacy of discrete national literatures and what seemed like their insular concerns, providing a framework for studying literature and culture in a transnational context that moved beyond the explicitly questioned older Eurocentric models of 'comparative' analysis." The transnational turn in literary studies thus "began in earnest when the study of minority, multicultural, and postcolonial literatures began to intersect with work done under the auspices of the emerging study of globalization."[31]

The transnational turn was not, then, a paradigm shift (in the Kuhnian sense of the term) that makes a claim to having overturned, invalidated, and superseded older models. While the metacritical "turn" and the scientific "paradigm shift" share the notion that the history of disciplines does not proceed on a linear principle of accretion, a "turn" in the humanities does not make an absolute and exclusive claim to truth in the way "paradigms" do in the sciences. Although a critical turn may put certain perspectives in or out of vogue, even to the point of dominance of one over another perspective, such dominance is based not on a claim to superior explanatory power of the object of inquiry or to being more "true" than a previous one based on a new empirical "discovery"; rather, it is the result of critical debate and "dialogue," as Gadamer pointed out, that puts considerations of subject positions at its front and center.[32]

If Kuhn's notion of a paradigm shift in the natural sciences has limited value for understanding critical turns in the humanities, it has opened the history of science to critical historicist analysis as practiced in the humanities by undermining the apocalyptic progressivist accounts of earlier generations of historians of science.[33] More important for my present purposes, by applying the historicizing impulse of the humanities to the history of science, it has enabled us to think historically about the relationship between the natural sciences and the humanities. How did it come to be, for example, that the modern natural sciences—their methods and hermeneutics of discovery—were able to arrogate to themselves an exclusivist and totalizing claim to truth after the break-up of Renaissance humanism—to the detriment, as Gadamer lamented, of the truth claims of the humanities' hermeneutics of recognition? And why is it that, after the breakup of Renaissance humanism, the modern natural sciences came to be organized transnationally while the modern humanities came to be organized nationally? Although these are obviously not questions that can be answered comprehensively here, I want to suggest some of the ways the interdisciplinary encounter between critical science studies and transnational literary scholarship on the early Americas can make significant contributions to our understanding of the history of the scientific "paradigm" and its ability to make an absolutist claim to truth in modern Western culture. In particular, I want to suggest that the sixteenth-century European conquest of the Americas played a crucial role in the modern elevation of the empirical method—only one among many in premodern scientia—to a position of transnational hegemony at the expense of the scholastic and humanist epistemologies that had previously laid the ground rules of scientific inquiry in the Latin West.[34]

Science, Humanities, and the Transnational
Turn in Early American Studies

The classic accounts following in the wake of Kuhn's *Structure* were, of course, the works of Michel Foucault, who did not confine himself to the natural sciences proper but attempted a more ambitious account of the history of the entire organization of Western knowledge; instead of Kuhnian "paradigms," he therefore proposed the more comprehensive term "episteme." Yet Foucault's works, like Kuhn's *Structure*, remained decidedly Eurocentric in their perspective, neglecting to consider in a sustained way the role European expansionism and colonialism played in the history of scientific or epistemic change. Thus, as Edward Said has suggested, much of what Foucault wrote "makes greatest sense not as an ethnocentric model of how power is exercised in modern society, but between Europe and the rest of the world," of the way Europe produced, occupied, ruled, and exploited the non-European world.[35]

The recent works of anthropologists of science such as Serres and Latour have followed up on the postcolonial critique of the history of knowledge. Latour, for example, has theorized the hegemony of the empirical sciences in modern Western culture as the result of an interplay between two ideological processes he calls "purification" and "hybridization" (the latter term appearing interchangeably in his work with "translation" or "mediation"). While "purification" separates nature from culture (mute things from speaking citizens, objects from subjects), "hybridization" re-mixes them in cunning ways; that is, it redeploys "nature" in the realm of culture and "culture" in the realm of nature. "Modernity," Latour argues, is a sort of "Constitution" that depends on the covert *collaboration* of the two processes of purification and hybridization even while it ostensibly *separates* the two by obscuring the latter. "The essential point of this modern Constitution is that it renders the work of mediation that assembles hybrids invisible, unthinkable, unrepresentable. . . . *The modern Constitution allows the expanded proliferation of the hybrids whose existence, whose very possibility it denies*" (34). In other words, the more modern Western culture insists on purification and disavows hybridization, the more it actually proliferates hybrids. If the covert connections between purification and hybridization are exposed, modernity and all its promises—progress, objectivity, historicism, and so on—vanish into the thin air they have been all along. (Hence, Latour's argument that "we have never been modern.")

For the most part, Latour argues, the moderns have been remarkably successful in their cunning duplicity of hiding the hybrids that purification spawns. In recent history, however, hybrids have proliferated to the point of creating a crisis in the modern project. While some of these recent historical developments have still been easily assigned to the modern notion of "progress" or its enemy ("declension")—the Internet and the Iranian Revolution respectively, for example—others cannot unequivocally be assigned to either one—the atom bomb or "surgical" drone strikes, for example. It is this crisis—resulting from proliferating hybrids mixing the "pure" realm of science with politics, ethics, religion, and so on—that has exposed modernity to the possibility of ethnographic description: "Modernization consists in continually exiting from an obscure age that mingled the needs of society with scientific truth, in order to enter into a new age that will finally distinguish clearly what belongs to atemporal nature and what comes from humans, what depends on things and what belongs to signs. Modern temporality arises from a superposition of the difference between past and future with another difference, so much more important, between mediation and purification" (71). Thus, the moderns want to have it both ways: "they can mobilize Nature at the heart of social relationships, even as they leave Nature infinitely remote from human beings; they are free to make and unmake their society, even as they render its laws ineluctable, necessary and absolute" (37).

Latour has provided here a useful conceptual model for understanding the modern hermeneutics of discovery undergirding the scientific "paradigm" in terms of purification and hybridization. Moreover, he has called attention to the *colonial nexus* in which modernity's "Constitution" emerged: "Native Americans were not mistaken," he writes, "when they accused the Whites of having forked tongues. By separating the relations of political power from the relations of scientific reasoning, while continuing to shore up power with reason and reason with power, the moderns have always had two irons in the fire. They have become invincible." Thus, Latour argues, the separation of mediation (hybridization) and purification is only one of the two "Great Divides" by which modernity legitimates itself—the "Internal Great Divide." The other, the "External Great Divide," is that between the moderns ("Us"), who distinguish between nature and culture, and those premoderns ("Them") who do not: medieval and non-Western people. "The Internal Great Divide accounts for the External Great Divide," he writes,

> we are the only ones who differentiate absolutely between Nature and Culture, between Science and Society, whereas in our eyes all the others—whether they are Chinese or Amerindian, Azande or Barouya—cannot really separate what is knowledge from what is Society, what is sign from what is thing, what comes from Nature as it is from what their cultures require. Whatever they do, however adapted, regulated and functional they may be, they will always remain blinded by this confusion; they are prisoners of the social and of language alike. Whatever we do, however criminal, however imperialistic we may be, we escape from the prison of the social or of language to gain access to things themselves through a providential exit gate, that of scientific knowledge. The internal partition between humans and nonhumans defines a second partition—an external one this time—through which the moderns have set themselves apart from the premoderns. For Them, Nature and Society, signs and things, are virtually coextensive. For Us they should never be. Even though we might still recognize in our own societies in madness, children, animals, popular culture and women's bodies, we believe our duty is to extirpate ourselves from those hor-

rible mixtures as forcibly as possible by no longer confusing
what pertains to mere social preoccupations and what pertains
to the real nature of things. (99–100)

While calling our attention to the colonial dimension of the modern
Constitution, Latour does not elucidate the specifics of the relationship
between the Internal and the External Great Divides he theorizes. Indeed, he suggests that the latter was merely an "exportation" of the former: "If Westerners had been content with trading and conquering, loot-
ing and dominating, they would not distinguish themselves radically
from other tradespeople and conquerors. But no, they invented science,
an activity totally distinct from conquest and trade, politics, and morality" (97). He seems to assume, in other words, that the modern hermeneutics of discovery in the natural sciences legitimated colonial conquest, rather than colonial conquest the modern hermeneutics of
discovery. Thus, he elaborates his notion of a modern "Constitution" in a
brilliant reading of Stephen Shapin's and Simon Schaefer's seminal *Levi-
athan and the Airpump* (1985), a socio-historical study of the confrontation between Robert Boyle and Thomas Hobbes during the English Civil
War over the relationship between science and politics, as well as over
the status of experimental science, which form (in Latour's view) the beginning of the modern divide between scientific objects and political
subjects: while Hobbes resorted to mathematical demonstration, Boyle
employed empirical eyewitness testimonies of the "natural" effects artifi-
cially produced in his vacuum pump, which, he claimed, were "matters
of fact" that spoke for themselves.

> The natural power that Boyle and his many scientific descen-
> dants defined in opposition to Hobbes, the power that allows
> mute objects to speak through the intermediary of loyal and dis-
> ciplined scientific spokesperson, offer a significant guarantee: it
> is not men who make Nature; Nature has always existed and has
> always already been there; we are only discovering its secrets. . . .

> Boyle and his countless successors go on and on both construct-
> ing Nature artificially and stating that they are discovering;
> Hobbes and the newly defined citizens go on and on construct-
> ing the Leviathan by dint of calculation and social force, but they
> recruit more and more objects in order to make it last. (30–31)

Thus, Latour posits Boyle and Hobbes as the Founding Fathers of sorts of
the modern "Constitution" that he sees as the root of modernity. But while
he goes on to trace the history of this Constitution through the modern
Western philosophical tradition (from Kant to Hegel, Habermas, and
Derrida), he fails to address the question of the *prehistory* of the double
"Great Divides" he theorizes. Nor does he offer any specifics about either
Boyle's or Hobbes's interest in or commitment to the colonial project.

In fact, Boyle was not only the "father" of modern experimental science but also a director of the East India Company and governor of the
Society for Propagation of the Gospel in New England.[36] Likewise,
Hobbes was not only the "father" of modern political philosophy but
also an heir to a line of theorists of mercantilist economics that reaches
back to the sixteenth-century Spanish Empire in America.[37] The colonial
nexus from which Latour's modern Constitution emerged is evident in
the omnipresent reference to the New World in the iconography with
which the empiricist paradigm of the "new" (i.e., Baconian) sciences was
articulated in the seventeenth century. Thus, Boyle's contemporary and
fellow Fellows in the Royal Society of London, the alchemist Noah Biggs,
described his investigations into the structure of matter as an inquiry
into the "America of nature."[38]

Perhaps the visually most poignant image capturing the modern
quest for purification comes in the frontispiece of Andrés García de Céspedes' *Regimiento de navegación* (Madrid, 1606), from which the design
for Bacon's (much more famous) plate in his frontispiece of the *Instauratio Magna* (1620) was quite obviously lifted (see Figures 5.1 and 5.2),[39] a
sixteenth-century Spanish galleon passing through the Pillars of Hercu-
les into the pure realm of nature in the New World, leaving behind all

Figure 5.1. Frontispiece, Andrés García de Céspedes, *Regimiento de Navegación* (Madrid, 1606). Courtesy of the John Carter Brown Library at Brown University.

tradition, society, politics, and culture in the Old. But there is perhaps not a more memorable image exposing the hybridization proliferated by the modern project of purification than that of the same sixteenth-century Spanish galleon found three hundred years later in the South American jungle by the nineteenth-century Spanish American patriarch, José Ar-

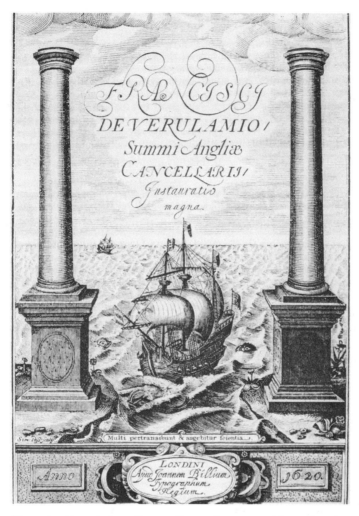

Figure 5.2. Frontispiece, Francis Bacon, *Instauratio Magna* (1620).

cadio Buendía, in Gabriel García Márquez's great twentieth-century masterpiece, *A Hundred Years of Solitude*. On a mad quest to find an opening to the Pacific Ocean, "Always, following a compass,"

> he kept on guiding his men toward the invisible north so that they would be able to get out of that enchanted region. It was a

thick night, starless, but the darkness was becoming impreg-
nated with a fresh and clear air. Exhausted by the long crossing
they hung up their hammocks and slept deeply for the first time
in two weeks. When they woke up, with the sun already high in
the sky, they were speechless with fascination. Before them, surrounded by ferns and palm trees, white and powdery in the silent morning light, was an enormous Spanish galleon. Tilted
slightly to the starboard, it had hanging from its intact masts the
dirty rags of its sails in the midst of its rigging, which was
adorned with orchids. The hull, covered with an armor of petri-
fied barnacles and soft moss, was firmly fastened into a surface
of stones. The whole structure seemed to occupy its own space,
one of solitude and oblivion, protected from the vices of time
and the habits of the birds. Inside, where the expeditionaries
explored with careful intent, there was nothing but a thick forest
of flowers. The discovery of the galleon, an indication of the
proximity of the sea, broke José Arcadio Buendía's drive. He
considered it a trick of whimsical fate to have searched for the
sea without finding it, at the cost of countless sacrifices and suffering, and to have found it all of a sudden without looking for
it, as it lay across his path like an insurmountable object.[40]

Having grown convinced that the place he chose for his New World settlement of Macondo is actually a peninsula, surrounded by water but
without any orientation for where to turn next, Buendía falls into a deep
despair: "We're going to rot our lives away here," he says to his wife,
"without receiving the benefits of science." Yet all of it had had such aus-
picious beginnings. Thus, the gypsy alchemist Melchíades began the history of the New World village of Macondo with the assertion that America was a world "so recent" that "many things lacked names and that in
order to indicate them, it was necessary to point" (1). He holds out the
wonders of "pure" science in a "New World" that incite the male members of the Buendía family in their mad quest for outlandish technologi-

cal devices for the detection of gold and weapons of solar warfare—mad quests that all come to naught with the final realization that their fate had been scripted all along for the apocalypse, a "biblical hurricane" (422), by the alchemist-narrator Melchíades.

García Márquez's novel reminds us that Latour's Great Modern Divides (nature/culture, premoderns/moderns) did not begin with the debate between Boyle and Hobbes; rather, its prehistory reaches back at least to the Spanish conquest of America during the sixteenth century. Indeed, as is well known among Latin Americanists, one of the primary sources of inspiration for García Márquez's masterpiece was roughly a contemporary of Francis Bacon and one of Bruno Latour's most perceptive seventeenth-century precursors to turn the anthropological gaze from "Them" to "Us," thereby exposing the many hybrids that the modern project of purification proliferates. When the colonial creole and minor bureaucrat from Bogotá Juan Rodríguez Freyle (1566–1640) sat down in 1636 to write his gossipy picaresque history of the New Kingdom of Granada (roughly, present-day Colombia) he looked back at the first hundred years of a colonial society in America from which had sprung the extraordinary violence and ordeals of conquest. Three conquerors had arrived independently and more or less simultaneously in quest for the legendary empire of "El Dorado," the golden king whose kingdom was located, according to Native American lore, somewhere in the highlands of Bogotá. Rodríguez Freyle entitled his unofficial history of these events and the colonial society that sprang from it *not* (in keeping with most "official" histories of the day) "the discovery and conquest of . . ." but rather "The Conquest and Discovery of the New Kingdom of Granada (*Conquista y descubrimiento del Nuevo Reino de Granada de las Indias Occidentales del Mar Océano*). America was conquered first, he suggests, and "discovered" only later. After providing a brief survey of the indigenous peoples and their wars before the arrival of the Spaniards, Rodríguez Freyle relates the Europeans' mad hunt for the elusive El Dorado, as "the Spaniards made forays over the whole territory, uncovering its secrets." Akin to the Buendías' monomaniacal quest for finding weapons of solar warfare, they devise outlandish schemes in the hunt for gold, such as the conqueror Antonio de Sepúlveda's harebrained idea to drain a lake in order to get at the gold:

> The persistent report that there was gold treasure to be found in all these lakes, and particularly in Guatavita, later led Antonio de Sepúlveda to come to an arrangement with His Majesty Philip II over draining it. He cut a first canal, which can still be seen, and affirmed that, as the level fell, he recovered gold to the value of over twelve thousand *pesos* merely from the shores. Long afterwards he tried draining it further at another spot, but without success, and in the end he wore himself out and died in poverty. Many others have tried their hand since and given up, for it is an interminable enterprise calling for vast expenditure of money and labour, in view of the depth of the lake and the amount of slime.[41]

Our author confesses to having himself caught the golden bug when he once went on a treasure hunt for a golden alligator that was allegedly hidden in a nearby lake.

> One who had been a priest of the sanctuary guided me to the lake, but no sooner had we come within sight of it than he fell face downward on the ground, and nothing I could do would make him get up again or address another word to me. So I came away empty-handed, with all my expenses for nothing. . . . Great is the attraction of gold and silver that lures young and old alike and leaves them always wanting more. (50)

The silent resistance of Rodríguez Freyle's native guide to the Golden Alligator gives our narrator pause to ponder the modern project of discovery from the Native American point of view:

The natives of these parts could well have spoken of the pre-conquest period as *their* golden age, of what came after as the age of iron, and of this present age as that of iron and steel. And what steel! For of all the earlier native population there survive today only a few handfuls to be found in the district of Santa Fé [de Bogotá] and in that of Tunja, and even of these . . . But no; it were better to keep silence. (56)

Keeping silent from this point onward about the consequences of the colonial project for New Granada's indigenous population, Rodríguez Freyle turns his close ethnographic look at the underbelly of colonial society. Not surprisingly, his text only circulated in manuscript throughout the colonial period under the popular title "El Carnero" (meaning "ram" or "sheep") until its first publication in Bogotá in 1859.[42] While there have been several interpretations of the significance of this popular title, the literary historian Roberto González Echevarría has maintained (based on the archival work of Susan Herman) that "carnero . . . is derived from *carnarium* and alludes by analogy to the place where discarded papers were thrown. "Carnero" meant the wastepaper basket at the Santa Fe de Bogotá *audiencia*, the bin where the textual remnants of a variety of legal cases were discarded."[43] In other words, our colonial auto-ethnographer Rodríguez Freyle dug around colonial society's trash, left outside the official seat of the Spanish Empire in northern South America, in order to expose the many hybrids that official imperial policy of purification had spawned and suppressed—the countless illegitimate "mestizo" offspring that had been proliferated by *limpieza de sangre* (blood purity) laws as well as the secret practices of "witchcraft" proliferated by Inquisition. In the old days, Rodríguez Freyle writes, only good Catholics and "Old Christians" (Christians, like his parents, not recently converted from Judaism or Islam) could come to the Indies, as Spanish colonial policy was intent on keeping the Indians pure of European heresies. This law "was in effect for a long time. Nowadays anybody can come. It must have gotten lost." One of the ironic consequences of *limp-ieza de sangre* required by the state in granting permissions for travel to the Indies was colonial society's disproportionate reliance on Native American and (increasingly African slave) labor, hereby spawning an entirely new sort of hybridization that had to be concealed—hybridiza-tions proliferated not only by purified blood but also by purified knowl-edge. Thus, he relates the scandalous story of a "young and pretty" wife who commits adultery while her husband is away on business in Spain. Finding herself pregnant and believing her husband's return to be immi-nent, she "took her problem to a friend, one Juana García, a freed ne-gress." This Juana García "was something of a witch" who uses a water tub to conjure up images of the itinerant husband showing him, far from intent on returning home, in the amorous company of another lady in Santo Domingo. With her magic, Juana is even able to snatch a sleeve from the mistress's dress, which the young wife keeps for evidence with which later to blackmail her husband. On the latter's return some years later (after the wife's illegitimate child had been born and was now old enough to be passed off as an adopted orphan), he is confronted with the evidence snatched by magic. Wife and husband eventually reconcile, but poor Juana has the worst of it when the husband "took the sleeve and went off with it to the bishop. . . . and told him the whole story" (211–212):

> He [the bishop] being also chief inquisitor . . . called the wife before him and took from her a declaration, in which she con-fessed frankly to the incident of the tub of water. Juana García the negress likewise confessed everything . . . . Her statement implicated various other women, and report had it that quite a number were caught in the net, ladies of quality among them. In the end Jiménez de Quesada [the governor] himself waited on the bishop with other citizens of rank and besought him to quash the proceedings, saying that the kingdom was still in its infancy and they must not cast a slur on its fair name. Such was their insistence that the bishop gave way, refusing only to ab-

solve Juana García. On her he imposed a penance that she stand on a raised platform in Santo Domingo church at the hour of high mass with a halter round her neck and a lighted candle in her hand. And there she lamented amid her sobs, "We were all in it, all of us, and I alone am made to pay!" (214)

Rodríguez Freyle's story of Juana García illuminates the colonial context from which one particular hybrid emerged in the early modern project of purification: the hybrid of witchcraft emerging from the purification of magic. Magic—the mixture of nature and culture—had had a long tradition in medieval Europe, but its purification—its split into Christian knowledge and demonic superstition—was the project of the early modern science of demonology, in its Reformation and Counter-Reformation varieties, that took place in the context of the European close encounters with religious otherness. Thus, the year 1492 notoriously marked not only the European "discovery" of America, but also the expulsion of the Jews from Spain and the completion of the Christian so-called re-conquest of the Iberian Peninsula from the eight-hundred year rule of Islam. The expulsion and re-conquest gave rise to the purifying project of the Spanish Inquisition, whose purpose was to suppress the remainders of Islam and Judaism within Christian society on the peninsula. Similarly, the conquest of the New World promised to offer a purely Christian—a messianic—solution for procuring the technological and material means that would bring about a re-conquest of Jerusalem, a Christian world empire, a global Reformation, and a universal scientific revolution.

The above can only begin to focus our attention on the *colonial history* of the "paradigm" in the empirical sciences, as it originated from the breakup of Renaissance humanism, the emergent gulf between the humanities and the natural sciences, as well as the subsequent hegemony of the empirical method in modern Western culture. Perhaps the most iconic piece of evidence testifying to the colonial and transnational history of this modern hegemony would come in the form of Francis Bacon's

"House of Salomon," the fabulous academy of science in his utopian treatise *The New Atlantis* (1627). Whereas the inhabitants of the original uto-
pia in Thomas More's prototype, published a hundred years earlier, were
still pagan Epicureans, Bacon's inhabitants of "Bensalem" were Spanish-
speaking Christians. Their scientific Epicureanism was derived not from
pagan philosophy or poetry (such as Lucretius's poem *De rerum natura*,
rediscovered in 1417 by Poggio Bracciolini), but rather from Christian
revelation, particularly the Apocalypse of John, a copy of which had mi-
raculously found its way to Bensalem. Bacon's "House of Salomon" was
modeled on the Spanish House of Trade (*Casa de contratación*), the
clearing house for all information about the New World established in
Seville in 1505. It combined empirical inquiry with Christian mission for
the purpose of "secret" knowledge production in the imperial Habsburg
state, as the natural secrets of the New World turned into the secrets of
state and the New World explorer into the modern secretary.[44]

The patent interest some of the key figures of the so-called Scientific
Revolution in England such as Bacon had in the Spanish imperial model
of empirical knowledge production betray the crucial role that the conquest of the New World played in the making of modern Western scientific culture. As Stephen Gaukroger has argued, the "reasons commonly
adduced for the success of a scientific culture in the West in the wake of
the Scientific Revolution—its use of adversarial non-dogmatic argument, its ability to disassociate itself from religion, its technological benefits—are mistaken and cannot explain this success." Indeed, one of the
distinctive features of the Scientific Revolution in seventeenth-century
Europe was, according to Gaukroger, "that, unlike other earlier scientific
programs and cultures, it is driven, often explicitly, by religious considerations: Christianity set the agenda for natural philosophy in many respects and projected it forward in a way quite different from that of any
other scientific culture." It was, thus, the amalgamation—rather than the
separation—of naturalist inquiry with religion that set the stage for what
Gaukroger sees as the "anomalous" path that Western scientific culture
has taken since the seventeenth century, when the "traditional balance of

interests" between cognitive practices characterizing pre-modern and non-Western societies was "replaced by a dominance of scientific concerns, while science itself experiences a rate of growth that is 'pathological' by the standards of earlier cultures, but is ultimately legitimated by the cognitive standing that it takes on" and no longer open to "refutation from outside."[45] The crucial difference between earlier ("medieval") and early modern attempts to fully amalgamate science with religion was that in the latter case this amalgamation was, for the first time, underwritten and promoted by both the imperial state and the imperial church in the context of the conquest of America, chronicled by colonial American archives in multiple languages.

Gaukroger's analysis sheds light then on one particular form of hybridization that was crucial in the history of the natural sciences' epistemological hegemony in modern Western culture, a hegemony that he sees as "pathological" and that philosophical hermeneutics (Gadamer) as well as recent critical science studies (Serres, Latour) have set out to deconstruct. From the point of view of critical science studies, however, it was the elaboration of Kuhn's notion of the "paradigm" in the 1960s—a concept he borrowed from the humanities—that was foundational in opening up the history of science—which had previously been immunized from critique "from outside" by its own progressivist logic—to analysis customary in the humanities, attuned as it is to issues of cultural, historical, and social context, representation, and power. In turn, modern humanists, who had by and large been ensconced in national archives and languages, as well as focused on modern "literary" discourses privileged by the New Criticism, were increasingly exposed to transnational archives traditionally considered to be outside the realm of "literature" proper—archives such as Linnean natural history, for example, or modern anthropology, which now became central objects of literary and rhetorical analysis in the postcolonial and New Historicist versions of transnational and comparative scholarship.[46] In this sense, Kuhn's analysis in the 1960s played a crucial role in enabling us not only to think historically about the modern organization of knowledge—thus opening up the empirical sciences to critique "from the outside"—but also to re-think literary and cultural studies in transnational terms. We might say that, though the transnational turn in the humanities was not a Kuhnian paradigm shift, both ideas are similarly the product of cross-fertilization between the humanities and critical science studies, as concepts migrate between here and there, reminding us that no step, turn, or shift will ever be a leap beyond history.

Chapter 6

◠

The Geopolitics and Tropologies
of the American Turn

MONIQUE ALLEWAERT

A turn suggests a change in direction that might be rendered as a curved line that stops short of a full circling. A *turn* does not cntail a completed action in time, as the governing metaphor of *revolution* used by older Americanist scholarship tended to suggest. Figuring thc turn as a curved line gives it a geometry, which implies at least an abstract temporality and spatiality but does not anchor the turn in a specific geography. And while it offers the possibility of movement, which implies temporality, it implies no teleology. In short, the metaphor of the turn evokes a partiality that does not promise a trajectory or telos. It is, then, is a metaphorical vehicle without a clear metaphorical target, a trope that gains its energy not from its completion, but from veering toward a frame that does not yet exist.

The indeterminacy and not-quite-yet-ness of the trope of the turn might make the critical metaphor seem oriented away from this world. Yet scholarship of the postnational turn's implicit attention to tropology emphasizes the centrality of metaphors—whether strong or slight ones—to materializing the frames that structure critics' organizations of the world.[1] If the trope of the turn calls attention to the material significance of metaphors, such a materialist account of figuration (and of the literary more broadly) was equally at work in the eighteenth and nineteenth centuries. Amanda Goldstein lays out three senses of figuration's materiality that undergird eighteenth and nineteenth century tropologies and our own: first, the "uncaused trope, turn, or swerve (clinamen)" that brings untouching bodies into relation; second the joining of these now-touching things into "composite con-figurations" (Geoffrey Sanborn's chapter in this volume takes up similar affiliations); third, these configurations' production of a historical atmosphere that gives and decomposes the persons and things that make up a moment.[2] By such accounts, tropology participates in processes by which writers and texts are produced by, ventriloquize, and pass into milieus, thereby materially changing the fields in which they move. This chapter will follow out this materialist sense of figuration in what might seem an unlikely place: the anonymous "Theresa—A Haytien Tale" (1828), one of the earliest stories about the Haitian revolution, and a story whose efforts, potentials, and aftereffects come more clearly into focus by interpreting the revolution's geopolitical and social significance in terms of its figurations.

In this chapter I show how the metaphors of turning in "Theresa" participate in its effort to produce a geopolitical form that puts Africans in the diaspora into a cosmopolitan global frame. As part of its effort to express Afro-American cosmopolitanism, "Theresa" proliferates catachrestic metaphors that ultimately redirect this project.[3] While catachreses in "Theresa" suggest the failure of its tropology to materialize the cosmopolitan global frame to which it aspires, this failure gives rise to an alter-materiality. Ultimately, catachreses in "Theresa" indicate that micro-level figural processes can reorient scholarship of the American turn from a global orientation that gives onto the existing totality of one world, to an archipelagic orientation that gives onto the emerging totality produced by the relation between many islands.

⤺

The claim that tropology was conceived as material in the eighteenth and nineteenth centuries is not new, as is evident from recalling the French

materialist tradition that influenced Marx as well as the empiricist eigh-
teenth- and nineteenth-century Anglophone criticism and pedagogies
used in American classrooms deep into the nineteenth century.[4] These
materialist and empiricist rhetorics circulated widely in nineteenth-
century cultures, shaping the production of famous literary figures as
well as that of anonymous scribes, and giving rise to an understanding of
figure and the literary as productive of an atmosphere equally taken in by
persons and poets outside of the high cultural literary production typi-
cally associated with rhetorical analyses. For instance, an early issue of
Freedom's Journal reprinted "A Fragment" concerned with how the presence or absence of a loved object changes an atmosphere. The story,
which tracks the protagonist's movement from joy to despair upon the
loss of the object, aims to pass on this affective and atmospheric change
to its readers, as though the literary artifact's function were to replicate
and pass on the affective and atmospheric effects it describes.[5] Despite
the pervasiveness of materialist accounts of figure and the literary in the
period, such analyses have not been taken up in early Americanists' critical approaches. Materialist theories of figuration have been particularly
overlooked by scholars who approach geopolitical problems through
structural, sociological, and political models, rather than through aesthetic methods other than formalisms such as genre analysis.[6]

In fields focused on geopolitical problems, postcolonial and colonial
analyses have, to date, made the most of materialist theories of figuration, particularly Gayatri Spivak's account of catachresis as a concept
metaphor without an adequate referent (for instance, the subaltern that
has no proper existence as such) that nonetheless haltingly manifests itself in geopolitics.[7] Working in this theoretical lineage, Srinivas Aravamudan proposes that catachresis describes processes of misnaming
through which eighteenth-century tropicopolitans (a term he uses to
describe the inhabitants of the tropics in the colonial era) "rework . . .
colonial discourse" (x). Recalling the centrality of the period's materialist
accounts of the literary and drawing together Spivak's and Aravamudan's
analyses allow us to posit trope, particularly catachresis, as a central critical

problem for geopolitical analyses emerging from attention to colonialism. Interpreting the tropologies of the period is necessary to engaging the practices of tropicopolitans who take in and turn the tropological performances that compose their atmospheres. In so doing, they inflect existing patterns of Atlantic relations, whether in desired ways—as when Aravamudan argues that Toussaint Louverture claims, ironizes, and expands the forms of agency circulating in Atlantic metropoles—or, as we shall see, haphazardly and out of necessity.

To consider how deepening the tropological orientation named by the trope of the turn might contribute to American studies focused on postnational geopolitics, consider the anonymously published (the author is identified only as "S") short story, "Theresa—A Haytien Tale," which appeared in four installments in January and February of 1828 in the New York-based African American periodical *Freedom's Journal*, which was edited by Jamaican-born and Bowdoin-educated John Russworm as well as (for part of its run) Delaware native Samuel Cornish.[8] *Freedom's Journal* cast itself as a medium in which Africans in the diaspora could argue on their own behest as well as "a medium of intercourse between our brethren in the different states of this confederacy."[9] If the aim of the paper is clearly to produce a black counterpublic, the inaugural issue names three geopolitical topoi as especially important to this public: news about Africa, news about Haiti's "progress in all the arts of civilization," and news of South American revolutionary movements (1). In addition to these topics that are routinely covered in original articles and reprints from other newspapers, *Freedom's Journal* published original pieces, reprints, and commentaries related to domestic and international news as well as history, short stories, poems, and advertisements. It explicitly encouraged and imagined itself as contributing to the project of educating the African American counter-public that it aimed to produce, particularly in reading, writing, history, and science (1). That "Theresa" takes place in revolutionary Haiti and appeared in a New York periodical whose audience included free African Americans in the northeast United States, enslaved African Americans in the southern United States, as well as a far-flung and racially diverse audience in Haiti, England, and Canada, brings into focus the sub- and supra-national geopolitical frames so central to American studies associated with trope of the turn.[10]

"Theresa" chronicles the adventures of three women, Paulina and her two daughters, Theresa and Amanda, and is set at some unspecified point during Toussaint Louverture's command of the troops (1792–1802) in the revolutionizing colony of St. Domingue (which achieved independence in 1804 and was given the postcolonial name *Haiti* in 1805). Its ornate plot, broadly concerned with the women's effort to flee from the warzone to safety, veers from contingent event to contingent event, which makes it difficult to interpret the story thematically.[11] Its characterization is nearly nonexistent since its characters are not persons in any ordinary sense but amalgamations of divergent types ranging from the rustic and simple woman of the folktale, to the virtuous woman of the Cult of True Womanhood, to the masculinized female patriot of revolutionary rhetoric, to the sentimental heroine of the nineteenth-century novel, to the republican mother of early national literatures. Rather than plot, theme, or character, the story's main interest is in presenting and producing its setting, which it does through elaborate, even hyperbolic figures.[12] Its account of the protagonists' flight through the revolutionary terrain emphasizes the island's beauty and bounty as much as it does the ongoing revolution. Consider, for instance, the story's odd overlay of landscape encomium and the events of the war: "Every tree kissed by the zephyrs, that ruffled its leaves, was an army approaching, and in the trunk of every decored mahogany, was seen a Frenchman in ambush— not less alarming to the fugitives, were the ripe fruit that frequently fell to the earth" (641).[13] In the midst of this account of the revolutionary warzone, the author emphasizes that although the tropical heat is "oppressive" it is not in the least malignant because it "render[s]" "the air . . . fragrant with the variety of aromatic shrubs, that grew spontaneously in this grove of peace" (641). In fact, this heat is further described as a fecundating force that gives rise to the "majestic spreading Guava" and "the humming bird skipping capriciously from blossom to blossom, display[ing] its magnificent plumage (641). As though it aimed to cover over the historical event that it takes as its context, the story piles figure on top of figure to attempt a lush description of the island's "dusky hills," "delightful" valleys, "beautiful" rivers, whispering zephyrs, groves of Pimento trees, colorful birds, as well as the coconuts, lemons, oranges, and "luxurious" mangoes the island bears in "spontaneous abundance."

If this fabulous burnishing of setting recalls colonial encomiums to tropical bounty and anticipates the coming touristic rhetoric through which the Caribbean has come to be integrated into global economies, we needn't interpret this as evidence of the story's neocolonialism. Rather, this tropology suggests an effort, whether intentional or not, to deploy a tropology that produces an alternate *non*colonial past for the terrain.[14] The means through which the story moves to this end is the sort of ornamental description of setting noted above. However, the story's interest in manufacturing a noncolonial past is also evident in its catachreses. That the story's sequence of events is set into motion by the ongoing Haitian Revolution indicates its recognition of the colonial history that gave rise to the revolution that ultimately yielded the first sovereign black state in the Western hemisphere, and the only state to reject slavery, racism, and—under Jean-Jacques Dessalines' administration (1805–6)—colonialism and imperialism as well. Yet if "Theresa" evokes the colonial history covered in detail in earlier issues of *Freedom's Journal*, from the first lines of the story onward the territory is identified as Haiti, and not by its colonial name, St. Domingue.[15] At a climactic point, Theresa, "as if aroused by some internal agent, exclaimed, 'Oh Hayti!'—be independent, and let Theresa be the unworthy sacrifice offered to that God, who shall raise his mighty arm in defense of thy injured children" (643).[16] Although there is a tension between the consistent appellation of the state as already existing under the name Haiti and Theresa's prophetic apostrophizing of Haiti as an independent state, in both cases the revolutionary state is designated by its postcolonial name, a tendency that is not in keeping with other articles in *Freedom's Journal* that generally use historically appropriate names in historical pieces, including those on focused on Haiti.[17]

A linked set of catachreses describes the colonial past as a scene of idyllic village life. Theresa longs for the "endeared village of her innocent childhood; still dear to her, though now it was become a theatre of many tragic scenes" (639) and again, later in the story, expresses nostalgia for the "village of her happiest days" (642). The colonial past of brutal exploitation is gone and instead "Theresa" presents plantations and their fields as "flourishing," "delightful," and above all economically profitable operations that testify to the West Indies' superfecundity. The brutality of colonial racism is tacitly acknowledged when the protagonists lament that their village homes have become "a theatre of . . . tragic scenes." And this racism implicitly structures a charade put on by the story's protagonists in order to pass beyond, and gain information from, French troops: Paulina performs as an officer (presumably, white) and presents her daughters as prisoners of war (presumably, black). Moreover, that the protagonists' male relatives are fighting for "liberty" might recall that in St. Domingue the opposite of liberty is not death but slavery. However, in "Theresa" liberty seems an ideal without any proper referent in actual historical slavery, as there is no explicit reference to racism, slavery, or colonialism in this story; it seems more interested in burnishing landscape than in chronicling revolution. In her critique of dominant enlightenment philosophies that treat slavery as a metaphorical instead of an actual condition, Susan Buck-Morss suggests that the proper critical response is to turn attention from metaphorical to actual slavery. However, this "Haytien story" veers toward the opposite strategy, for it attempts to cover over actual slavery, racism, and colonialism and in its place presents the village idyll and a slavery that seems almost entirely as abstracted as that of dominant enlightenment thought.[18] This raises a key question: what is the story's investment not only in naming Haiti before its proper existence but also in abstracting the colonial past, including colonial slavery (the most significant cause of the revolution), and putting in its place a past of village life that is entirely devoid of specificity?

To some extent, the answer to this question is simple. In posing the existence of Haiti before its proper existence, the story makes Haitian revolutionary nationalism like other new nationalisms by granting it a long, in fact immemorial existence that covers over its newness and vulnerability.[19] However, while the North Americans and the French named and idealized specific earlier historical moments (for instance, Noah Webster's idealization of England under the reign of Queen Anne, Thomas Jefferson's idealization of Anglo Saxony, or Robespierre's idealization of the Romans) and then blamed more recent political structures for destroying this historical tradition and its virtues, this Haitian story idealizes not an earlier historical moment but the generic past of the village idyll that could be anywhere and have emerged at anytime.[20] And because it offers few references to the brutalities of colonialism, plantation slavery, and racism, it offers no reason why a break with the past was necessary. It is as though it wants to present revolution as a pure restoration not of a particular past moment (as the United States tended to, as the French did too, and as Dessalines's purported naming of Haiti for the island's earlier Arawak inhabitants did), but of an entirely generic past.[21]

Here we might hazard a fuller response to the question posed above. The presentation in "Theresa" of a past of generic village life attempts to break with Haiti's colonial past in order to produce an account of sovereignty that is not predicated on racism and subalterity, a position consistent with *Freedom's Journal*'s efforts to orient its readers to stories that document African civilization in ways that resist casting Africa either in the racist terms of Anglo-European history and philosophy or as reactions against these racist terms. Moreover, this production of Haiti's generic past covers over and abstracts the anti-colonialism and revolutionary violence that had produced Haiti as a post- and anti-colonial state, but had also led most other American and European powers to close Haiti out of the emerging modernity of revolutionary nationalism and embargo it from global trade (Trouillot, Fischer).[22]

In the years leading up to the publication of "Theresa," Haitian president Jean-Pierre Boyer propagandized the state's immense agricultural output and economic potential so as to incline foreign powers to open trade relations with the state (it was Boyer who agreed to pay France reparations to normalize trade relations with it). This propagandistic presentation of the state also aimed to recruit blacks from elsewhere in the American hemisphere to Haiti, where they were promised that agricultural labor yielded an easy profit and where, according to the editors of *Freedom's Journal*, "the Man of Colour is seen in all the dignity of man."[23] Insofar as *Freedom's Journal* and other venues advocating for Haiti in the 1820s turned sustained attention to the colonial past and the reasons for the revolution, they called attention to the fact that the emergence and continued existence of Haiti challenged the colonialism, slavery, and racism that continued to structure the world economy in the period. For writers and politicians advocating on behalf of Haiti this was a problem, as the existence of Haiti threatened a global economy that was still structured by slave labor and the cheap wage labor of disenfranchised persons. Seemingly aware of this problem, the editors of *Freedom's Journal* sometimes tried to make the case against slavery by advancing economic arguments meant to appeal even to those with a vested interest in the plantocracy. For instance, the May 25, June 1, and June 8, 1827 issues reprinted articles that made the case for emancipation using Adam Smith's argument that slave labor was more expensive than wage labor, suggesting that turning slave laborers to wage laborers would work to the advantage of capitalists. Given that Haiti's challenge to colonialism, slavery, and racism posed a problem to those advocating for Haitian sovereignty, it is likely that the story's catachrestic naming of Haiti as always existing and having an utterly generic past indicates an effort, whether conscious or not, to cover over a brutal colonial past and a quite exceptional revolution that could only remind black as well as white audiences of why Haiti was closed out of global trade.[24]

If production in "Theresa" of a generic past indicates how the story (as well as *Freedom's Journal*) was shaped by, and attempted to give shape to, the historical forces of racism and colonialism that inflected its production, its way of routing the generic is quite specific. While the story's tropologies attempt to produce Haiti as a generic revolutionary nationalism, its tropologies trade in Haiti's hyperfecundity and its West Indian specificity.[25] Thus, the story traffics in two different processes of specification. On the one hand, "Theresa" participates in discourses producing a West Indian regional specificity that began developing in the natural history produced in the colonial era and that emphasizes the region's fecundity and its supposed effects, from the plantation-based economic system to putatively exotic fruits and persons. On the other hand, the story's elimination of this colonial history so as to produce the colony's generic past participates in discourses that produced the geopolitical specificity of revolutionary nationalism, which was being developed by other post-revolutionary states like France, Britain, and the United States, all of which were, not incidentally, existing or emerging global powers.[26] Actuating these two distinct claims for specificity, the tropology of "Theresa" codes the tropical particularities that were sometimes seen by metropolitan writers as detrimental to civilization as having a positive value because they spurred an agricultural output that was to form the basis of an economic and political system of exchange with other post-enlightenment and post-revolutionary nation-states whose economic and political systems were rational, republican, and, by 1828, increasingly democratic.

The story has difficulty managing these two kinds of specification, which is particularly evident in another of the story's catachreses, one in which a tension in the metaphorical vehicle misdirects the tenor. Early in the story, Theresa's mother contemplates her daughters, who "in the morning of life, were expanding, like the foliages of the rose into elegance and beauty" (640). Here the story recirculates an Anglo-European metaphor that equates female beauty with roses (as most famously articulated in Robert Burns's Scottish ballads). That this metaphor compares Haitian women to roses need not be interpreted as indicating that the writer fails to see that roses, which are not native to the West Indies, are not the proper vehicles for describing West Indian women. Rather than revealing that the author labors under a colonial psychology, this metaphor assays a generic tropology that suggests that the author's effort, insofar as we can deduce it, is to trade in the conventional: the metaphor mobilizes an Anglo-European typicality to produce Theresa and her sister Amanda as generic daughters of a generic revolutionary nationalist state. Yet this metaphor, rising from the generic tropologies that composed the literary atmosphere of the era, nonetheless reroutes the tropology of the metropole to turn cosmopolitan modes of specification with West Indian ends. The metaphor's vehicle is not in fact roses but foliages, which are modified as the foliages of roses. In making the vehicle intended to describe Haitian women into the leaves of rose bushes, this metaphor slides toward the rhetoric of West Indian hyperfecundity that, as we have already seen, the story also activates. That this metaphor's vehicle aims at once toward a global English tropology and a West Indian one produces a notably odd tenor: woman as fast growing tropical vegetation of English provenance. This oddity testifies to a tension between the story's expression of the specificity of revolutionary nationalism (one that from the periphery is produced, in part, by tropes that stereotype the metropole) and its desire for a West Indian specification (one produced, in part, by producing geographically and regionally specific tropes that are also advertisements for West Indian goods that might circulate on a global market). Recalling that tropologies are spun from and press back on the milieux in which they circulate, we might say that the story's mixed metaphors arise from a world system in which sovereignty is increasingly produced via revolutionary nationalisms like that of states like the United States, France, England, and emerging South American republics, and where the economic potential of the West Indies was linked to its agricultural output. In telling the story of what is cast as a generic revolution of a people with a generic past, yet carefully drawing a setting that emphasizes tropical products (although notably not sugar cane), the story actuates potentialities moving through the milieu from which it arises in an effort to instantiate what was then a scarcely possible referent: a sovereign and economically robust Haiti.

This tension between the geopolitical specificity of the revolutionary nationalist state and the regional specificity of the peripheral state also occurs in North American literature produced contemporaneously with

"Theresa." For instance, James Fenimore Cooper's *The Last of the Mohicans* (1826) begins by distinguishing the delicacy and brilliant paleness of Colonel Munro's English daughter Alice Munro from the strength and darkness of his mixed race American daughter Cora Munro.[27] In Cooper's novel, the geopolitical and regional specificities that "Theresa" presents together are divided and then managed when Cora dies and Alice, who survives, is set to marry the Virginian Captain Duncan Haywerd. Cooper's novel enacts a process of sublation whereby that which is eliminated—the racial mixing and créolité common to the Americas from the Canadian wilds to the West Indies—is purified and given a new form when the English daughter is set to become an American wife. Here one daughter typifies the cosmopolitan tradition that peripheral nationalisms needed to evoke to articulate revolutionary nationalism, a second typifies regional particularly, and by the story's close the cosmopolitan figure has encoded and transformed the regionally particular, both of which disappear in the face of a new national form that has metabolized both the racial legacy of the Americas and the cosmopolitan inheritance of England. However, in "Theresa," where these two kinds of typicality are not synthesized, we have neither the production of the stereotype nor a process of sublation, as we see in Cooper, but an unresolved tension between geopolitical and regional specificities.

The tension between these different specificities contributes to the story's proliferating catachreses, which are likely not intentional, but rather failures of style that we might attribute to the journal's and the story's efforts to participate in the project of producing national literatures from the perspective of the periphery. The catachreses emerge also from the attempt to produce a referent for a sovereign Haiti that, even for a black readership, was only haltingly possible in a period in which other revolutionary nationalist states had not recognized Haiti as a sovereign state. In short, the tropology of "Theresa" emerges in conditions in which the perspective of the periphery is not possible, and in which the possibility of a politically and economically sovereign Haiti is only partially thinkable. Yet if these catachreses indicate the impossibility of the referent the story assays, these are important failures that we might draw on to press further the tropological mode of inquiry latent in American studies of the postnational turn.

⤚

To investigate how attending to the tropologies arising by heed and hazard from American peripherics might deepen twenty-first-century critical approaches associated with the trope of the turn, it is worth considering "Theresa" in terms of the geopolitical frames evoked by postnational Americanist work. Literary critics of the postnational American turn working with Wallersteinian and cosmopolitan models have replaced the totalizing frame of the nation with that of the globe.[28] For instance, Elizabeth Maddock Dillon's exemplary essay "Slaves in Algiers" argues that early American nationalism emerges on a global frame that makes internationalism the framework and necessary condition through which nationalism emerges. Moving onto this global framework, we might note that the tropologies of "Theresa," including its two unsynthesizable processes of specification, indicate an ambition of writing Haiti into the existing world system, an ambition quite clearly expressed in the attention paid by the editors of *Freedom's Journal* to Haiti's economic potential, and in articles posing Haiti as a state in which people of color can assert personhood in an abstract, universal sense. Should Haiti and its allies like *Freedom's Journal* have succeeded in writing the state into the existing world system—and to some extent Boyer's administration, at least, was successful since it succeeding in lifting French sanctions against Haiti—Haiti's inclusion in the global system would change its existing operations, since it would require that racism become a secondary instead of a primary motive determining the relation between nation-states.[29]

The desire by the Boyer administration, *Freedom's Journal*, and "Theresa" for Haitian inclusion into the system of modern nation-states and the incorporation of persons of African descent into a universal history of man is unfulfilled by history. This is not surprising, since despite *Free-*

dom's Journal's explicit challenges to color prejudice, the racism of the then dominant nation states demanded that things African be closed out of the movement of history. That the tropology of "Theresa" affects no syntheses, then, is a failure we could assign to the racism and imperialism that became increasingly central to the nationalisms being developed by post-revolutionary nation-states. This reading implies that syntheses such as that achieved by Cooper could not emerge in "Theresa" because the nation-states that largely determined the terms on which other states were admitted into global relations were both imperialist and racist and had little interest in recognizing a free black state as anything other than a subordinate power. The racism and imperialism of post-revolutionary nation states is evident in the French government's requirement that if Haiti were to be recognized as a sovereign nation state, the Haitian government must pay France reparations for the losses incurred from the slave revolution. This policy undermined the Haitian sovereignty it supposedly bestowed since it mandated that free blacks in Haiti continue to render economic benefits to whites in the metropole, while at the same time redirecting capital that might have been put to developing manufacturing and the agricultural economy.

If it is entirely possible to put this analysis of catachresis in "Theresa" into the service of the global and cosmopolitan line of postnational American studies, and if such an analysis deepens our understanding of the writings and perspectives of American peripheries, then the limitation of this interpretation is that it does not yet yield new knowledge about the field evoked by the trope of the turn. After all, from the beginning of the analysis—even before scholars began working on supra- and subnational frames of the postnational turn—Americanist scholars were aware of the appeal of cosmopolitanism to those dispossessed of rights. They were aware, as well, of the racism and imperialism of dominant nineteenth-century nation-states, and mindful that this racism and imperialism produced the shape of the global such that certain regions were shut outside of history and consigned to economic dependency and environmental degradation.

Yet the fact that the tropology of "Theresa" produces only incommensurate modes of specification points toward an analytic that departs from the global frame of the systems theory and cosmopolitan analyses that have dominated Americanist scholarship following the postnational turn. We might note that the juxtaposition in "Theresa" of the coordinates of regional and geopolitical specificities creates a tenor that further diversifies each of these specificities. The coordinates of tropical regionalism come to include the perversion of cosmopolitanism when, in the metaphor discussed above, the English rose passes into tropical foliage. In tropicalizing the English rose, the story's production of the coordinates of the regional comes to include unnatural growth that is not intrinsic to the region, but rather comes from the grafting of the metropolitan type onto a set of tropical coordinates to quicken an unwieldy new formation whose components pull apart and remain in tension instead of resolving into synthesis.

Moreover, the story's production of a generic past that eliminates any particular past sets it apart from contemporary literary expressions of revolutionary nationalism, which themselves circulated particular pasts, and which increasingly posed these particular pasts as the basis of nationalism (Cooper's frontier narratives, Irving's Dutch folk mythology, Hawthorne's Puritan New England). While we might interpret the story's oddly closed relation to any past, whether Haitian or not, as resulting from the fact that Haiti was closed out of the set of revolutionary nationalisms precisely because of its revolutionary past, and while we might interpret this as evidence that Haiti's past was too brutal to allow for the sort of looking backward that shaped other revolutionary nationalisms, we might flip this interpretation to propose that the story's production of a generic past allows for a different mode of revolutionary nationalism. In doing so, we might see that in putting the generic in the place of the actual past "Theresa" produces a revolutionary nationalism that cuts its relation to the past. In this sense it departs from other early nineteenth-century revolutionary nationalisms' idealization of particular pasts, and of historiography more generally. If this is almost certainly a revolution-

ary nationalism articulated by hap, we might note that more than familiar revolutionary nationalisms, "Theresa" veers toward Marx's call for a
revolution that sheds historical drag to become capable of producing a
genuinely new tongue. While neither the tongue nor the tropology are
fluent, their haltingness lend them a viscosity by which the generic ma-
terializes a different frame for postnational American studies.[30]

If the catachreses in "Theresa" do not produce their impossible referent, they do offer the conditions of possibility for an archipelagic approach
that counters cosmopolitan and global approaches to postnational American studies. The catachrestic metaphors' pluralization of existing terms
(the tropicalization of the Anglo European and the cosmopolitanization
of the tropical) anticipate the characteristic move of the archipelagic approach that emphasizes the relation among diverse connected but also
disconnected regions whose relation changes the shape of the totality in
which they participate. Instead of the unified totalities of the nation or
the globe that contains them, archipelagic approaches propose that totality cannot be reduced to one—the nation or the globe or the world—
since it is produced through relays between many islands that give rise to
alternate modernities that are in relay with, yet also exceed, existing totalities, whether globe or nation.[31] What we might, following Gilles
Deleuze as well as Édouard Glissant, call *disjunctive synthesis* produces a
pluralization of each of the specificities brought into relation.[32] This is
the disjunctive synthesis that emerges from the failed tropology of "Theresa." If this tropology does not achieve its goals, it nonetheless shows
that pushing scholarship of the postnational American turn to the tropological yields an analytic by which peripheral writings pass beyond
minoritarian-majoritarian models through the accumulating material
effect of the figures that crowd the aesthetic field and slowly change the
atmosphere. Taking in this atmosphere yields an analytic by which peripheral writings pass from center-peripheral models and move into the
open totality of the archipelago.

Chapter 7

ᔕ

The Caribbean Turn in C19 American Literary Studies

SEAN X. GOUDIE

The year 1992 was the quincentennial anniversary of the moment when Columbus's ill-fated voyage to the Indies took an unplanned West Indian turn. The anniversary of the year when the Caribbean became the original site in the hemisphere of Native American genocide, of the enslavement of captured Africans and their descendants, and of European colonialism and settlement coincides with, and bears an indirect relation to, what this essay argues was a Caribbean turn in nineteenth-century American literary and cultural studies. While no single anniversary or critic or event, we shall see, is responsible for generating such a turn, this chapter's first section identifies several key figures, texts, and developments that inspired a Caribbean turn two decades ago by scholars of nineteenth-century American literature and culture. Then, in the second section, I draw on examples from my current research to suggest the possibilities and limitations of various kinds of Caribbean turns practiced by scholars in the field. In so doing, I demonstrate how our relatively recent fascination with the Caribbean is, more accurately put, a *return* to a long nineteenth century of still largely unexamined Caribbean-North American literary and cultural relations. By limning the range of phenomena shaping over two decades of Caribbean turning in the field and showing how we might treat the past in the service of a more ethical present and future, this essay models a multidimensional way of turning to the Caribbean in nineteenth-century American literary and cultural studies. Specifically, by recognizing U.S. interdependence with the Caribbean on historic, economic, cultural, and other levels, such an approach can challenge oppressive imperial logics that enable and sustain prolonged exploitative conditions providing for Caribbean indebtedness to the United States while simultaneously disavowing U.S. dependence on, and indebtedness to, the Caribbean both imaginatively and otherwise. In such a way we might ensure that the Caribbean turn in the field is not just a passing fad or an ironically U.S.-centered critical tendency but a sustained, far-reaching, multidirectional, and interdynamic study of Caribbean American literary and cultural relations across space and time.

The Caribbean and C19/92

A few decades ago, or in or around 1992, nineteenth-century American literary and cultural studies took a Caribbean turn. This was due to a number of interrelated developments. First, with the announcement that year that St. Lucian poet, playwright, and critic Derek Walcott had won the Nobel Prize for Literature—a first for a West Indian writer—Anglophone Caribbean literature took a turn towards the canonical. Given Walcott's long career as a professor living and working in the United States and the Caribbean American regional settings of many of his poems, the prize seemed to affirm the migrant route toward the U.S. academy and away from Europe that Walcott and many of his Caribbean contemporaries pursued as artists and intellectuals in the mid-twentieth-century. Walcott's epic poem *Omeros*, published just two years before the awarding of the Nobel, pays homage to the substantial influence of the poem's two namesakes—the poet Homer and the *other* Homer, painter Winslow Homer—and to U.S. poets like Walt Whitman, Hart Crane, and, much less flatteringly, novelist and poet Herman Melville. In such a way,

Walcott's Nobel Prize took on added significance as a touchstone in the long, entangled history of U.S.-Caribbean literary and cultural relations.

Related to that development, Francophone and Hispanic Caribbean literature in translation, as well as a full complement of Caribbean "diaspora" women writers, became fixtures on multiethnic literature publishing lists. Moreover, a number of these writers authored metahistorical works of fiction centered on revising iconic U.S. figures, works, and events from a distinctly Caribbean point of view. In so doing, these authors were suggesting to their readers ways in which they themselves might reenvision the too narrowly understood historic, geographic, temporal, and aesthetic dimensions of American history—and American literary history—writ large. Two prominent examples include Maryse Condé, whose novel *I, Tituba, Black Witch of Salem*, first published in English in 1992, rewrites the Salem Witchcraft Trials and Hawthorne's *The Scarlet Letter* from the eponymous Black Caribbean woman's point of view. A year later, Jamaican writer Michelle Cliff published *Free Enterprise: A Novel of Mary Ellen Pleasant,* which retells the story of John Brown's Raid—and much else in U.S. history and literary history—from the point of view of two co-conspirators of Brown's, including the title character and the Jamaican immigrant Annie Christmas, effectively queering Caribbean American regional history across space and time. As the above authors and their texts became visible on course syllabi in the U.S. academy, many teachers and students—including scholars of nineteenth-century American literature drawn to the above titles' revisionist engagements with canonical nineteenth-century American authors, characters, texts, figures, and/or events—began to turn to the Caribbean in ways that exceeded the touristic gaze that Walcott critiqued so severely in his Nobel Lecture *The Antilles: Fragments of Epic Memory* (1992). Likewise they learned how to turn American literary history inside out according to a Caribbean way of seeing otherwise.

Coincident with these advancements in the literary world was the sudden prominence in the U.S. academy of Caribbean-based critics and theorists, scholars whose works indelibly altered the course of urgent scholarly conversations across disciplines, time periods, and geographies. For example, there was much renewed attention to the works of Trinidadian novelist, cultural critic, and political theorist C. L. R. James; the oft-cited *C. L. R. James Reader*, a primer for the uninitiated, was first published by Duke University Press in 1992, and many of James's other works were republished in new editions during the ensuing decade by Duke and other university presses. Scholar of the Haitian Revolution, aficionado of cricket, admirer of Walt Whitman and Herman Melville, and critic of U.S. civilization, James, upon his works becoming more widely available to a new generation of readers, modeled for scholars based in the U.S. academy a multiply situated form of postcolonial critique, at once within and outside the Caribbean and United States, that helped to facilitate their own Caribbean turns in the late twentieth century. Likewise, twentieth-century Martinican philosopher, theorist, and novelist Édouard Glissant's classic collection of essays *Le Discours antillais* (*Caribbean Discourse*) was published for the first time in English in 1992 by the University of Virginia Press. In lyrical and engaging prose, Glissant's writings ushered in foundational ideas about creolization and poetic relations in the Americas—aesthetic, political, cultural, and historical. Finally, Antonio Benítez-Rojo's landmark study *The Repeating Island: The Caribbean and the Postmodern Perspective* was published— you got it—in 1992. Benítez-Rojo's work employed chaos theory to argue for the figure of the plantation as a paradoxical phenomenon according to which continuity and discontinuity shape and inform one another in non-antithetical ways, a sort of (post)modern Caribbean archipelagic complex that pulsates outward, across the Americas. Studies by Caribbean-affiliated theorists such as James, Glissant, and Benítez-Rojo, among many others, thus hugely influenced not only Caribbean studies but also American studies broadly defined over the ensuing decades. If anything, their influence is more palpable today than it was when their writings first began appearing in the last decade of the twentieth century.

The turn by scholars of nineteenth-century American literary studies in particular toward the Caribbean during the 1990s was a byproduct of many other developments as well, including the emergence of postcolonialism as a dominant methodology in literary and cultural studies. Of particular relevance here were questions posed by some of its leading practitioners in the early 1990s, figures such as Peter Hulme and Ella Shohat, about why, to that point in time, the United States had somehow been exempted as a site of postcolonial critique. Further, scholars wondered about how properly to conduct a "postcolonial" analysis of the United States across various epochs in its history—whether by treating the nation as postcolonial, neocolonial, imperial, and/or something else. The landmark collection *Cultures of United States Imperialism* (1993) took up these questions in compelling terms, and a few of the essays specifically treated U.S. imperialism in the Caribbean, including one by co-editor Amy Kaplan focused on the threat posed by Black troops on San Juan Hill to white efforts "in the wilderness of empire . . . to displace, appropriate, and incorporate the agency of nonwhites both in empire and at home."[1] Likewise, foundational works in Latin@ Studies provided paradigms for rethinking national, political, economic, cultural, and epistemic borders. Especially noteworthy in this vein are José Saldívar's *The Dialectics of Our America* and the collection *Criticism in the Borderlands*, both published by Duke University Press in 1991. Like Kaplan's attention to Black heroism and participation in the War of 1898, Saldívar's works recognized and responded to the centennial anniversary of Cuban patriot and exile José Martí's *Nuestra América/Our America* (1891), evoking Martí's inter-American revolutionary viewpoint to challenge scholars across American Studies areas to reconsider their nation-bound assumptions about literary and cultural formation.

In addition to the centennial of the War of 1898, another anniversary loomed large by 1992. With the bicentennial celebration of Haitian Independence in 2004 a little over a decade away, and anniversaries marking the Revolution itself already underway, scholars launched projects that would look anew at the significance of the Haitian Revolution and its aftermath. Key works in this vein include Michel-Rolph Trouillot's *Silencing the Past: Power and the Production of History* (1995)—whose central argument first appeared in print in article form in 1991.[2] Trouillot's study asked a simple question that was remarkable for its penetrating insight: how was it that the Haitian Revolution came to be disavowed in and by the West during the nineteenth century and beyond? Over the next two decades, scholars sought to respond to Trouillot's question by reexamining nineteenth- and twentieth-century historical records and cultural artifacts to show how an active silencing or disavowal of the Haitian Revolution in the archives has been at the heart of Western modernity, not least in the nineteenth-century United States. Joan (now Colin) Dayan's *Haiti, History, and the Gods*, published the same year as Trouillot's study, suggested how scholars might examine not only how the West actively sought to silence and disavow Haiti as part of the making of the modern nation state but also how Caribbean-based cultural forms such as Haitian vodoun—nontraditional, vernacular archives as it were—served as repositories for the reconfiguration of powerful myths of white domination into narratives of violence, seduction, and resistance. Intent on broadening the nineteenth-century U.S. literary archive as well, Dayan's study provided an influential estimation of a then little-known novel by Philadelphia-based author Leonora Sansay entitled *Secret History; or, the Horrors of St. Domingo* (1808) that led to its becoming required reading in nineteenth-century American literary studies.

As we have seen, 1992 saw the quincentennial of Columbus's landing in the West Indies, Walcott win the Nobel Prize for Literature, James's, Glissant's, and Benítez-Rojo's works become available in English, Conde's "Caribbean American" novel published, and critical work in postcolonialism, Latin@ Studies, and Caribbean Studies affecting the U.S. academy in far-reaching ways. Likewise, a year later two landmark studies were published that sought to reorient how scholars fundamentally understood race and the formation of nineteenth- and early twentieth-century U.S. literature and culture—and, relevant for our purposes here, the Caribbean's crucial relation to these important questions. In "Part I. Slavery, Revolution, Renaissance" of Eric Sundquist's magisterial *To*

Wake the Nations: Race in the Making of American Literature (1993), win-
ner of the James Russell Lowell Prize from the MLA, the Caribbean plays
a major role. Texts like Melville's "Benito Cereno" (1853), *The Confessions
of Nat Turner* (1831), and Martin Delany's *Blake; or the Huts of America*
(1865), Sundquist suggests, cannot be properly understood without considering their entanglement with, and deft meditations on, radical anti-
slavery in, and U.S. expansionist designs on, the Caribbean. Of especial
significance to U.S. literary and cultural formation during the antebellum period, Sundquist argues, are the Haitian Revolution and filibustering expeditions to and from Cuba according to competing pro- and an-
tislavery visions for U.S. empire building. Yet even as Sundquist seeks to
awaken his reader to Caribbean influences on Turner, Delany, and Melville, the Caribbean, or more precisely Caribbeans, never emerge in his
study as figures making "American" literature and culture worthy of
study. That is, Caribbean scenes and events, keenly identified and re-
hearsed by Sundquist, productively complicate nation-based frames of
reference for understanding how race and slavery imbue the nineteenth-
century American literary imaginary without causing the reader to re-
think the national boundaries of the canon itself.

That certainly is not the case with Paul Gilroy's *The Black Atlantic:
Modernity and Double Consciousness*, also published in 1993, which ag-
gressively challenges national estimations of "African American" or "Caribbean" or "British" literature and culture in arguing for the formation
of a uniquely transatlantic Black culture in the wake of slavery and its
aftermath, a culture not bound to any one location but drawing on, and
commingling, all of them in a glorious act of Black countermodernity.
While he seizes on the phenomenon of migrant Afro-Caribbean black
musical forms such as Hip Hop to make his case, Gilroy focuses, as many
critics have noted, almost exclusively on the transatlantic dimensions of
African American writers like W. E. B. Du Bois, Frederick Douglass, and
Richard Wright across his study. Gilroy's Black Atlantic methodology,
which values "mutation, hybridity, and intermixture en route to better

theories of racism and of black political culture than those so far offered by cultural absolutists," flows most often according to an east-west horizontal axis and less on a north-south vertical one.[3] Ultimately Gilroy awkwardly explains away the absence of Caribbean critics (with the notable exception of Glissant), authors, and texts (beyond the musical) in the study by suggesting that most of these figures and texts would fit his pattern anyway—as if one could not be modern and Black in the Atlantic world, whether in North America, the Caribbean, and/or Latin America, without first traveling imaginatively and otherwise to Europe. Anticipating and attempting to head off challenges to the selectiveness of his case studies, Gilroy ends his "Preface" by suggesting his project is "too massive and its history so little known that I have done scarcely more than put down some preliminary markers for more detailed future investigations"—in effect conceding that perhaps the scale of his project is at once too widely and too narrowly drawn.[4]

What, then, was the precise nature of the Caribbean turn being made by critics like Sundquist and Gilroy in the early 1990s? As a first-year graduate student, I remember being impressed by the awarding of the Nobel Prize to Walcott in 1992. Walcott was a poet and playwright I had admired for a number of years; I first came across his work while teaching at the sixth form level in Belize, specifically his well-known autobiographical poem "A Far Cry from Africa" (1962), which Caribbean students read in an anthology of poems in preparation for their A-level exams. The poem is a meditation on the mixed-race poet's inability, or unwillingness, to choose to turn to either his British or African cultural inheritances alone as opposed to turning to both for poetic inspiration:

> I who am poisoned with the blood of both,
> Where shall I turn, divided to the vein?
> I who have cursed
> The drunken officer of British rule, how choose
> Between this Africa and the English Tongue I love?[5]

Sundquist and Gilroy were addressing a related sort of question in their studies, if from somewhat distinct vantage points: is it possible to understand the making of American literature and culture in the long nineteenth century without considering the constitutive role not only of race but also of the Caribbean?

Since the early 1990s, American literary criticism has persisted in making a turn toward the Caribbean. Nowhere has this been more prominent in recent years than in studies of regionalism, perhaps especially in Southern Studies, attentive to the shared history of plantation economies in the U.S. South and the Caribbean. Yet even as scholars turn more and more toward the Caribbean, or more precisely toward Caribbean presences in the making of nineteenth-century American literature, they have often done so in unidirectional ways. Indeed, much scholarship produced in nineteenth-century American literary studies from the 1990s to the present time, richly provocative and important as it is, might best be characterized as making a Caribbean "half turn." By Caribbean "half turn," I mean to suggest how scholars and critics, in treating Caribbean presences in works authored by U.S. authors, turn to the Caribbean according to a North-South trajectory to spy out influence without ever relocating themselves according to a South-North directionality, a reality that reflects their and their field's institutional location, hierarchies of assumption, and investments.

Put differently, as nineteenth-century Americanist scholarship continues to make a "Caribbean turn," we might ask who is making the turn, from where to where, to whom or to what, and to what end? Conversely, who or what is not turning or being turned to and why? Does one have a choice about whether to turn or not turn? Ultimately, drawing on the poet-speaker's sentiment in "A Far Cry from Africa," I want to suggest the value of a full "Caribbean turn" that is not so much a turn in one or the other direction but a both/and, *a turn from America to the Caribbean* and *from the Caribbean to America* in nineteenth-century American literary and cultural studies.

Caribbean American Regionalism(s) at the C19/C20 Turn

In 1884, New England regionalist painter Winslow Homer's career took a Caribbean turn when he set out on the first of many winter excursions to the Caribbean, travels that would revolutionize his oeuvre in far-reaching ways. As such, critics have been almost universal in recognizing the invigorating, lightening effects that the Caribbean—its tropical landscapes, its variegated seas—had on Homer's aesthetics. One of Homer's best known works from his Caribbean period, *The Gulf Stream* (1899) (Figure. 7.1), challenges critical notions that Homer mechanically reproduces the picturesque discourse underwriting a burgeoning tourism industry in his West Indian watercolors, though to some extent he surely does, as in *On the Way to Market* (1885) (Figure 7.2).

Among several fascinating anecdotes I have come across in my research is testimony from a family friend that Homer hung his Caribbean watercolors in a newly opened lodging house near his Prout's Neck, Maine, studio once the tourist industry took hold there in the late nineteenth century. Not unlike a number of U.S. regionalist writers in New England, the South, and elsewhere treated in my larger project, Homer thus seeks to inculcate touristic desire in, at one and the same time, the Caribbean and Maine as twinned tourist destinations by trafficking in Caribbean "things." Such complexities point to the multidirectional ways in which U.S. expansionism in the late nineteenth and early twentieth centuries—as carried forth by proliferating multinational corporations like United Fruit Company, whose steamships conveyed high-paying tourists like Homer above deck to and from the Caribbean—transformed landscapes, seascapes, peoples, and cultures across the Caribbean and North America. As I have argued in greater detail elsewhere, writers, artists, and intellectuals across North America and the Caribbean responded to this phenomenon, and by so doing were participating in a field of literary and cultural production I have termed *Caribbean American regionalism.*[6] Such a field is not bound exclusively to the objects of study for scholars working in Latin American or Caribbean stud-

Figure 7.1. Winslow Homer, *The Gulf Stream* (1899), The Metropolitan Museum of Art, Catharine Lorillard Wolfe Collection, Wolfe Fund, 1906 (06.1234). The Metropolitan Museum of Art. All rights reserved.

Figure 7.2 Winslow Homer, *On the Way to Market* (1885), Brooklyn Museum of Art. Gift of Gunnar Maske in Memory of Elizabeth Treadway White Maske (69.50). All rights reserved.

ies or in U.S. regionalist traditions, even as it acknowledges and extends from innovative scholarship in these and other areas. Likewise, rather than ignoring competing usages and definitions of the terms "region" and "regionalism" across locales and disciplines, my research allows such definitions to sit uneasily alongside and in productive friction with one another as distinct and, at times, countervailing modes of configuring the time-space coordinates of region within the Caribbean American regional system.

Notwithstanding the less than progressive tendencies on Homer's part, Homer's West Indian paintings cannot be categorized according to a single representational mode or ideological orientation—a racialist, parasitically consumptive, heteronormative Caribbean picturesque, for example. Rather, these artworks display an array of aesthetic practices reflective of the dynamic operations of cultural texts in Caribbean American regionalism writ large produced during the late nineteenth and early twentieth centuries. Consistent with such a critical awareness, even as Homer decorated the walls of his Prout's Neck guest cottage with his picturesque West Indian watercolors, he came to recognize that *The Gulf Stream* would be a most inhospitable presence hung in such a place given its depiction of a perilously threatened Black sailor adrift on a damaged boat surrounded by blood seeking sharks in the turbulent waters of a stormy Gulf Stream. As Homer instructed his agent, "Why do you not try and sell the 'Gulf Stream' to . . . some other public gallery? No one would expect to have it in a private house."[7] The painting's unsuitability for private American interiors suggests the ways an art buying elite actively disavowed their connection to the violence—both literal and figurative—the painting represents, the violence upholding the world-changing historical moment in which Homer painted, whereby a dying European colonialism was giving way to a rising U.S. imperialism in the hemisphere. More precisely, Homer's lasting reputation as a visual artist owes itself to the intricate set of aesthetic practices animating his Caribbean artworks, which register, albeit in oblique and frequently misestimated ways, his emergent sensitivity to the ways U.S. claims to hemispheric exceptionalism during this time pivoted on a disturbing irony. At exactly the moment when the United States relied on immigrant and ex-slave labor at home and West Indian colonial labor abroad for its capitalist and territorial expansionism, white Americans turned ever more resolutely to supremacist attitudes to justify this trend. Homer's Caribbean artworks reflect and critique that Caribbean American regional reality in highly imaginative ways.

Thus when two prospective female buyers of *The Gulf Stream* inquire about what Homer intends by portraying a black sailor in such a precarious state, Homer's reply amounts to a dis-identification with the buyers' picturesque sensibility; instead, he affiliates with, even as he runs the risk of co-opting, his suffering subject's plight. Satirizing their hypocritical yearning for a sentimental resolution to the epic struggle for African American and Afro-Caribbean recognition, resources, and freedom across space and time that the oil painting conveys on formal and figurative levels, Homer pens the following response to his critics via his agent: "The criticisms of the Gulf Stream by old women and others are noted. You may inform these people that the Negro did not starve to death. He was not eaten by the sharks. The waterspout did not hit him. And he was rescued by a passing ship which is not shown in the picture."[8] Fascinatingly enough, Homer did add the merchant ship to the background of the painting *after* learning of such criticisms. Such a retroactive insertion might support the argument that the artist was caving in to critique, thereby compromising the work's artistic and ideological integrity. On the contrary, Homer's addition of an indifferent or at least unaware, rather than rescuing, commercial vessel seems to mock his critics' picturesque sentimentality while simultaneously laying bare the exploitative, inhospitable nature of U.S. expansionism in and around the Caribbean. Such contestation registers itself anew in a representation of *The Gulf Stream* during production, a staged photograph of an indifferent Homer looking away from, and thereby redoubling the pose of, the imperiled Black sailor (Figure 7.3). In the photograph, the only one known to exist that shows Homer at work in his Maine studio, artist and subject rebuff the con-

Figure 7.3 Winslow Homer in his Prout's Neck Studio, beside *The Gulf Stream*, ca. 1900. Bowdoin College of Art, Brunswick, Maine. Gift of the Homer Family (1964–69:179–9).

sumptive gaze of the viewer by turning away from the viewer and each other and toward, Janus-faced, the margins of the photograph.

Homer's capacity to sympathize with the plight of laboring Blacks haunted by their condition of un-freedom in the Caribbean American region, whether in the post-Reconstruction U.S. or in the decolonizing Caribbean, together with the impulse to see and not see and to mimic and mock, characterize the design structure underpinning a painting composed two decades prior to *The Gulf Stream*. In 1876, Homer traveled to Virginia on the eve of the nation's centennial celebration of independence and its catastrophic abandonment of Reconstruction to sketch freedmen and women. In *Dressing for Carnival* (1876), Homer locates himself and the viewer behind a fence near where a Black family prepares to celebrate Jonkonnu, a holiday imported from the West Indies according to which slaves were given license during the Christmas holidays to act as if they were free and did so by dressing up and dancing in

Figure 7.4. Winslow Homer, *Dressing for Carnival* (1876), The Metropolitan
Museum of Art, Amelia B. Lazarus Fund, 1922 (22.220). The Metropolitan
Museum of Art. All rights reserved.

ways that mimicked and mocked the styles, attitudes, and behaviors of
their white masters (Figure 7.4) Art historians wonder whether Homer
"knew" about the tradition of Jonkonnu depicted in the painting. That
he locates himself *behind* the fence barring this family—and others like
it—from participating in July 4 celebrations and a state of unconditional
freedom and mobility suggests Homer likely witnessed and discussed
the celebration with its Black participants.

In their most progressive forms—the West Indian watercolors that
complicate without transcending the touristic mode in which they are
drawn, the haunting naturalism of *The Gulf Stream*, and the thickly descriptive realism of *Dressing for Carnival*—Homer's Caribbean artworks
gesture toward, without necessarily arriving at, the sort of *unconditional*
laws of hospitable relations that might have allowed for all parties in the
multiple locales of the Caribbean American region to renegotiate the
boundaries of their identities, values, ideals, and assumptions according

to mutually enabling terms, providing for a more ethical and sustainable future. This, however, is not the sort of future provided for by the investors, agents, and representatives of U.S. empire building in the Caribbean at the turn of the century.

The turn-of-the-century photograph shown in Figure 7.5 is one of thousands produced by the Isthmian Canal Commission (ICC) coterminous with the building of the Panama Canal (Figure 7.5). The photograph depicts within its frame the voiceless mass of Black West Indian laborers necessary to build the epic Canal project as sign and symbol of U.S. exceptionalism in the hemisphere. Our line of sight here is that of the sovereign photographer looking down at the nameless laborers. How do we occupy their vantage point? Indeed, we have precious few first-hand accounts by West Indian laborers about their experiences working amid inhospitable conditions in the segregated canal zone. Louis S. Meikle's *Confederation of the British West Indies versus Annexation to the United States of America* (1912) is a "canal" narrative in an oblique sort of way. Meikle was a U.S.-trained medical professional who, like so many brown and black West Indian peoples, migrated outside of his home colony of Jamaica in search of gainful employment owing to the depressed economic conditions of the West Indies in the late nineteenth and early twentieth centuries. On receiving his medical degrees from Howard University, he worked throughout the United States and the Caribbean on behalf of U.S. interests, including several years as part of the massive West Indian labor contingent helping to build the canal. Meikle was thus well positioned to diagnose the root cause of America's unrest in the Canal Zone and of West Indian laborers seeking freedom and self-government everywhere.

In his text, Meikle authorizes a poetics and politics for a federated "United West Indies," a blueprint for a more hospitable, viable, and just brown and black future—a "West Indies for West Indians . . . *federated* as one body with *self-government*," as he puts it—against which both sides of the Anglo-American imperial divide—the declining British Crown Colony government and the ever-widening U.S.-controlled Caribbean American regional system—conspired.[9] Many U.S. writers advocated

Figure 7.5. "Arrival at Cristobal of S.S. Ancon with 1500 Laborers from Barbados," 2 September 1909. Courtesy National Archives.

against U.S. annexation in the West Indies as well across various genres and texts. Yet whereas they often employ the specter of Black rebellion in a gothic mode to ward off U.S. annexation in the West Indies so as to resist becoming mired in another "Hayti," Meikle mobilizes the specter of an inhospitable *white* United States to urge the British against accepting U.S. annexation in the West Indies.

According to Meikle's first-hand account living and working in the segregated Canal Zone, what makes the U.S. annexation of the West Indies so objectionable is the inability of the U.S. colonizer to creolize himself—to embrace a kind of postcolonial conduct as the guest of other Creole hosts in the hemisphere—rather than persisting in imperial hostility: "he will not readily adapt himself to conditions found outside of his own country, and as a result, his actions in this new sphere have been characterized as the man who—literally speaking—takes the bull by the horns as the simplest and easiest method for overcoming resistance."[10] Thus, Meikle's narrative, at once a protest and an appeal, and the many U.S. texts that existed alongside it (as, for example, the ICC photograph above) evince a richly variable, if paradoxically contingent, inter-imperial aesthetics that form themselves according to past, present, and future conditions of Caribbean American regional relations—the latter protective of a white nationalism within the context of an ever-expanding U.S. informal empire in the Caribbean, the former suggestive of an emergent business of brown and black Caribbean nationalisms amidst an inhospitable, irrepressible U.S. expansionist presence that threatens to derail them, a phenomenon hauntingly depicted, albeit obliquely, in Homer's *The Gulf Stream* and *Dressing for Carnival*.

Like Meikle, Eric Walrond witnessed first hand the building of the Panama Canal and he is unique among the many West Indian-born writers and intellectuals who inspired the Harlem Renaissance for having labored in the Canal Zone. Born in British Guiana in 1898, Walrond relocated with his mother to Barbados at age eight and then to Panama in 1911, where he finished his schooling before working as a journalist on a Panamanian newspaper. He later migrated to New York City, where he wrote the ten loosely related experimental stories of *Tropic Death* (1926), perhaps Walrond's greatest fictional contribution to forging a collective awareness in his readers about the extreme servitude and suffering endured by the laboring classes across the Caribbean. Such suffering is nowhere present in the expensive lithograph authorized by the United Fruit Company in 1904 reproduced in Figure 7.6. In it, an adoring Hindu

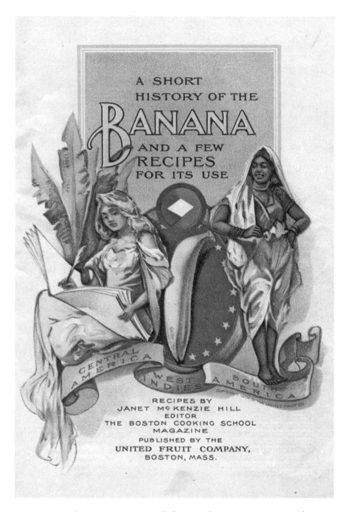

Figure 7.6. United Fruit Company lithograph. Front cover, *A Short History of the Banana and a Few Recipes for Its Use* (Boston: United Fruit Company, 1904), frontispiece.

woman turns to a loosely dressed white U.S. woman across an erotically charged banana divide and gives her culinary secrets freely. The labor providing for tropical fruit production and transportation disavowed in the lithograph are Walrond's focus in his story "The Yellow One" in *Tropic Death*. In "The Yellow One," Walrond writes through and across the banana divide of the UFC lithograph, resisting its unidirectional, imperial poetics from a relational viewpoint.

The yellow object that lends an erotic charge in Walrond's story is not a phallic banana—though bananas lie everywhere above and below decks—but the eponymous figure, a mestizo woman from Honduras "idealized" as la madurita. Maduro, feminized into Madura, means ripe and mature—as in fruits, cigars, and wines. By adding the diminutive ending "ita," Walrond suggests not only smallness but affection. Anticipating the rebranding in mid-century of United Fruit as "Chiquita," the diminutive form of "chica," or girl, Walrond exploits, albeit in indicting ways, the connection made across islands and continents between ripe, mature fruit and eroticized female bodies, as in the UFC lithograph. Accordingly, la madurita rouses the desire of all deck hands on the *Urubamba*, a U.S.-operated banana boat traveling from Honduras to Jamaica. Brown and black laborers alike stare at la madurita with lust, and white American crew members grab at her with "flesh-crazed hands."[11]

Language plays a central role in the sexually driven rivalry on board the *Urubamba*. Where the challenges of translation are mystified according to the romantic relations between the white American woman and her Hindu informant in the UFC lithograph, Walrond's story exposes, and by so doing confronts, the imperial violence underpinning such a gesture. More precisely, when "the yellow one" talks to her Jamaican partner Alfred or the white U.S. crew members, she speaks in a Jamaican creole that is so densely rendered by Walrond as to be almost indecipherable to metropolitan-based readers who would seek to consume it like the Hindu woman's Caribbean recipes. Yet when la madurita communicates with Jota Arosemena, a "mestizo" of "Latin" extraction who aids her and her ailing baby on board the ship, their "ready means of communication" is Spanish, a tongue that is said, much like their budding affair, to have sprung "spontaneously up between them" (51).

Ultimately the story culminates in a tragically violent confrontation between the Cuban-born Arosemena and Hubigon, a black "son of the Florida Gulf" (60) who recalls Homer's central figure, their bitter rivalry as automatic as the affection between Arosemena and la madurita, who recoils at the "black and ugly" dock hands loading bananas onto the *Urubamba*. Hubigon's anger boils over when he reflects on how he is subjected to U.S.-style segregationist laws and customs on and off the American-managed banana boat whereas the Cuban Arosemena, whom Hubigon mockingly calls "Porto Rico," enjoys a social mobility denied Hubigon despite their occupying the same laboring class on board the ship. Such privileges include spontaneous affairs with mestiza women like la madurita and drinking sessions with the ship's chef, a "freckle-faced Carolina 'cracker,'" and the "baker's assistant, a New Orleans creole," in cafés that "barred jet-black American Negroes" (60).

In condensing racial and economic inequalities and embodied rage into a murderous conflict between two kitchen workers on board, "The Yellow One" suggests the broken pieces of Antillean history famously described by Walcott in his Noble Lecture. But unlike Walcott's optimistically rendered vision, such shards remain fragmented rather than reassembled. Likewise, the *Urubamba* resembles a kind of "Open Boat," "a womb abyss," to evoke Edouard Glissant, an impossible yet historically factual space where life and death converge.[12] The possible future of a "West Indies for West Indians" that Meikle calls for, or that Puerto Rican Rámon Emeterio Betances, a founding figure in the "antillanismo" movement, envisioned in the Spanish Caribbean context as early as 1866, remains tragically deferred as Jamaica's "dead blue hills" (66) appear on the horizon at story's end—not unlike the oppressive white storm clouds that hover over the imperiled Black sailor in Homer's *Gulf Stream*.

By treating Homer's paintings alongside Meikle's political tract and Walrond's short story and plotting a field of literary and cultural production that we might term Caribbean American regionalism, I have endeavored to demonstrate the potential value awaiting scholars willing to make a full Caribbean turn in nineteenth-century American literary and cultural studies. Ultimately, such a project aims to inspire scholars working within and across would-be discrete areas and fields to collaborate with one another on mapping a new cultural history and geography of transdisciplinary, transregional space and time in the service of more equitable and just Caribbean American regional relations and futures for all stakeholders.

‌‌‌

To evoke Gilroy once more, the "massive" project of making a full Caribbean turn in nineteenth-century American literary and cultural studies has indeed been a collaborative one. Since the field began turning to the Caribbean in the early 1990s, what was once the "early national" or "post-Revolutionary" period in nineteenth-century American literary studies no longer makes categorical sense if used to describe the literary and cultural tradition of any one nation—not only because scholars have painstakingly shown how entangled the early U.S. was with the colonies and emergent nation states of the Caribbean on political, economic, and other levels, but also because there were other "early national" and "New" republics emerging simultaneously in the hemisphere, not least of all Haiti. Furthermore, if in 1992 scholars based in the U.S. academy endeavored to identify Caribbean influences on *the* American Renaissance— meaning singular—in order to enrich our appreciation of it, scholars since then have undertaken path-breaking work to show how that American Renaissance did not exist independent or exclusive of multiple, overlapping, and frequently competing American Renaissances unfolding across the Americas, including the Caribbean.[13] So, too, where once we thought of authors as being bound to one "national" context, renewed scholarly attention to authors and/or their texts migrating to and away from North American and the Caribbean, whether by force or choice, across epochs in the long nineteenth century has made it impossible to assign many of them to a fixed geographic locale or national context— figures like Olaudah Equiano and Leonora Sansay; José María Heredia and Mary Seacole; José Martí and Marcus Garvey; and Pierre Faubert and Frederick Douglass. This is the result of innovative Caribbean-based paradigms like "Black cosmopolitanism," "Black Empire," and "Caribbean Middlebrow,"[14] and "ambassadors of culture," "the *Filibustero*," and "*Nuestra América*/Our America."[15] Likewise, nineteenth-century Americanists are actively seeking out Caribbean primary and critical sources for study that have led them to devise influential concepts like "creole complex," "ecological personhood," "the American Mediterranean," and many others.[16] Finally, the Caribbean turn has provided for and been enabled by other paradigms not tied exclusively to the Caribbean— major concepts like the circum-atlantic, the transnational, and the hemispheric—and new ways of understanding period and time, genre and aesthetics, geography and space, economics and ecology, translation and archives, and religion and science, among other fertile topics currently in vogue in nineteenth-century American literary studies, have helped to produce a Caribbean turn even as the Caribbean turn has ushered in new methods and approaches in these areas of study.

I began this essay by imagining an anniversary year—1992—as the moment when a Caribbean turn in nineteenth-century American literary studies got underway. I might just as well have cited 1998 (1898) or 2004 (1804), among many others. But to return to 1992, that was also the year Barbadian writer and critic George Lamming's *The Pleasures of Exile* (1960) was reissued in a new edition by the University of Michigan Press. In that classic study of decolonization, Lamming insists that Caribbean peoples have "always been mixed up in America's business," a phenomenon Lamming was discovering anew as he visited New York City for the first time. [17] So, too, we might say that C19 American literary and cultural studies is now all mixed up in the Caribbean's business, and it is a safe bet that it always will be. If, as we have seen, scholars in nineteenth-century American literary studies have been turning to the Caribbean in increasing numbers since 1992, the anniversaries that, in part, prompted that exciting development in the field remind us of the perpetual need to re-turn to foundational myths and events in order to re-tell them in less univocal ways, or in the context of this essay, Caribbean-wise—hence Michelle Cliff's John Brown story, or Condé's playful tale about Hester Prynne and Tituba. The turn to the Caribbean in nineteenth-century American literary studies is, and always will be, then, a *re*-turning, a perpetual search for a more just past future of Caribbean American regional relations. Such an ethical calling is consistent with Lamming's eloquent appeal in, fittingly enough, a chapter in his study entitled, "Ishmael at Home": "America is one island only . . . the less money and the more islands, the better it may be for America herself."[18] Put another way, it is always the right time for nineteenth-century Americanists to be making a Caribbean (re-)turn.

Chapter 8

⟿

Oceanic Turns and American Literary History in Global Context

MICHELLE BURNHAM

An unusual map titled "Atlantic Ocean, Toscanelli, 1474" appeared in
J. G. Bartholomew's 1911 *Literary and Historical Atlas of America*. This
composite map superimposes onto a modern cartography of the Atlantic
world Toscanelli's premodern map of that same space. The earlier 1474
map was drawn, of course, without any knowledge of the existence of
the Americas, and the effects of combining pre-Columbian with post-
Columbian geography are both fascinating and disorienting. The large
island of Japan (then called Cipangu) hovers over the western half of
Mexico, the enormous landmass identified as Cathay (or Northern
China) swallows the Aleutians and shoulders its way onto southern
Alaska, while a busy constellation of East Indian islands fills up the sea
between Manji (or Southern China) and Japan, as well as much of what
we now recognize as the Rocky Mountain time zone. Perhaps the most
interesting effect of this blended map, however, is the peculiar confusion
it creates between the Atlantic and Pacific oceans, which appear here to
compete for exactly the same water: when we look from the land on the
west (or left side of the map), we automatically recognize the Pacific;
from the land on the east (or right side), we instantly register that same
water as the Atlantic.

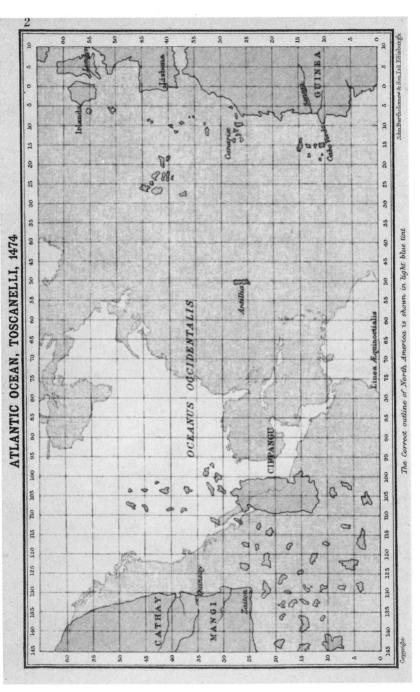

Figure 8.1. "Atlantic Ocean, Toscanelli, 1474." J. G. Bartholomew, *A Literary and Historical Atlas of North and South America* (London: J.M. Dent, 1911; rev. 1930), 201.

Narratives of American literature and history like to begin with what was wrong about this older map, and scholars such as Peter Hulme and others have taught us to understand that it was the power of maps like Toscanelli's that convinced Columbus that Cuba was really Cathay, and that Hispaniola must be Japan.[1] Anecdotes about Columbus's cartographic and continental confusion now usually circulate as humorous early modern warnings about the failure to ask for directions or the humiliating consequences of bad geography. But this perspective only encourages students and scholars alike to ignore what is perhaps most revealing about this story—the incredible intensity of Europe's desire to reach Asia, not only in 1492 but also for centuries after. It is as if the East Indies literally fall off the map as soon as the West Indies appear on them. As a result, the Eastern hemisphere has essentially been exiled from accounts of American literary and cultural history, as a space too impossibly distant and irrelevant to matter. Narratives of American literature conventionally begin with this simultaneous temporal and spatial reorientation set off by the unexpected landfall of 1492, for the historical clock also gets re-set once this geographical space is re-mapped. Recognizing the Americas, in other words, has long meant forgetting Asia—despite the fact that Europe's encounter with America continued in many ways to be managed, understood, and recorded through its sustained interest in reaching the products and markets of the East. This chapter asks what it might mean to recover this wider, transhemispheric, global context for American literary studies, and how a turn toward the oceans might help us get there.

Precisely because the sea offers an alternative dimensionality, what Hester Blum has described as a "methodological model for nonlinear or nonplanar thought," it has the capacity substantially to reorient both the maps and the narratives we use to study, teach, and understand American literary history.[2] As I noted above, the name and identity of the ocean on Bartholomew's map shifts entirely depending on which continental coast one stands on and looks out from. But what if one is positioned instead at sea? How might such an oceanic perspective bring a global dimension to a literary history that has always been framed in terrestrial terms?

Narrative

The Atlantic world framework that has so powerfully reoriented the field of American studies over the past several decades has already given a new kind of centrality to the ocean. Or so it would seem. As several scholars have pointed out, the apparently aquatic focus on the Atlantic remains in many ways undermined by a residual terrestrialism. Despite Atlanticism's shift from the nation to the ocean, the paradigm is nonetheless sustained by a land-based imaginary in which the ocean figures predominantly as a liquid road that connects solid pieces of land to each other—what Philip E. Steinberg describes as "a space of connection that merely unifies the societies on its borders." The result is too often an Atlantic in which one "never gets wet" or an approach to oceanic studies that, in Kären Wigen's words, "rarely peers beneath the waves."[3] This Atlantic model limitation might be extended to its Pacific and Indian Ocean counterparts, each of which likewise positions a major ocean at the liquid center of a transnational, transcultural, and multilingual world, rimmed and held together by a container of land.[4] Indeed, these models might be better labeled with Felipe Fernández-Armesto's term "rimlands" to describe those stretches of "land at the water margin," spaces devoid of that "complex, four-dimensional materiality" so evocatively tied to oceanic space itself.[5] But another result of this rimlands emphasis is to disconnect the oceans from each other, an especially strange effect considering that the movement of oceanic water mostly merges, melds, and mixes with more water—with bays and inlets, with rivers, gulfs and seas, but also with other oceans. Alison Games has insisted that "It is time to restore the ocean to Atlantic history," and I suggest that the best way of doing so may be to restore the Atlantic itself to its global transoceanic connections.[6]

The extraordinary appeal of Atlantic studies might be identified less with its ocean, then, than with the ready-made transnationalism its rimlands focus makes possible. Unlike an earlier nation-centered model of literary history, transatlanticism positions America within an Atlantic rimland characterized by an extraordinary multiplicity of national, cultural, and linguistic traditions. The effect of this reorientation is especially visible in the by now routine inclusion of translated colonial Spanish, French, Dutch, and Portuguese texts alongside colonial English writings in anthologies of American literature. But as Ralph Bauer has noted, there is a curious partiality to these selections, for they are invariably limited to descriptions of lands that would later come to be part of the current United States, excluding work (even sometimes by the same author or from the same text) describing lands that are now outside U.S. boundaries.[7] In other words, beneath the apparent transnationalism of our current anthologies persists a residual nationalism. This residual nationalism cooperates, I suggest, with the residual terrestrialism Steinberg identifies in current Atlantic studies work, for anthology selections that favor depictions of U.S. lands obviously already favor depictions of land itself, despite the fact that a large number of these early texts are taken up by extensive passages describing sea travel. My point here is not really one about narrative inclusion but rather one about narrative dimensionality. A shift from a rimlands to a transoceanic context would exchange a linear or planar narrative for a multidimensional one that emphasizes America's ongoing material connectedness with the rest of the globe.

The limitations of linear terrestriality as a framework for American literary history become even more evident in those anthology sections devoted to representing texts published after the colonial period, when the non-English texts and traditions that enrich the early pages of most contemporary American literature anthologies disappear altogether. As one approaches, more or less, the magical date of 1776, these transnational and multilingual beginnings suddenly become moored on the familiar monolinguistic and nationalist sandbar of the American Revolution. Bauer observes that the multilingual and transnational representation of colonial texts "vanishes into thin air after the initial phase of the European discoveries and conquests has been completed," a disappearance that moreover implies the absence of non-English-speaking peoples and their experiences from subsequent American literary and cultural history.[8] In other words, American literary history is at once grounded by a spatial imagination that is land-based and tethered to a temporal logic that remains nation-centered in large part because its central narrative remains revolution-centered. As I have argued elsewhere, revolution itself is routinely narrativized in almost exclusively national terms.[9] Indeed, the American Revolution functions something like the temporal counterpart to American continental space on Toscanelli's map: it is an obstacle as much as an opportunity, a highly productive resource that is also an astonishingly blinding roadblock. Together, the terrestriality of the continent and the temporality of the Revolution ground a fundamentally linear national narrative that both retrospectively and prospectively shapes the story of American literary and cultural history.

The traditional classroom pedagogical tools used to teach American literature—the survey and the anthology—both still overwhelmingly bear the residual armature of this older, linear narrative dominated by the nation, however many multicultural and transnational modifications have since been surgically grafted onto it.[10] Sarah Rivett identifies what is at stake in this persistence when she notes that the traditional narrative about American exceptionalism continues to be happily claimed and reinforced by the political Right in the United States, perhaps especially in the absence of any compelling alternatives to it. She argues that scholars and teachers of American literature currently

> see the arc from the Puritans to the present day as potentially useful in the classroom but too teleological and too singular for our scholarship. Narrative and genealogical histories of America from the colonial period to the present day have become increasingly elusive with the transnational, hemispheric, Atlantic, and comparative conceptual frameworks that we have all

come to accept as not only more historically accurate but also politically efficacious.[11]

Rivett's observation suggests that while these newer models have allowed for various *remappings* of American literature, history, and culture, they have not yet generated any postnational *narratives* of American literary history in its long form; we've not yet translated these maps into story (see Martin Brückner's chapter in this volume on critical "remappings"). Doing so, I suggest, requires not just changing the protagonist of this story (replacing the nation with, for example, religion) but changing its narrative form. What if our literary and cultural histories of America began not with the "discovery" of land but with the movement of water? What if we emphasize not what was wrong about Toscanelli's older map, but what may be unintentionally right about Bartholomew's disorientingly layered map, which presents us with an image of transoceanic connection over the space of an America that is both in the middle of it all and yet not quite there?[12] A focus on transoceanic connection across a half-present continent might provide a way into an alternative narrative that accounts for the movement of and resistance to global empires by tracking the transportation and translation of goods, bodies, and texts through and across terraqueous space.

A global framework that acknowledges the intercontinental and transoceanic context for American literature and culture would emphasize that sea travel has materially connected continents, peoples, and products from the colonial period to the present day; that the Atlantic, Pacific, and Indian oceans (as well as the Caribbean and Mediterranean Seas) were tied to each other through exploration, empire, and commerce; and that indigenous peoples both participated in and vigorously resisted all three. A transoceanic turn that moves toward imagining American literary history in the context of the planet's multiple, and interconnected, oceans might change the way we think about space, about archives, about materiality, textuality, and translation. But it might also allow us to position American literature within a global literary history by narrating a story about the connections between America and its writing with the rest of world.

Geography

An American literary history framed within a transoceanic global context would combine the materialist commitments of world-systems theory and global history with the maritime emphasis of oceanic studies and empire studies. As historian Peter Coclanis observes, the "degree of separation between the 'Atlantic World' and the rest of the world is chronically overstated," and in a recent interview titled "Are We All Global Historians Now?" David Armitage more specifically suggests that "one of the futures of Atlantic history is precisely joining it to other oceanic and trans-regional histories" in order to "think about the interrelations between these oceanic arenas and how in some sense they add up to a global or proto-global history." Americanist scholars like Jorge Cañizares-Esguerra and Antonio Benítez-Rojo have begun to point in this direction by recognizing the ways in which the administrative coordinates and material networks of early modern empires linked multiple oceans—as Spain, for example, moved resources extracted from both the Atlantic and the Pacific through Mexico and the Caribbean.[13] The work of global historians makes it clear that connections between the Atlantic, Caribbean, and Pacific waterworlds were moreover forged and maintained as a way of reaching another ocean altogether—the Indian Ocean, whose trading networks, ports, and goods dominated global trade not only at the time of Columbus's voyages but for centuries beyond. As Robert Marks puts it, it was the Indian Ocean that at this time figured as "the most important crossroads for global exchanges of goods, ideas, and culture, with China, India, and the Islamic Near and Middle East meeting there as the major players, and Europe a peripheral, marginal player trying desperately to gain access to the sources of wealth generated in Asia." Enrique Dussel likewise emphasizes that Europe's eventual cen-

trality within the modern/colonial world-system arrived only as an unexpected result of its desperate efforts to reach China and India by a
western oceanic route that happened to lead Europeans into resource-
rich continents they hadn't known existed. Such accounts offer an important geographical and historical extension to a Wallersteinian model
of a capitalist world-system that is often assumed only to begin spatially
with Europe and temporally in 1492.[14]

In fact, even when astonishing mineral resources were discovered in
the Americas, they were primarily of interest as a ticket that finally
gained Spain access to highly coveted Asian ports and trade goods.[15] The
Spanish galleon trade that connected the Atlantic and Pacific as early as
1565 transported silver mined in Mexico or Peru and exchanged it in the
Philippine markets of Manila or Cavite for products like silks, spices, and
porcelain that arrived there from China and India. The ships that carried
these sought-after goods from the East also carried Chinese, Filipino,
and Indian sailors and slaves, at least some of whom ended up in the
Americas, in locations like Mexico or Louisiana or California.[16] The
Spanish galleon trade generated two centuries of histories and archives
of writing that have hardly begun to be recovered, much less read together with literatures of the Spanish Americas or of the British and
Dutch Atlantic slave trades.

Spain was hardly alone among European nations in persisting in its
goal of reaching Asia by connecting oceans. The transoceanic voyages of
sixteenth- and seventeenth-century privateers like Francis Drake,
Woodes Rogers, and William Dampier pursued, on behalf of the English
crown, the wealth transported from Asia on Spanish ships. These journeys documented movements between such far-flung sites as Puerto
Rico, Virginia, the Bahamas, Mexico, Panama, Campeachy, Peru, California, Guam, the Molucca islands, China, Australia, Sumatra, Juan Fernandez Island, Ecuador, and the Bahamas. But as they did so they occupied a largely liquid terrain whose nameless locations were (and still
remain) nearly impossible for readers to imagine or differentiate from
each other outside the abstract orientations of latitude and longitude.

Similarly, seventeenth-century Dutch explorers like Jacob Roggoveen, Willem Shouten, and Jacob LeMaire generated accounts of maritime exploration to and between the Falkland Islands, Cape Horn, Chile, Easter Island, and Indonesia. Russians arrived in the north Pacific in the early eighteenth century and eventually reached as far as Fort Ross in northern California in pursuit of the fur trade with China, inspiring Spain's response in the form not only of competing voyages but the California mission system's attempts to lay claim to Pacific coast territory and control over the region's indigenous peoples. Subsequent French and English expeditions finally tapped into the riches of the East by virtue of this lucrative Pacific fur trade, facilitated by northwest coast natives and Aleutian and Kodiak islanders, to trade with the Chinese for the fine porcelains, silks, and teas that ended up in markets, shops, homes, and books throughout the Americas as well as Europe.

Accounts of such exchanges and discoveries circulated widely in the many eighteenth- and early nineteenth-century reprints and translations of global circumnavigations by the Englishmen Cook and Vancouver, the French expeditions by Lapérouse and Bougainville, and Spanish voyages by Maurelle and Bodega. These were in turn followed up by countless commercial voyages from Europe and the United States in pursuit of such oceanic commodities as fur, whales, sandalwood, and sea cucumber. The texts that document this laborious and often violent movement of bodies, goods, and ships represent a centuries-long transnational archive of waterlogged writing that remains excluded from a simultaneously terrestrialized and nationalized American literary history. These unfamiliar texts moreover provide access to the materialist transoceanic contexts for much more familiar writing, for those texts that we have in many cases been looking at for a long time. Jim Egan, for example, has identified a profound engagement with the East in the texts of such colonial writers as John Smith and Anne Bradstreet, while Geoffrey Sanborn has brought to light the Pacific influences on and context for James Fenimore Cooper's otherwise landlocked novel *Last of the Mohicans*.[17] Such transoceanic movement can be inscribed in as mundane a moment as the description in Catherine Maria Sedgwick's 1824 historical romance *Hope Leslie* of John Winthrop's Boston home, which contains "great looking-glasses, turkey carpets, window-curtains and valance, picture and a map, a brass clock, red leather back chairs, a great pair of and-irons," and whose pantry is stuffed with "Madeira wine, prunes, marmalade, silver-tankards and wine-cups."[18] Governor Winthrop dines here with his family, several recently arrived English colonists, the Narragansett chief Miantonomo, his councilors, and an interpreter. In this brief passage, global relations between laborers, traders, sailors, financiers, and consumers are embedded in the imported foreign objects among which local New England colonial negotiations take place. What kinds of linguistic contacts, acts of force and violence, and financial mechanisms across oceans brought these objects and people to John Winthrop's imagined dining room? How might that thick network of contacts, exchanges, and movements provide a context in which to understand literary genre, linguistic style, prose aesthetics, and book form?

This long history of transoceanic, global empires also suggests why—even three centuries after the Columbian arrival—nearly every European nation was still sending ships to find the imagined route of a "Northwest passage" through the North American continent to the Pacific. Although the late eighteenth century is routinely associated with revolution and nation-building in the Atlantic, it was also characterized by an enormous surge in Pacific voyages. In the South Pacific as well, those same European nations continued, for far longer than was reasonable, to seek a fabled "great Southern continent" whose resources and commercial value were expected to eclipse that of the American colonies. Like the account of Columbus asking an Arawak Indian how to get to the Chinese palace of the Grand Khan, these stories tend to get dismissed as ridiculous navigational follies and geographical fantasies, but in fact they provide striking evidence of the extraordinary commercial commitments by early modern global empires to reaching the markets and products of the East, efforts that folded the Americas—and writing about the Americas—into transoceanic networks. American literary history has been dominated by a land-revolution-nation matrix whose almost gravitational force has kept scholars from recognizing an alternative ocean-empire-globe paradigm. Along the way, it has also prevented us from asking what revolutionary nation-building and transoceanic commerce-building might have to do with each other.

Recently, planetary models for an American literary history have offered compelling alternatives to the global, in part by adding to this extensive horizontal reach a vertical dimension that takes into account the biospheric interrelations of human with other life forms, expanding to include that dimension Robert Cox describes as constituting a "thin envelope encompassing the planet from the upper atmosphere to the seabeds." Joyce Chaplin, for example, argues that the recent focus on globalization has prevented our attention to the history of planetary awareness that dates back to the circumnavigation narratives of the 1500s. In contrast to a global emphasis on the social, she advocates for a planetary focus on the physical that might supplant a possessive nationalism and lead Americans instead to take "the physical Earth seriously as an expression of its world-wide obligations and privileges."[19] Chaplin's advocacy of a planetary over a global turn allows her to emphasize the ecological concerns of the former too often clouded by the economic emphasis of the latter.

Wai Chee Dimock similarly advocates a planetary model for American literary study that quickly distinguishes its orientation from the global approaches of Wallerstein, whose focus on the capitalist world-system she eschews for "other phenomena, not reducible to capitalism." Dimock zooms in from Franco Moretti's distance reading approach to engage with "the phenomenal world of particular texts," locating a stunning history of global textual exchange, influence, and translation, especially among nineteenth- and twentieth-century texts.[20] But as Gretchen Murphy has pointed out, the networks of books and readers that emerge from this planetary phenomenalism leave out both those "forms of culture that might not make it onto library shelves and the material forces that channel circuits of culture." The resulting model is one that risks engaging in what Trish Loughran describes as a "transhistorical act of reading across space and beyond local time" and that comes to resemble the detached and transcendent qualities of Emerson's transparent eyeball.[21] In other words, an exclusive emphasis on the histories of reading and the movement of texts overlooks the multidimensional oceanic materiality to which world-systems theory and global history remain committed.

Indeed, one might argue that this contest between global and planetary frameworks is a false one that asks scholars to choose between ecological and economic orientations, when the two forces remain fundamentally and critically intertwined. It is, of course, impossible to separate the social and economic relations of a capitalist world-system from the mechanisms by which some books (and not others) get transported onto library shelves around the world, just as it is impossible to separate the environmental destruction Chaplin and others are so right to deplore from the economic relations that lead to such results. Recent news stories about the movement of predatory air breathing Asian fish into the waterways of New York or the arrival of a Japanese dock encrusted with radioactive sea life on the coast of Oregon point toward the combination of economic and environmental, manmade and natural, forces that tie the social and the physical worlds to each other. Global history and world-systems theory can bring an oceanic materiality to bear on an otherwise transcendental textuality, making the stories we tell about America and the maps on which we chart them far more watery ones than they have been.

Translation

A more specifically oceanic literary history would draw attention not only to the transportation of commodities, bodies, and raw materials (and to the residues of that movement left behind in character, setting, plot, and theme) but to the material movement and circulation of texts.

Oceans are spaces with little regard for the coherence of national languages or claims to textual originality, and a more aquatic (or at least
more amphibian) orientation to literary history demands our engagement with underexplored archives, with translations, with reprints, with
periodical circulation. Meredith McGill recognizes a reprint culture in
which "authorship is not the dominant mode of organizing literary culture" and in which "texts with authors' names attached take their place
alongside anonymous, pseudonymous, and unauthorized texts." Reprint
studies aim to recover those texts that evade terrestrial boundary lines
and inhabit the submerged underside of the "author-centered literary
nationalisms" with which literary history has traditionally been preoc-
cupied.[22] Reprints, abridged editions, and pirated texts are the literary
historical versions of sunken ships, drowned bodies, jetsam. Translations, too, are akin to textual castaways left behind for their presumed
lack of authenticity in relation to an "original," to whose language and
meaning they can be quite egregiously unfaithful. Because translations
say as much if not more about the translator than they do about the text
translated, they have traditionally invited scholarly skepticism and
avoidance. But these textual categories gain new relevance if we understand literary history in the way James Clifford has taught us to think
about cultures: not only as fixed in place, like continental land, but as
moving about like a ship or like the unstable multidimensionalities of
water, whose currents, waves, and tides possess at once regularity and
unpredictability. Clifford argues that anthropology has privileged the village as the authentic site of a culture, ignoring the often far-flung reaches
of a culture's own travels. If we think of a textual original as the literary
historical equivalent to Clifford's "authentic" anthropological village,
then that text's many translations, reprints, and rogue editions are the
equivalent of his hotel lobbies and airport terminals (or, in oceanic
terms, ship decks, holds, and ports) around the globe—sites through
which texts (like cultures) travel, and in response to which they change
in selective and adaptive ways. Epeli Hau'ofa has made precisely this argument in describing Pacific cultures as continually traversing "national

boundaries, the international dateline, and the equator," moving through "seaports and airports throughout the Central Pacific." Hauʻofa's vision of Oceania as a "sea of islands" recognizes the oceanic multidimensionality of a "universe comprised not only [of] land surfaces but the surrounding ocean as far as they could traverse and exploit it, the underworld with its fire-controlling and earth-shaking denizens, and the heavens above with their hierarchies of powerful gods and named stars and constellations that people could count on to guide their ways across oceans."[23]

Of course, it bears remembering that our current anthologies already traffic considerably in translation, nowhere more than in their colonial selections. Colleen Boggs compellingly argues for the centrality of translation to a transnational American literature, and emphasizes the ways translation "may defamiliarize the domestic and erode the very borders of linguistic distinction."[24] This framework might be extended to include transoceanic networks between Atlantic, Pacific, and Indian waterworlds that in turn transport texts and inspire translations, of which we have many. Such a perspective also offers a reprieve to scholarly objections that the limits of our linguistic competence and geographical knowledge impede any rigorous transatlantic or hemispheric approach.[25] Those concerns would seem only to be impossibly exacerbated by a global transoceanic scope that includes not only Spanish and French (the more traditional Atlantic partners to English), but Russian and Chinese and Dutch texts as well as the astoundingly diverse oral cultures of native peoples—from the Kamchatka peninsula in Siberia, to Cavite in the Philippines, the Hawaiian islands, the Pacific northwest coast, Acapulco, Chile, Polynesia, New Zealand, Goa, as well as equally far-ranging Atlantic locations. Rather than resign before the stumbling blocks of linguistic facility or geographical expertise, we might turn to the paired oceanic practices of translation and transportation as productive responses to them.[26]

Christopher Columbus's fifteenth-century confusion between Asian and Antillean islands might be ascribed to the botched spatial translation embedded in Toscanelli's map. But as Elizabeth DeLoughrey observes, this interoceanic Atlantic-Pacific overlap was repeated many times over, perhaps most famously by Daniel Defoe's 1719 *Robinson Crusoe*.[27] The English story of Alexander Selkirk (first told by privateer Woodes Rogers) is usually nominated as Defoe's crucial predecessor. But unlike Crusoe, Selkirk was discovered not in the Atlantic or Caribbean but in the Pacific, on the island of Juan Fernandez off the coast of Chile. To complicate matters even farther, Selkirk's story was preceded by an earlier one recorded by William Dampier about his crew's recovery of a Mosquito Indian who had been abandoned, also on Juan Fernandez Island. A more comprehensively global literary history, however, would have to begin even earlier and farther away, with a fourteenth-century Arabic text by Ibn Tufayl that tells the story of a "self-taught philosopher" who grew up alone on a deserted island in the Indian Ocean. *Hayy Ibn Yaqzan* was translated into Latin and Dutch before appearing in several English translations in the late seventeenth and early eighteenth centuries, after which it generated an extraordinary number of imitations, revisions, and adaptations—including such Atlantic stories about shipwrecks and islands as Ambrose Evans's 1719 *The Adventures, and Surprizing Deliverances, of James Dubordieu and His Wife*, Penelope Aubin's 1721 *The Strange Adventures of the Count de Vinevil and His Family*, and the anonymous 1767 *The Female American*. An even longer and wider literary history, however, would be compelled to track the drifting and turbulent locations for these water-soaked stories into the Indian and Pacific oceans.[28]

It may seem that these texts simply pick up their islands and move them from one ocean to another. But the experience of reading these texts alongside each other suggests a different dimensionality of movement altogether, one in which the islands stay in place while the globe repeatedly turns around them, situating each story within a new body of water. Read within an oceanic rather than terrestrial logic, these texts escape both the stable fixity provided by anchors and the satisfying linearity of the chains or ropes that hold them; instead, their relations collaborate in a literary history whose form emphasizes the fluidity, mobility, and inconsistency of water over the firm certainty and singularity of land. Such a narrative engages with the shifts and spirals of what Kaumu Brathwaite describes as tidalectics when he sees a Jamaican woman ritually sweeping her doorstep and suddenly recognizes her as walking on water rather than sand, "travelling across that middlepassage, constantly coming from where she had come from—in her case Africa—to this spot in North Coast Jamaica." The spatial and temporal curvature of this tidalectic movement is "like the movement of the ocean she's walking on, coming from one continent/continuum, touching another, and then receding ('reading') from the island(s) into the perhaps creative chaos of the(ir) future."[29] DeLoughrey describes Brathwaite's tidalectics as "an 'alter/native' historiography to linear models of colonial progress" that resist "the synthesizing telos of Hegel's dialectic by drawing from a cyclical model, invoking the continual movement and rhythm of the ocean" and argues that it is precisely such a model that is needed to read transoceanic archives. Translations and adaptations similarly traffic in the indeterminate regions outside definitive authorship, beyond the anchored certainties of geographical location, national identity, and determinate authorship. The relations between these texts compose an international, multilingual, and transoceanic narrative in which categorical belonging and national groundedness dissolve in an oceanic logic of shift and flux that refuses the "myth of island isolation."[30]

Some may argue that such global reach has dangerously spongelike properties that threaten to absorb into American literary history a great many texts that belong instead to other national traditions of writing. Such a claim would be right if "American" signals a national identity governed by a terrestrial logic. Of course, American literary history already violates this national-territorial logic by including in current anthologies colonial writers, many of whom wrote in places other than America and in languages other than English, and few if any of whom identified as American. But "American" might signal instead a particular spatial orientation within a global geography governed by a logic of oceanic movement, by a dynamics of blending and flux rather than one of boundaries and possession. Indeed, texts like the diaries of Christopher Columbus, the narratives of the *Jesuit Relations*, or the novels of Susanna Rowson bear just such an oceanic and imperial, rather than a terrestrial or national, relation to America. Importing transoceanic multidimensionalities into a globalized American literary history is neither to assign to texts some kind of American identity nor to claim some kind of American possession of them (for indeed they simultaneously belong to other globalized literary histories that remain centered elsewhere), but it is to insist on the complex material connections that entwine America with the world. Only by attending to the transoceanic movement of ships, labor, and books might we understand, for example, how the East Indian man in Susanna Rowson's remarkably nonlinear novel *The Inquisitor* came to be begging on the streets of London, much less how this narrative later circulated in Philadelphia when it was published there in 1793. Such a perspective also brings into view a forgotten text like *The Adventures of Hildebrand Bowman*, written and published anonymously in England in 1778, which describes an Englishman's fantastical travels through the South Pacific. This novel does not take place in America, was never printed in America, and does not include any characters who identify as American, but it does include a scarcely veiled allegory of the American Revolution in its account of an uprising by the imaginary Pacific colony called Armoseria against the empire of Luxo-volupto. While neither terrestrially bound to the continent nor politically bound to the nation in the way we imagine the contemporaneous writings of, say, Benjamin Franklin or Phillis Wheatley to be, *The Adventures of Hildebrand Bowman* bears a transoceanic relation to America that has something critical to say about empire, revolution, and American literary and cultural history.

Global models for American literary history have often been met with concerns about categorical absorption on the one hand and categorical dissolution on the other. The first worries about the potential disappearance of the rest of the world within an expanding category named America, while the second worries about the disappearance of America as a distinct and meaningful category. The first can be thought of as the "we are the world" problem, or the sense that global expansion is a disciplinary expression of American empire, yet another American act of claiming ever more of the world for itself. The second wonders instead whether there is any longer a discernible America or American literature, as the boundaries between it and the rest of the world and its texts become increasingly blurred. In response to both of these anxieties, we might turn again to Bartholomew's strange map to see the shadowy presence of the Americas beneath conjoined oceanic waters as a visual representation of a globalized literary history in which the nation is decentered, the continent itself half drowned. The map's orientation alone gives it an American perspective, a perspective that might easily be rotated or adjusted to align with a different geographical perspective (an English or African or Chinese literary history, for example) and its attendant aquatic contexts. But much like the island castaway stories described above, these literary histories invariably overlap, blend, and mix.

Miles Ogborn has offered three epistemological approaches to Atlantic studies that might also be seen as three modes of narration: the survey, the network, and the trace. The survey attempts to encapsulate or accommodate the whole, and depends on territorialized maps of continental land. The network depends instead on the work of comparison, and replaces the "surveyor's map" with "a skein of lines and points" that represent routes and ports—a version, perhaps, of the rhizomatic or fractal designs several scholars have advocated for Atlantic or global studies. The trace, on the other hand, is a kind of microhistory in which small-scale intimacies and large-scale developments intersect—stories, for instance, of the slave trade, or naturalists, or political radicals. Atlantic traces are for Ogborn underscored by "violence, friendship, love, and labour" and are characterized by what Joseph Roach has termed "surrogation," or collective attempts to fill in the narrative and material spaces left vacant by death, loss, and departure.[31] Transoceanic narratives of literary history might be thought to locate such traces of historical surrogation while also continuing the work of surrogation—not to fix literary history into any final or even definitive form, but to add new dimensions and materialities that may well deform the familiar or the stable. Matt Matsuda has argued that "refashioning" the narratives of Pacific history "will be the work that runs below and through islands and continents connected by water, spaces, times, and places that in their multiple conjunctures define the histories of an Oceanic Pacific," and we might simply stretch this claim and its image across the globe and its waters.[32]

A transoceanic American literary studies does not insist that there is anything particularly or uniquely American about the texts it studies, but it does insist that this larger archive and context must be taken into account in any attempt to rewrite American literary history in relation to the globe. It asks us to imagine America as both there and not there, at once central to and yet profoundly decentered from the globe and its connections, part of both Atlantic and Pacific waterworlds that are in turn linked to other seas and oceans. Monique Allewaert has suggested that the image of a continentally coherent North America has dominated conceptions of American literary history, and offers in its place the image of a dissolving continent, a landmass that is instead fragmented by "a liquefying natural world."[33] I would like to think of Bartholomew's map as one representation of that possibility. A transoceanic version of American literary history might accommodate some of the best features of both the Atlantic studies and the hemispheric paradigms. It might also allow the multinational and multilingual commitments of earlier, colonial American literary history to be sustained not only on the other side of the American revolution, but right through it, much as the merged waters of the Atlantic-Pacific on Bartholomew's map have a certain blithe disregard for the continent. If this model leaves America as a nation at times strangely displaced from its own narrative, it also ties America and its literature to the world through its materialist relations with the globe's often overwhelming and far-flung network of routes and relations. Steinberg argues that the sea is not "an abstract point on a grid" but must instead be recognized for the material relations otherwise obscured by precisely such a perspective.[34] An oceanic literary history must remain committed to recognizing and tracing those material relations, even and particularly when they do not conform to linear narrative forms.

In this chapter, I have nominated water as a material in which simultaneously to remap and renarrativize American literatures in global context. Whether we ultimately maintain or abandon the familiar tools of literary surveys and anthologies, we do need to challenge the assumption of both that any expansion of scope means covering, including, or accumulating more.[35] We need to replace a terrestrial model of stockpiling texts with an oceanic one of exploring them. Historian Thomas Bender writes that the global approach "is not in any way a brief for writing global histories"—or, I would add, in the case of English studies, for writing histories of world literature. "The point is not to displace the monograph," he continues, "only to thicken the layers of context it incorporates."[36] Bender's language of layering here might be supplemented with the drifting, blending, and mixing qualities of water, by the liquid properties of four-dimensional fluidity. It is not that we need to understand the world before we can understand a text, or that we should all now write histories of world literature. Instead, we should read a text so that we are able to locate the world, the materiality of intercontinental and transoceanic connection and circulation, within it. Doing so means heading into oceans, and recognizing the routes across as well as between them, their surfaces as well as their depths and dimensions. American literature is and always has been connected to the world—commercially, politically, and textually—and is bound in surprisingly intimate ways with places and peoples at great distances away. These material connections are recorded in the content, publication, and circulation of texts, and in the bodies, materials, and goods that circulate with them. Our task should be to locate and analyze the multidimensional materialities of these historical, cultural, and literary networks in order to tell stories about the connections between America and the rest of the world—what they have been, what they are now, and what they might be in the future.

Notes

༄

INTRODUCTION. ACADEMIC POSITIONING SYSTEMS

1. In addition to turning, scholars have made other directional moves in recent years, whether by rewriting history "from the bottom up" (a concept originating with historian Jesse Lemisch); "facing east from Indian country," in Daniel K. Richter's phrase, *Facing East from Indian Country: A Native History of Early America* (Cambridge, Mass.: Harvard University Press, 2001); making a "dorsal" turn in David Wills's proposal, by which all deviations are toward the back, *Dorsality: Thinking Back Through Technology and Politics* (Minneapolis: University of Minnesota Press, 2008); venturing the planetary turn invited by Wai Chee Dimock, *Through Other Continents: American Literature Across Deep Time* (Princeton, N.J.: Princeton University Press, 2006); and Gayatri Chakravorty Spivak, *Death of a Discipline* (New York: Columbia University Press, 2003), and expanded on in the collection *The Planetary Turn: Art, Dialogue, and Geoaesthetics in the 21st Century*, ed. Amy J. Elias and Christian Moraru (Evanston. Ill.: Northwestern University Press, 2015); or thinking in oceanic terms, as contributors to a *PMLA* Theories and Methodologies cluster on "Oceanic Studies" and others have proposed, *PMLA* 125, 3 (May 2010): 657–736, to give just a few examples.

2. This is related to their etymological link with the word for "lathe" in ancient Greek. Judith Surkis, "When Was the Linguistic Turn? A Genealogy," *AHR* 117, 3 (2012): 704.

3. Richard Rorty, ed., *The Linguistic Turn: Essays in Philosophical Method* (Chicago: University of Chicago Press, 1967).

4. Just a few recent examples include Caroline F. Levander and Robert S. Levine, eds., *Hemispheric American Studies* (New Brunswick, N.J.: Rutgers University Press, 2008); Wai Chee Dimock and Lawrence Buell, eds., *Shades of the Planet: American Literature as World Literature* (Princeton, N.J.: Princeton University Press, 2007); Kirsten Silva Gruesz, *Ambassadors of Culture: The Transamerican Origins of Latino Writing* (Princeton, N.J.: Princeton University Press 2002); Anna Brickhouse, *Trans-*

american Literary Relations and the Nineteenth-Century Public Sphere (Cambridge: Cambridge University Press, 2004); Rodrigo Lazo, *Writing to Cuba: Filibustering and Cuban Exiles in the United States* (Chapel Hill: University of North Carolina Press, 2005); and Sean X. Goudie, *Creole America: The West Indies and the Formation of Literature and Culture in the New Republic* (Philadelphia: University of Pennsylvania Press, 2006).

5. See in particular Martin Brückner, *The Geographic Revolution in Early America: Maps, Literacy, and National Identity* (Chapel Hill: University of North Carolina Press, 2006) and Hsuan Hsu, *Geography and the Production of Space in Nineteenth-Century American Literature* (Cambridge: Cambridge University Press, 2010).

6. Notable works in temporal studies include Dana Luciano, *Arranging Grief: Sacred Time and the Body in Nineteenth-Century America* (New York: New York University Press, 2007); Lloyd Pratt, *Archives of American Time: Literature and Modernity in the Nineteenth Century* (Philadelphia: University of Pennsylvania Press, 2009), and Dimock, *Through Other Continents.*

7. Consider Jordan Alexander Stein and Justine S. Murison's special issue, "Methods for the Study of Religion in Early American Literature," *Early American Literature* 45, 1 (2010); Joanna Brooks, *American Lazarus: Religion and the Rise of African American and Native American Literatures* (Oxford: Oxford University Press, 2007); Jürgen Habermas, "Notes on a Post-Secular Society," www.signandsight.com, 2008; and John Lardas Modern, *Secularism in Antebellum America* (Chicago: University of Chicago Press, 2011).

8. Recent collections on the topic include Cindy Weinstein and Christopher Looby, eds., *American Literature's Aesthetic Dimensions* (New York: Columbia University Press, 2012), and Samuel Otter and Geoffrey Sanborn, eds., *Melville and Aesthetics* (New York: Palgrave Macmillan, 2011).

9. Essays foundational to these conversations include "Paranoid Reading and Reparative Reading: or, You're So Paranoid, You Probably Think this Introduction Is About You," Eve Kosovsky Sedgwick's introduction to *Novel Gazing: Queer Readings in Fiction* (Durham, N.C.: Duke University Press, 1997), 1–37, and Bruno Latour, "Why Has Critique Run Out of Steam? From Matters of Fact to Matters of Concern," *Critical Inquiry* 30, 2 (Winter 2004): 225–48. A special issue of *Representations* coedited by Stephen Best and Sharon Marcus entitled "The Way We Read Now" elaborates on "surface reading" as a critical practice, 108, 1 (Fall 2009).

10. Franco Moretti is arguably most associated with distant reading practices; see also recent essays by Heather K. Love, including "Close but not Deep: Literary Ethics and the Descriptive Turn," *New Literary History* 41, 2 (Spring 2010): 371–91.

11. In addition to pioneering theoretical works by Eve Kosovsky Sedgwick, Gilles Deleuze, Feliz Guattari, Michael Hardt, and Brian Massumi, see the work of

Americanist scholars such as Christopher Castiglia, *Interior States: Institutional Consciousness and the Inner Life of Democracy in the Antebellum United States* (Durham, N.C.: Duke University Press, 2008); Peter Coviello, *Intimacy in America: Dreams of Affiliation in Antebellum Literature* (Minneapolis: University of Minnesota Press, 2005); and Sianne Ngai, *Ugly Feelings* (Cambridge, Mass.: Harvard University Press 2005).

CHAPTER 1. TURN IT UP: AFFECTS, STRUCTURES OF FEELING, AND FACE-TO-FACE EDUCATION

1. Elizabeth Grosz, *The Nick of Time: Politics, Evolution, and the Untimely* (Durham, N.C.: Duke University Press, 2004), 26.

2. F. Scott Fitzgerald, *The Great Gatsby* (New York: Scribner, 2004), 40–41.

3. Elizabeth Grosz, *Becoming Undone: Darwinian Reflections on Life, Politics, and Art* (Durham, N.C.: Duke University Press, 2011), 38.

4. Sianne Ngai, *Ugly Feelings* (Cambridge, Mass.: Harvard University Press, 2009), 74.

5. Ibid., 52.

6. Ibid.; Raymond Williams, *Marxism and Literature* (Oxford: Oxford University Press, 1977), 132.

7. My sense of the importance of the present participle as a signifier of ongoing experience derives from the work of Samuel Weber. See in particular *Theatricality as Medium* (New York: Fordham University Press, 2004), 15–20.

8. Williams, *Marxism*, 132, 128.

9. Ibid., 132; emphasis in original.

10. Pete Seeger, "Turn! Turn! Turn!" *The Bitter and the Sweet*, 1962, Columbia Records, cd.

11. Nathaniel Hawthorne, *The Scarlet Letter* (New York: Norton, 2005), 163; William Faulkner, *Absalom, Absalom!* (New York: Vintage, 1986), 303.

12. Samuel Weber, *Benjamin's -abilities* (Cambridge, Mass.: Harvard University Press, 2008), 66.

13. I am borrowing this illustration from Grosz, *Becoming*, 39.

14. Fitzgerald, *Gatsby*, 99.

15. Grosz, *Becoming*, 38.

16. Gilles Deleuze and Felix Guattari, *What Is Philosophy?* trans. Hugh Tomlinson and Graham Burchell (New York: Columbia University Press, 1994), 17.

17. Richard Rushton, "What Can a Face Do? On Deleuze and Faces," *Cultural Critique* 51 (2002): 228.

18. Ibid., 225.

19. Ibid., 38.

20. Ralph Waldo Emerson, "Circles," in *Nature and Selected Essays* (New York: Penguin, 2003), 238.

21. Emerson, "Self-Reliance," in *Nature and Selected Essays*, 190.

22. Ibid., 190.

23. Grosz, *Nick of Time*, 11.

24. Williams, *Marxism*, 133; emphasis in original.

25. Emerson, "Self-Reliance," 191.

26. Seeger, "Turn! Turn! Turn!"

CHAPTER 2. LITERARY HISTORY, BOOK HISTORY, AND MEDIA STUDIES

1. For a history of the emergence of the concept of the "text" in the 1960s and '70s, see John Mowitt, *Text: The Genealogy of an Antidisciplinary Object* (Durham, N.C.: Duke University Press, 1992).

2. There are, of course, exceptions to this rule. Leading book historians who teach in schools of Media or Communication include Ronald Zboray (University of Pittsburgh), David Paul Nord (Indiana University), and John Nerone (University of Illinois), the latter two arriving at the field through the history of journalism. Others pursue book history scholarship from their perch in libraries, having established their expertise through training in rare book librarianship. And yet most book history scholars are trained as historians or literary critics and teach in schools of Arts and Sciences. Under the influence of media studies, book historians have begun to pay more attention to modern mass media's impact on the book trade. However, volumes 4 and 5 of *A History of the Book in America* (Chapel Hill: University of North Carolina Press, 2009) still hew pretty closely to the story of the development of print, with only sidelong glances at the larger mass media environment. For considerations of twentieth-century book production and reception in the context of other media, see in volume 4 (*Print in Motion: The Expansion of Publishing and Reading in the United States, 1880–1940*, ed. Carl F. Kaestle and Janice A. Radway), Ellen Gruber Garvey, "Ambivalent Advertising: Books, Prestige, and the Circulation of Publicity," 170–89, and in volume 5 (*The Enduring Book: Print Culture in Postwar America*, ed. David Paul Nord, Joan Shelley Rubin, and Michael Schudson), Donald A. Downs, "Government Censorship Since 1945," 135–50, John B. Thomson, "U.S. Academic Publishing in the Digital Age," 361–75, and Priscilla Coit Murphy, "The Silent Spring Debate," 447–58.

3. The University of Wisconsin's rechristening of its "Center for the History of Print Culture in Modern America" as the "Center for the History of Print and Digital Culture" is exemplary of this trend. Media archaeology, an emerging subfield of media studies, is an antiteleological approach to media history that attends to failed uses and lost lineages of communications technology, emphasizing the resilience of the outmoded and the impress of imagined technological capacities on media history. While the boundaries of the subfield are contested, Jussi Parikka introduces the various strands of thought that comprise the field in *What Is Media Archaeology?* (Malden, Mass.: Polity, 2012). See also Erkki Huhtamo and Jussi Parikka, eds., *Media Archaeology: Approaches, Applications, and Implications* (Berkeley: University of California Press, 2011). Matthew Gold's *Debates in the Digital Humanities* (Minneapolis: University of Minnesota Press, 2012) collects numerous short essays that represent the wide range of work that falls under the rubric Digital Humanities.

4. "Paper or Me, You Know . . . (New Speculations on a Luxury of the Poor)," in Jacques Derrida, *Paper Machine*, trans. Rachel Bowlby (Stanford, Calif.: Stanford University Press, 2005), 41–65. In discussing the transformation of the cultural status of paper by the digitization of writing, Derrida notes that he prefers to use the term "withdrawal" (retrait) "since this word can mark the limit of a structural or even structuring, modeling hegemony, without that implying a death of paper, only a reduction" (46).

5. N. Katherine Hayles and Jessica Pressman call for the integration of the study of digital and print culture under the banner of "Comparative Textual Media" in a recent collection of essays. See their introduction to *Comparative Textual Media: Transforming the Humanities in the Postprint Era*, ed. Hayles and Pressman (Minneapolis: University of Minnesota Press, 2013), vii–xxxiii.

6. Robert Darnton, "What Is the History of Books?" *Daedalus* 111 (1982): 65–83. This essay has been reprinted widely, including in Darnton, *The Kiss of Lamourette: Reflections in Cultural History* (New York: Norton, 1990), 107–35, and David Finkelstein and Alistair McCleery, *The Book History Reader*, 2nd ed. (London: Routledge, 2006), 9–26, from which I quote below. *The Book History Reader* also includes Thomas R. Adams and Nicolas Barker's revisions to Darnton's schema, "A New Model for the Study of the Book," 47–65. See also Darnton's reevaluation of his influential model, "'What Is the History of Books?' Revisited," *Modern Intellectual History* 4, 3 (2007), 495–508.

7. Roger Chartier, "Intellectual History or Sociocultural History, The French Trajectories" (1982), reprinted in *Histories: French Construction of the Past*, ed. Jacques Revel and Lynn Hunt (New York: New Press, 1995), 287–97.

8. David D. Hall gives a helpful overview of the history of the discipline of bibliography in his contribution to volume 5 of *A History of the Book in America*, "Bib-

liography and the Meaning of 'Text,'" 245–55. G. Thomas Tanselle has written the definitive history of the discipline; see his *Textual Criticism Since Greg: A Chronicle, 1950–2000*, expanded ed. (Charlottesville: Bibliographical Society of the University of Virginia, 2005). A shorter version of this history appears as the first chapter of Tanselle's *Bibliographical Analysis: A Historical Introduction* (New York: Cambridge University Press, 2009), 6–30. Useful overviews can also be found in *The Cambridge Companion to Textual Scholarship* ed. Neil Fraistat and Julia Flanders (New York: Cambridge University Press, 2013). See in particular David Greetham, "A History of Textual Scholarship," 16–41, and Kathryn Sutherland, "Anglo-American Editorial Theory," 42–60.

9. Tanselle, *Bibliographical Analysis*, 29.

10. I discuss this history at greater length in "Echocriticism: Repetition and the Order of Texts," *American Literature* 88, 1 (March 2016). Jeanne Boydston has examined the editorial standards for texts approved by the MLA Center for Editions of American Authors and it successor organization, the Committee for Scholarly Editions. See her "Standards for Scholarly Editing: The CEAA and the CSE," *Text: Transactions of the Society for Textual Scholarship* 6 (1994): 21–33.

11. W. W. Greg, "The Rationale of Copy-Text," in *Bibliography and Textual Criticism: English and American Literature, 1700 to the Present*, ed. O. M. Brack, Jr., and Warner Barnes (Chicago: University of Chicago Press, 1969), 41–58, 43.

12. Fredson Bowers, "Some Principles for Scholarly Editions of Nineteenth-Century American Authors," in Brack and Barnes, *Bibliography and Textual Criticism*, 194–201, 195.

13. Much of the following paragraph is taken from the introduction to Meredith L. McGill, *American Literature and the Culture of Reprinting, 1834–1853* (Philadelphia: University of Pennsylvania Press, 2003), 5–6.

14. "Printers of the Mind: Some Notes on Bibliographical Theories and Printing House Practices" was first published in *Studies in Bibliography* 22 (1969): 1–75, but is perhaps most easily found in the posthumously published collection *Making Meaning: "Printers of the Mind" and Other Essays*, ed. Peter D. McDonald and Michael Felix Suarez (Amherst: University of Massachusetts Press, 2002).

15. Jonathan Rose, *The Intellectual Life of the British Working Classes* (New Haven, Conn.: Yale University Press, 2001), 466, n21.

16. See for example Patricia Crain, *The Story of A* (Stanford, Calif.: Stanford University Press, 2000), which concludes with a treatment of Hawthorne's *Scarlet Letter*; Thomas Augst, *The Clerk's Tale*, which arrives at a reading of Melville's "Bartleby the Scrivener" in its final chapter (Chicago: University of Chicago Press, 2003); and my own *American Literature and the Culture of Reprinting*, which closes with a reading of Hawthorne's *House of the Seven Gables*.

17. For a polemical treatment of the importance of paratexts to classic works of scholarship in book history, see Michael Gavin, "Writing Print Cultures Past: Literary Criticism and Book History," *Book History* 15 (2012): 26–47.

18. See Geoffrey Batchen, "Electricity Made Visible," in *New Media, Old Media: A History and Theory Reader*, ed. Wendy Hui Kyong Chun and Thomas Keenan (New York: Routledge, 2006), 27–44, as well as his *Burning with Desire: The Conception of Photography* (Cambridge, Mass.: MIT Press, 1997). See also Lisa Gitelman, *Always Already New: Media, History and the Data of Culture* (Cambridge, Mass.: MIT Press, 2006), and *Scripts, Grooves, and Writing Machines: Representing Technology in the Edison Era* (Stanford, Calif.: Stanford University Press, 1999).

19. For an account of the emergence of the media concept out of an encounter between the system of fine arts and modern communications technology, see John Guillory, "Genesis of the Media Concept," *Critical Inquiry* 36 (2010): 321–62.

20. *Georgic Modernity and British Romanticism: Poetry and the Mediation of History* (New York: Cambridge University Press, 2004).

21. Whitney Anne Trettien, "A Deep History of Electronic Textuality: The Case of *English Reprints Jhon Milton Areopagitica*," *Digital Humanities Quarterly* 7 (2013).

22. This effort is matched by his concomitant attempt to wrestle formal similarities and allusions to other works into a story of influence that preserves the originality and the identity of the text.

23. Bonnie Mak has examined the material history of the EEBO digital scans, which originate in World War II era attempts to microfilm all the titles listed in the Short Title Catalog. Mak argues that the digital presentation of these images suppresses this history, eliding intermediary material formats, and encouraging readers instead to imagine that they offer improved, intimate access to the original printed sources. See her "Archaeology of a Digitization," *Journal of the American Society for Information Science and Technology* 65, 8 (August 2014): 1515–26. Heavy users of Google Books will have noticed the disproportionate online presence of nineteenth-century reprints— British versions of American texts and American editions of British ones—kept out of Special Collections due to their presumed bibliographical irrelevance, and therefore left on open shelves for Google to scan. Like the zombie Milton editions Trettien examines, they have begun to appear with distressing regularity in the classroom.

CHAPTER 3. THE CARTOGRAPHIC TURN AND AMERICAN LITERARY STUDIES: OF MAPS, MAPPINGS, AND THE LIMITS OF METAPHOR

1. To reconstruct "map" related terms see *MLA International Bibliography* and *America: History & Life*, both hosted online by EBSCO Industries, Inc.; and *Arts &*

Humanities Citation Index, hosted by Thomson Reuters "Web of Knowledge," accessed March 2013.

2. See the entries for "turn" as noun and verb in the OED, accessed online March 30, 2013. Also, a forum published in *American Historical Review* has scrutinized the conceptual model of "turns" (historiographic, linguistic, and cultural), providing a survey of critical debates while also testing the model's usefulness. See in particular Judith Surkis, "When Was the Linguistic Turn? A Genealogy," *AHR* 117, 3 (June 2012): 700–722; and Gary Wilder, "From Optic to Topic: The Forclosure Effect of Historiographic Turns," *AHR* 117, 3 (June 2012): 723–45.

3. On the danger of overusing the cartographic terminology in literary studies, see Denis Cosgrove, ed., *Mappings* (London: Reaktion, 1999), 3; on cartographic anxiety in other disciplines see Derek Gregory, *Geographical Imaginations* (London: Blackwell, 1994), 70–205; Denis Wood, *Rethinking the Power of Maps* (New York: Guilford, 2010), 111–215.

4. Instead of listing key authors who shaped the spatial turn during the 1980s and 1990s, see the overviews offered by John A. Agnew, David Livingstone, and Alisdair Rogers, eds., *Human Geography: An Essential Anthology* (Oxford: Oxford University Press, 1996); Phil Hubbard and Rob Kitchin, eds., *Key Thinkers on Space and Place* (London: Sage, 2004); and the selection on time and space in Simon During, *The Cultural Studies Reader* (London: Routledge, 2007).

5. Michel Foucault, "Questions on Geography," in *Power/Knowledge: Selected Interviews and Other Writings, 1972–1977*, ed. Colin Gordon (New York: Pantheon, 1980), 70.

6. Henri Lefebvre, *The Production of Space*, trans. Donald Nicholson-Smith (Cambridge: Blackwell, 1991); David Harvey, *Justice, Nature, and the Geography of Difference* (London: Blackwell, 1996); Michel de Certeau, *The Practice of Everyday Life* (Berkeley: University of California Press, 1984); Gilles Deleuze and Félix Guattari, *A Thousand Plateaus: Capitalism and Schizophrenia*, trans. Brian Massumi (Minneapolis: University of Minnesota Press, 1987); Fredric Jameson, *Postmodernism or, The Cultural Logic of Late Capitalism* (Durham, N.C.: Duke University Press, 1990).

7. Neil Smith and Cindi Katz, "Grounding Metaphor: Towards a Spatialized Politics," in *Place and the Politics of Identity*, ed. Michael Katz and Steve Pile (London: Routledge, 1993), 68. For a recent survey of spatial approaches see Barney Warf and Santa Arias, eds., *The Spatial Turn: Interdisciplinary Perspectives* (London: Routledge, 2008).

8. Smith and Katz, "Grounding Metaphor," 70.

9. Edward Soja, *Postmodern Geographies: The Reassertion of Space in Critical Social Theory* (New York: Verso, 1989); Gregory, *Geographical Imaginations*; Denis

Cosgrove, *Social Formations and Symbolic Landscapes* (1984; Madison: University of Wisconsin Press, 1998); Doreen Massey, *Space, Place, and Gender* (Minneapolis: University of Minnesota Press, 1994); John Brian Harley, *The New Nature of Maps: Essays in the History of Cartography*, ed. Paul Laxton (Baltimore: Johns Hopkins University Press, 2001); J. B. Harley and David Woodward, eds., *The History of Cartography*, vols. 1–3 (Chicago: University of Chicago Press, 1987); Denis Wood with John Fels, *The Power of Maps* (New York: Guilford, 1992); Christian Jacob, *The Sovereign Map: Theoretical Approaches in Cartography Throughout History*, trans. Edward Dahl (1992; Chicago: University of Chicago Press, 2006).

10. The debate lasted from the late 1980s to the mid-1990s and concentrated among other things on whether maps were textlike constructs obeying rules of signification and/or representation. Or, as Matthew H. Edney sums it up, "the aim of the new approaches is to de-naturalise the map . . . to break through the shell of objectivity with which our culture has surrounded the map in order to expose and then to study the map for what it is: a human practice." See his "Theory and the History of Cartography," *Imago Mundi* 48 (1996): 188; also see John Pickles, *A History of Spaces: Cartographic Reason, Mapping, and the Geo-Coded World* (London: Routledge, 2004).

11. Denis Cosgrove, *Geography and Vision: Seeing, Imagining, and Representing the World* (London: Tauris, 2008), 155.

12. Cosgrove, *Mappings*, 1.

13. Wood, *Rethinking the Power of Maps*, 19.

14. Mary Ellen Snodgrass, *Literary Maps for Young Adult Literature* (Englewood, Colo.: Libraries Unlimited, 1995); Matthew Wilkens, "The Geographic Imagination of Civil War-Era American Fiction," *American Literary History* 25, 4 (Winter 2013): 803–40.

15. Here I adapt and expand the synthesis of literary cartographies offered by David Cooper and Ian N. Gregory, "Mapping the English Lake District: A Literary GIS," *Transactions of the Institute of British Geographers* 36 (2011): 91–93.

16. Wayne Franklin, *Discoverers, Explorers, Settlers. The Diligent Writers of Early America* (Chicago: University of Chicago Press, 1979); Robert Lawson-Peebles, *Landscape and Written Expression in Revolutionary America* (Cambridge: Cambridge University Press, 1988); John Logan Allen, *Passage Through the Garden: Lewis and Clark and the Image of the American Northwest* (Urbana: University of Illinois Press, 1975).

17. Martin Brückner, *The Geographic Revolution in Early America: Maps, Literacy, and National Identity* (Chapel Hill: University of North Carolina Press, 2006); Hsuan L. Hsu, *Geography and the Production of Space in Nineteenth-Century American Literature* (Cambridge: Cambridge University Press, 2010).

18. Jane Tompkins, *Sensational Designs: The Cultural Work of American Fiction, 1790–1860* (New York: Oxford University Press, 1985); Bruce E. Harvey, *American Geographics: U.S. National Narratives and the Representation of the Non-European World, 1830–1865* (Stanford, Calif.: Stanford University Press, 2001); Martha Schoolman, *Abolitionist Geographies* (Minneapolis: University of Minnesota Press, 2014).

19. For example, see Hester Blum, *The View from the Masthead: Maritime Imagination and Antebellum American Sea Narratives* (Chapel Hill: University of North Carolina Press, 2008); Eric Bulson, *Novels, Maps, Modernity: The Spatial Imagination, 1850–2000* (London: Routledge, 2007); or *Melville's Marginalia Online* (melvilles marginalia.org).

20. Edlie L. Wong, "Around the World and Across the Board: Nellie Bly and the Geography of Games," in *American Literary Geographies*, ed. Martin Brückner and Hsuan L. Hsu (Newark: University of Delaware Press, 2007), 296–324.

21. See James F. Cooper, *Les Pionniers* (Paris: C. Gosselin, 1828); or, Edgar Allan Poe, *The Narrative of Arthur Gordon Pym of Nantucket*, ed. Frederick S. Frank and Diane Hoeveler (Peterborough, Ont.: Broadview, 2010), 30–31.

22. Phillip C. Muehrcke and Juliana O. Muehrcke, "Maps in Literature," *Geographical Review* 64, 3 (July 1974): 317–38.

23. For example, Peter Turchi, *Maps of the Imagination: The Writer as Cartographer* (San Antonio: Trinity University Press, 2007); Ricardo Padron, "Mapping Imaginary Worlds," in *Maps: Finding Our Place in the World*, ed. Robert Karrow and James Akerman (Chicago: University of Chicago Press, 2007), 255–87; Cynthia Sundberg Wall, *The Prose of Things. Transformations of Description in the Eighteenth Century* (Chicago: University of Chicago Press, 2007); Anthony Pavlik, "'A Special Kind of Reading Game': Maps in Children's Literature," *International Research in Children's Literature* 3, 1 (2010): 28–43.

24. De Certeau, 120; Deleuze and Guattari, 12; Jean Baudrillard, *Simulacra and Simulacrum*, trans. Sheila Faria Glaser (Ann Arbor: University of Michigan Press, 1994), 1.

25. Benedict Anderson, *Imagined Communities: Reflections on the Origin and Spread of Nationalism* (1991); Edward W. Said, *Culture and Imperialism* (New York: Vintage, 1993); Paul Gilroy, *The Black Atlantic: Modernity and Double-Consciousness* (Cambridge, Mass.: Harvard University Press, 1993); Wai Chee Dimock, *Through Other Continents: American Literature Across Deep Time* (Princeton, N.J.: Princeton University Press, 2008); Paul Giles, *The Global Remapping of American Literature* (Princeton, N.J.: Princeton University Press, 2011).

26. See the illustrated survey of "literary maps" by Martha Hopkins and Michael Buscher, *The Language of the Land: The Library of Congress Book of Literary Maps* (Washington, D.C.: Library of Congress, 1999).

27. Nina Baym et al., *The Norton Anthology of American Literature*, shorter 7th ed. (New York: Norton, 2008).

28. Franco Moretti, *Atlas of the European Novel* (London: Verso, 1998), 3; see also his *Graphs, Trees, Maps* (London: Verso, 2005).

29. See Wilkens; Cooper and Gregory.

30. The literature on the powers of the map gaze and its visuality is extensive. For example, see Cosgrove, *Geography and Vision* and his *Apollo's Eye: A Cartographic Genealogy of the Earth in the Western Imagination* (Baltimore: Johns Hopkins University Press, 2001); also see Jacob, *Sovereign Map*, esp. 66, 77, 114.

31. J. B. Harley, "The Map and the Development of the History of Cartography," in *The History of Cartography*, vol. 1, ed. Harley and Woodward, 3; Jacob, *Sovereign Map*, 11, 185.

32. Deleuze and Guattari, 21.

33. Jacob, *Sovereign Map*, 199.

34. Smith and Katz, 69. They cite J. H. Andrews, "Map and Language: A Metaphor Extended," *Cartographica* 27 (1990): 16.

35. Karl Popper, *Unended Quest: An Intellectual Autobiography* (London: Routledge, 1976), 77; E. H. Gombrich, *Art and Illusion: A Study in the Psychology of Pictorial Representation* (New York: Pantheon, 1960), 90; or Nelson Goodman, *Languages of Art: An Approach to a Theory of Symbols* (Indianapolis: Bobbs-Merrill, 1976).

36. Smith and Katz, 70.

37. Kenneth Burke, *A Grammar of Motives* (Berkeley: University if California Press, 1969), 503.

38. See Ernst Robert Curtius, *European Literature and the Latin Middle Ages*, trans. Willard R. Trask, Bollingen Series 36 (Princeton, N.J.: Princeton University Press, 1953), 128. Burke's and Curtius's understandings of metaphor anticipate interpretations by psychologists who explain metaphors as a process involving "information transfer" and "feature matching." See Patrick Hogan, *Cognitive Science, Literature and the Arts: A Guide for Humanists* (New York: Routledge, 2003), 87; and Andrew Ortney, "Metaphor, Language, and Thought," in *Metaphor and Thought*, ed. Andrew Ortney (Cambridge: Cambridge University Press, 1993), 1–19.

39. Jacob, *Sovereign Map*, 11.

40. Matthew Edney has called attention to an increased uncertainty surrounding academic and popular perceptions of maps: while "maps are now understood to possess fluid, ambiguous, highly partial, and persistently ideological meanings," he writes "we can no longer insist . . . that maps must be graphic in form; we now accept that they can be verbal, tectonic, gestural, or performative." See Edney, "Irony of Imperial Mapping," in *The Imperial Map: Cartography and the Mastery of Empire*, ed. James R. Akerman (Chicago: University of Chicago Press, 2009), 12.

41. When looking at the content of critical works bearing "map" titles it is striking to realize that only a small number of studies engages with actual maps, literary maps, or a defined mapping project. What is much more widespread, and this goes beyond critical work using "map" as a bibliographic referent, is the use of the verb form "to map" or the noun "map" as a metaphor for invoking—intentionally or accidentally—the map discourse function and its implied set of spatial concepts and analytical protocols.

42. Here I borrow from the critique offered by Alfred Korzybski, *Science and Sanity: An Introduction to Non-Aristotelian Systems and General Semantics* (1933; New York: Institute of General Semantics, 2000), 58.

43. Jacob, *Sovereign Map*, 306.

44. The exception was Gottfried Leibnitz, who conceived of space in relative terms, contending that space was nothing but a synchronic system of relations best imagined as a series of distance relations between coexisting realities. We are just beginning to wrestle with this kind of spatiality.

45. Jacob, *Sovereign Map*, 46.

46. W. J. T. Mitchell, *Picture Theory: Essays on Verbal and Visual Representation* (Chicago: University of Chicago Press, 1995), 31.

47. W. J. T. Mitchell, "Imperial Landscape," in *Landscape and Power*, ed. Mitchell (Chicago: University of Chicago Press, 1994), 5.

48. Lefebvre, *Production of Space*, 15, 85.

49. Cosgrove, *Geography and Vision*, 156.

CHAPTER 4. TWISTS AND TURNS

1. Eve Kosofsky Sedgwick, *Touching Feeling: Affect, Pedagogy, Performativity* (Durham, N.C.: Duke University Press, 2003), 113, 117.

2. Paul Ricoeur, *Freud and Philosophy: An Essay on Interpretation* (New Haven, Conn.: Yale University Press, 1977).

3. Theodor Adorno, "Something's Missing: A Discussion Between Ernst Bloch and Theordor W. Adorno on the Contradictions of Utopian Longing," in Ernst Bloch, *The Utopian Function of Art and Literature: Selected Essays*, trans. Jack Zipes and Frank Mecklenburg (Cambridge, Mass.: MIT Press, 1988).

4. Richard Chase, *Herman Melville: A Critical Study* (New York: Hafner, 1971), 301.

5. F. O. Matthiessen, *American Renaissance: Art and Expression in the Age of Emerson and Whitman* (New York: Oxford University Press, 1968), 372; Chase, *Herman Melville*, 292.

6. Amy Kaplan, "A Call for a Truce," *American Literary History* 17, 1 (2005): 141–47; Leo Marx, "On Recovering the 'Ur' Theory of American Studies," *American Literary History* 17, 1 (2005): 118–34. Subsequent references cited parenthetically in the text.

7. Matthew Cordova Frankel, "Tattoo Art: The Composition of Text, Voice, and Race in Melville's Moby-Dick." *ESQ* 53, 2 (2007): 115.

8. Ernst Bloch, *Literary Essays* (Stanford, Calif.: Stanford University Press, 1998), 340.

9. Ibid., 441.

10. Ibid., 341.

11. "The Rest of the World: A Conversation with Gayatri Spivak," in *Hope: New Philosophies for Change*, ed. Mary Zournazi (New York: Routledge, 2002), 173.

12. Bloch, *Essays*, 342, 345.

13. Ibid., 345, 344.

14. Ibid., 341.

15. "Carnival of the Senses: A Conversation with Michael Taussig," in *Hope*, ed., Zournazi, 54.

16. Ibid., 54.

17. "Hope, Passion, Politics: A Conversation with Chantal Mouffe and Ernesto Laclau," in *Hope*, ed. Zournazi. Subsequent references cited parenthetically in the text.

18. Lewis Mumford, *The Golden Day: A Study in American Literature and Culture* (Boston: Beacon, 1955), xxii. Subsequent references cited parenthetically in the text.

19. R. W. B. Lewis, *American Adam: Innocence, Tragedy, and Tradition in the Nineteenth Century* (Chicago: University of Chicago Press, 1955), 196. Subsequent references cited parenthetically in the text.

20. C. L. R. James, *American Civilization* (Oxford: Blackwell, 1992), 38, 30, 36.

21. Ibid., 31.

22. C. L. R. James, *Mariners, Renegades and Castaways: The Story of Herman Melville and the World We Live In* (Hanover, N.H.: Dartmouth College Press), 115.

23. Chase, *Herman Melville*, 63, 22.

24. Ibid., 283.

25. Newton Arvin, *Herman Melville* (New York: Grove, 2002), 37, 77.

26. Richard Chase, *The American Novel and Its Tradition* (Baltimore: Johns Hopkins University Press, 1957), 1–2.

27. Ibid., 19, 107.

28. Richard Poirier, *A World Elsewhere: The Place of Style in American Literature* (New York: Oxford University Press, 1966), 7. The phrase "foolish, preposterous, and

sexually irregular" appears in Poirier, "Worlds of Style," *Partisan Review* 33, 4 (1966): 514.

29. Poirier, *World Elsewhere*, 7.

30. Arvin, *Herman Melville*, 256.

31. Ibid., 263.

32. Brooks, Van Wyck, "On Creating a Usable Past," *The Dial: a Semi-monthly Journal of Literary Criticism, Discussion, and Information* 64, 7 (April 11, 1918): 339.

33. Taussig, "Carnival of the Senses," 44.

34. Eve Kosofsky Sedgwick, *Shame and Its Sisters: A Silvan Tomkins Reader* (Durham, N.C.: Duke University Press, 1995), 23.

35. Rita Felski, "Suspicious Minds." *Poetics Today* 32, 2 (2011): 215–34, 218.

36. Taussig, "Carnival of the Senses," 48.

37. Zournazi, "Introduction," *Hope*, 15; "Carnival of the Senses," *Hope*, 49.

38. Lewis, *American Adam*, 9–10.

39. Newton Arvin, *American Pantheon*, ed. Daniel Aaron and Sylvan Schendler (New York: Delacorte, 1966), 19.

40. Ibid., 31.

41. Chase, *Herman Melville*, vi.

CHAPTER 5. OF TURNS AND PARADIGM SHIFTS: HUMANITIES, SCIENCE, AND TRANSNATIONAL AMERICAN STUDIES

1. Shelley Fisher Fishkin, "Crossroads of Cultures: The Transnational Turn in American Studies—Presidential Address to the American Studies Association, November 12, 2004," *American Quarterly* 57, 1 (March 2005): 17–57 (my emphasis). For earlier uses of the phrase "transnational turn" in reference to American studies, see Robert A. Gross, "The Transnational Turn: Rediscovering American Studies in a Wider World," *Journal of American Studies* 34, 3 (December 2000): 373–93.

2. Paul Jay, *Global Matters: The Transnational Turn in Literary and Cultural Studies* (Ithaca, N.Y.: Cornell University Press, 2010), 4.

3. Priscilla Wald, "Mine Fields and Meeting Grounds: Transnational Analyses and American Studies," *American Literary History* 10 (1998): 199–218, 202, 200–201; my emphasis.

4. Aristotle, *Prior Analytics*, trans. with introduction, notes, and commentary by Robin Smith (Indianapolis: Hackett, 1989), 100.

5. Giorgio Agamben, "What Is a Paradigm," in *The Signature of All Things: On Method*, trans. Luca D'Isanto with Kevin Attell (New York: Zone, 2009), 9–32, 18–19. On the connection between Kuhn's "paradigm" and Foucault's "episteme," see also

Hubert Dreyfus and Paul Rabinow, *Michel Foucault: Beyond Structuralism and Hermeneutics: With an Afterword by and Interview with Michel Foucault* (Chicago: University of Chicago Press, 1983), 199.

6. See, for example, Wald's *Contagious: Cultures, Carriers, and the Outbreak Narrative* (Durham, N.C.: Duke University Press, 2008), 32.

7. For some critical assessments of the allegedly paradigmatic shift presented by the transnational turn in American Studies, see Winfried Fluck, "A New Beginning? Transnationalisms." *New Literary History* 42, 2 (Summer 2011): 365–84; and "American Literary History and the Romance with America," *American Literary History* 21, 1 (Spring 2009): 1–18; also Winfried Fluck, Donald Pease, and John Carlos Rowe, *Re-Framing the Transnational Turn in American Studies* (Hanover, N.H.: Dartmouth College Press, 2011).

8. Geoffrey Harpham, "Between Humanity and the Homeland: the evolution of an institutional concept." *American Literary History* 18, 2 (2006): 245–61, 250, 252, 257.

9. Wai Chee Dimock, "Scales of Aggregation: Prenational, Subnational, Transnational," *American Literary History* 18, 2 (Summer 2006): 219–28, 223.

10. Alfred Crosby, *The Columbian Exchange: The Biological and Cultural Consequences of 1492* (Westport, Conn.: Greenwood, 1972); see also Crosby, *Ecological Imperialism: The Biological Expansion of Europe* (Cambridge: Cambridge University Press, 1992); David Noble Cook, *Born to Die: Disease and New World Conquest* (Cambridge: Cambridge University Press, 1998), David Jones, *Rationalizing Epidemics: Meanings and Uses of Indian Mortality since 1600* (Cambridge, Mass.: Harvard University Press, 2004); Joyce Chaplin, *Subject Matter: Technology, the Body, and Science on the Anglo-American Frontier, 1500–1676* (Cambridge, Mass.: Harvard University Press, 2001); Cristobal Silva, *Miraculous Plagues: An Epidemiology of Early American Narrative* (Oxford: Oxford University Press, 2011); and Kelly Wisecup, *Medical Encounters: Knowledge and Identity in Early American Literatures* (Amherst: University of Massachusetts Press, 2013).

11. See Mary Louise Pratt, *Imperial Eyes: Travel Writing and Transculturation* (New York: Routledge, 1992); Susan Scott Parrish, *American Curiosity: Cultures of Natural History in the Colonial Atlantic World* (Colonial Williamsburg and Chapel Hill: University of North Carolina Press for Omohundro Institute of Early American History and Culture, 2006); Jorge Cañizares-Esguerra, *Nature, Empire, and Nation: Explorations of the History of Science in the Iberian World* (Stanford, Calif.: Stanford University Press, 2006); Christopher Iannini, *Fatal Revolutions: Natural History, West Indian Slavery, and the Routes of American Literature* (Colonial Williamsburg and Chapel Hill: University of North Carolina Press for Omohundro Institute of Early American History and Culture, 2012); Ralph Bauer and José Antonio Mazzotti,

eds., *Creole Subjects: Empires, Texts, Identities* (Colonial Williamsburg and Chapel Hill: University of North Carolina Press for Omohundro Institute of Early American History and Culture, 2009). In *The Cultural Geography of Colonial American Literatures: Empire, Travel, Modernity* (Cambridge: Cambridge University Press, 2003), I have attempted to describe the uneven development of literary and scientific discourses in the early modern Atlantic world in terms of the Wallersteinian World-Systems Theory of knowledge production I called a poetics of "epistemic mercantilism," which structured the production of knowledge in early modern natural history in geographical and geopolitical hierarchies.

12. I adopt the phrase "hermeneutics of discovery" from literary historian James Dougal Fleming. See his "Introduction," in *The Invention of Discovery: Humanism, Science, and Hermeneutics*, ed. James Dougal Fleming (Aldershot: Ashgate, 2011), 1–13, 7, 8; also his monograph, *Milton's Secrecy: And Philosophical Hermeneutics* (Aldershot: Ashgate, 2009), 1–4. Fleming coined the phrase "hermeneutic of discovery" to characterize the hermeneutical practices in the modern empirical sciences in his engagement with Hans Georg Gadamer, who defined the hermeneutical practices in the humanities as a "hermeneutic of recognition." On the humanist notion of discovery as a "hermeneutics of recognition," see Hans Georg Gadamer, *Truth and Method* (1960; New York: Continuum, 2004), esp. 113.

13. For an overview of recent hemispheric American studies scholarship, see Ralph Bauer, "Hemispheric American Studies," *PMLA* 124, 1 (January 2009): 234–250.

14. J. W. N. Watkins, "Against 'Normal Science,'" in *Criticism and the Growth of Knowledge*, ed. Imre Lakotos and Alan Musgrave (Cambridge: Cambridge University Press, 1970), 25–38, 28.

15. Thomas S. Kuhn, *The Structure of Scientific Revolutions*, 2nd ed. (Chicago: University of Chicago Press, 1970), 35–42.

16. Margaret Masterman claimed to have found twenty-one meanings of "paradigm" used in *The Structure of Scientific Revolutions*. See Masterman, "The Nature of a Paradigm," in *Criticism and the Growth of Knowledge*, ed. Imre Lakatos and Alan Musgrave (Cambridge: Cambridge University Press, 1970), 59–89.

17. Thomas Kuhn, "Postscript 1969," in Kuhn, *Structure*, 176, 180. See also Thomas Kuhn, *The Road Since Structure: Philosophical Essays, 1970–1993, with an Autobiographical Interview*, ed. James Conant and John Haugeland (Chicago: University of Chicago Press, 2000).

18. Peter Burke, "Paradigms Lost: From Göttingen to Berlin," *Common Knowledge* 14, 2 (Spring 2008): 244–57, 244.

19. Kuhn, *Structure*, 52–53.

20. See Lakatos and Musgrave, eds., *Criticism and the Growth of Knowledge*.

21. Eugene Garfield, "A Different Sort of Great Books List: The 50 Twentieth-Century Works Most Cited in the *Arts & Humanities Citation Index*, 1976–1983," *Current Contents* 16 (20 April 1987): 3–7. For more recent (and more charitable) assessments broth from within and without the history of science proper, see David Hollinger, "T. S. Kuhn's Theory of Science and its Implications for History," in Hollinger, *In the American Province: Studies in the History and Historiography of Ideas* (Bloomington: Indiana University Press, 1985), 105–29; and Allan Megill, "Coherence and Incoherence in Historical Studies: from the Annales School to the New Cultural History," *New Literary History* 35, 2 (2004): 207–31; Thomas Nickle, ed., *Thomas Kuhn* (Cambridge Cambridge University Press, 2003); Steve Fuller, *Thomas Kuhn: A Philosophical History of our Times* (Chicago: University of Chicago Press, 2000); Gary Gutting, ed., *Paradigms and Revolutions: Appraisals and Applications of Thomas Kuhn's Philosophy of Science* (Notre Dame, Ind.: University of Notre Dame Press, 1980).

22. Kuhn, *Structure*, 208.

23. Ibid., 162, 164.

24. See Michel Serres with Bruno Latour, *Conversations on Science, Culture, and Time*, trans. Roxanne Lapidus (Ann Arbor: University of Michigan Press, 1995); Serres, *Hermes: Literature, Science, Philosophy*, ed. Josué V. Harari and David F. Bell (Baltimore: Johns Hopkins University Press, 1982); and Latour, *We Have Never Been Modern*, trans. Catherine Porter (Cambridge, Mass: Harvard University Press, 1993), 10–15. Future references to *We Have Never Been Modern* are cited parenthetically in the text.

25. One might think here, for example, of Franco Moretti's overly polemical presentation of his introduction of quantitative methods of literary criticism—"we know how to read texts, now let's learn how *not* to read them"—and the visceral response by the literary-critical profession. See Franco Moretti, "Conjectures on World Literature," *New Left Review* 1 (January–February 2000): 54–68.

26. Carolyn Porter, "What We Know That We Don't Know: Remapping American Literary Studies," *American Literary History* 6, 3 (1994): 467–526, 468.

27. Ibid., 471.

28. Robert Levine and Caroline Levander, "Introduction," in *Hemispheric American Studies: Essays Beyond the Nation*, ed. Robert Levine and Caroline Levander (New Brunswick, N.J.: Rutgers University Press, 2008), 6.

29. Fluck, "A New Beginning," 366.

30. Ibid., 379.

31. Jay, *Global Matters*, 1–2.

32. Gadamer, *Truth and Method*, 113

33. See Paul Horwich, ed., *World Changes: Thomas Kuhn and the Nature of Science* (Cambridge, Mass.: MIT Press, 1993); Stefano Gattei, *Thomas Kuhn's "Linguistic Turn"*

and the Legacy of Logical Empiricism (Aldershot: Ashgate, 2008); and Brad Wray, *Kuhn's Evolutionary Social Epistemology* (Cambridge: Cambridge University Press, 2011).

34. I develop this argument in more depth in my current book project, *The Alchemy of Conquest: Discovery, Prophecy, and the Secrets of the New World.*

35. Edward Said, *The World, the Text, and the Critic* (London: Faber, 1984), 222; see also *Orientalism* (New York: Pantheon, 1978) and *Culture and Imperialism* (New York: Knopf, distributed by Random House, 1993).

36. On the colonial connections between the Royal Society's program in science and the Puritan missionary enterprises in the New World, see Sarah Rivett, *The Science of the Soul in Colonial New England* (Colonial Williamsburg and Chapel Hill: Published for the Omohundro Institute of Early American History and Culture by the University of North Carolina Press, 2011).

37. See Bauer, *Cultural*, 1–29; also Immanuel Wallerstein, *The Modern World System: Capitalist Agriculture and the Origins of the European-World Economy in the Sixteenth Century* (New York: Knopf, 1974); and *Geopolitics and Geoculture: Essays on the Changing World* (Cambridge: Cambridge University Press, 1991); also Lars Magnusson, *Mercantilism: The Shaping of an Economic Language* (London: Routledge, 1994), 10, 11–12.

38. Noah Biggs, *The Vanity of the Craft of Physick* (London: Giles Calvert, 1651), 57; my emphasis. On Biggs, see Allen G. Debus, *The Chemical Philosophy: Paracelsian Science and Medicine in the Sixteenth Century* (New York: Science History Publications, 1977), 499–512

39. See Juan Pimentel, "The Iberian Vision: Science and Empire in the Framework of a Universal Monarchy, 1500–1800," *Osiris* 15, 1 (2000): 17–21.

40. Gabriel García Márquez, *One Hundred Years of Solitude*, trans. Gregory Rabasa (New York: Harper and Row, 1991), 12. Future references to *One Hundred Years of Solitude* are cited parenthetically in the text.

41. Juan Rodríguez Freyle, *El Carnero*, prólogo, notas, y cronología Dario Achury Valenzuela (Biblioteca Ayacucho, 1979), 38. Future references to *El Carnero* are cited parenthetically in the text.

42. Dario Achury Valenzuela, "Prólogo," in *El Carnero*, 57.

43. Roberto González Echevarría, *Myth and Archive: A Theory of Latin American Narrative* (Cambridge: Cambridge University Press, 1990), 90.

44. Francis Bacon, *The New Atlantis*, ed. Brian Vickers (Oxford: Oxford University Press, 1996); on Lucretius and his subterranean life during the Renaissance, see Gerard Passannante, *The Lucretian Renaissance: Philology and the Afterlife of Tradition* (Chicago: University of Chicago Press, 2011); on the role of the Council of the Indies and the House of Trade in the making of the empirical state sponsored model

of science, see Maria Portuondo, *Secret Science: Spanish Cosmography and the New World* (Chicago: University of Chicago Press, 2009).

45. Stephen Gaukroger, *The Emergence of a Scientific Culture: Science and the Shaping of Modernity, 1210–1685* (Oxford: Clarendon, 2006), 161, 163, 165.

46. One key event in this development was the cross-fertilization between post-colonial cultural anthropology and comparative literary criticism in the aftermath of decolonization during the 1980s and 1990s in works such as Peter Hulme's *Colonial Encounters: Europe and the Native Caribbean* (New York: Methuen, 1986); Mary Louise Pratt's *Imperial Eyes*; James Clifford's and George Marcus's collection of essays *Writing Culture: The Poetics and Politics of Ethnography* (Berkeley: University of California Press, 1986); and James Boon's collection *Other Tribes, Other Scribes: Symbolic Anthropology in the Comparative Study of Cultures, Histories, Religions, and Texts* (Cambridge: Cambridge University Press, 1982). Another key event in this development was the rise of the Civil Rights and Red Power movements and the critiques of the social sciences they brought about in publications such as Vine Deloria's seminal *Custer Died for Your Sins* (Norman: University of Oklahoma Press, 1969).

CHAPTER 6. THE GEOPOLITICS AND TROPOLOGIES
OF THE AMERICAN TURN

1. *Turn* derives from the Greek *tornos*, a shaping of material on a lathe, whereas *trope* derives from the Greek *trepein*, or a turning or shift of direction linked to victory (the terms *trope* and *trophy* are etymologically linked, as though the direction of the trope were toward victory). Shaping on a lathe and shifting direction both describe a movement that effects a material transformation, whether the form that rises from the lathe's rotation or the redirection that comes from troping.

2. Amanda Goldstein, "Growing Old Together: Lucretian Materialism in Shelley's Poetry of Life," *Representations* 128, 1 (2014): 60–92. See also Natania Meeker, *Voluptuous Philosophy: Literary Materialism in the French Enlightenment* (NYC: Fordham, 2006); Marjorie Levinson, "A Motion and a Spirit: Romancing Spinoza," *Studies in Romanticism* 46, 4 (Winter 2007): 366–408; "Of Being Numerous: Counting and Matching in Wordsworth's Poetry," *Studies in Romanticism* 49, 4 (Winter 2011): 633–657; Jane Bennett, *Vibrant Matter* (Durham, N.C.: Duke University Press, 2010); Sara Guyer and Celeste Langan, "Romantic Materialities: Or, This is Not a Thing," *Romantic Circles* (February 2015). As Goldstein wonderfully puts it, these material configurations compose an atmosphere at in which the materiality of history and place swirl: "Persons 'Kindle invisibly' and are gradually 'extinguished'

under the impact" of this atmosphere that the poet and the material residue of his age "collectively generate and endure" (77). See also Goldstein, 84, note 15.

3. I use the term "Afro-American" to designate a hemispheric experience of diaspora that avoids the U.S. frame sometimes associated with the term "African American." I use the term "African American" when referring to an explicitly U.S.-based community of African descent.

4. On French materialisms see Meeker's *Voluptuous Philosophy*. Anglophone pedagogies leaned heavily on empiricist rhetorical tracts of the eighteenth century like Lord Kames's *Elements of Criticism*, which was commonly used, often in abridged form, in English and American classrooms until the middle of the nineteenth century, as well as those of his successor Hugh Blair's *Lectures on Rhetoric and Belles Lettres*, which remained a standard in American classrooms across the nineteenth century. Kames's and Blair's rhetorics influenced the most widely-used nineteenth-century grammars and writing manuals in the US, including Caleb Bingham's *The Columbian Orator*, Samuel Newman's *A Practical System of Rhetoric* (1835), and Henry Day's *Elements of the Art of Rhetoric* (1850). On the use of Kames and Blair in American pedagogy, see Nan Johnson, *Nineteenth-Century Rhetoric in North America* (Carbondale: Southern Illinois University Press, 1991), esp. Appendixes B and C. On the influence of Kames and Blair on American textbooks, see James A. Berlin, *Writing Instruction in Nineteenth-Century American Colleges* (Carbondale: Southern Illinois University Press, 1984), particularly 35–41.

5. *Freedom's Journal* 1, 2 (March 23, 1827): 1–2.

6. White and Drexler propose that early American literary studies have traditionally been so historical, economic, and sociological in focus that it has often reduced the literary to an expression of historical, economic, and sociological forces. Ed White and Michael Drexler, "The Theory Gap," *American Literary History* 22, 2 (2010): 480–94. My assessment here slightly revises White and Drexler's diagnosis, which claims that early American work has a weak sense of form as well. For at least forty years, early American literature has been deeply invested in generic or formal claims; a few instances: the sermon, the Jeremiad (Bercovitch and the many scholars in his wake) and the novel (Davidson, Armstrong and Tennenhouse, White, Dillon).

7. Here, catachresis is less explicitly a feature of the literary work and more precisely a practice of the critic who proceeds with an awareness of the simultaneous necessity and failure of catachrestic terms that name an impossible category. For Spivak's discussions of catachresis, see *Outside in the Teaching Machine* (New York: Routledge, 1993) and also *A Critique of Postcolonial Reason* (Cambridge, Mass.: Harvard University Press, 1997).

8. "Theresa—A Haytien Tale," *Freedom's Journal* 1, 43 (January 18, 1828); 1, 44 (January 25, 1828); 1, 46 (February 8, 1828); and 1, 47 (February 15, 1828). Frances

Smith Foster speculates that the author of "Theresa" "may have been Prince Saunders, a New England teacher of African descent who moved to Haiti after the Revolution to organize an education system (and to convert Haitians to Protestantism)" (636). Saunders's work on Haiti was published in London and Boston, and he was a vocal proponent of Afro-American colonization to Haiti even before Russworm's conversion to the colonization position. See Frances Smith Foster, "How Do You Solve a Problem like Theresa," *African American Review* 40, 4 (Winter 2006): 631–45.

9. *Freedom's Journal* 1, 1 (March 16): 182, 1.

10. The story, which Foster and Jean Lee Cole both present as the first Afro-American short story, does not focus on the life, culture, or suffering of enslaved Afro-Americans, which distinguishes it from the slave narrative that was the dominant form of Afro-American narrative writing at the time of its publication and that was generally directed to a white audience. For existing readings of the story as well as more on the context in which it circulated, see Foster, "How Do You Solve a Problem like Theresa"; Jean Lee Cole, "Theresa and Blake: Mobility and Resistance in Antebellum African American Serialized Fiction," *Callaloo* 34, 1 (2011): 158–75. For a history of *Freedom's Journal*, see Jacquelyn Bacon, *Freedom's Journal: The First African American Periodical* (Lanham, Md.: Lexington, 2007). For *Freedom's Journal's* circulation see Bacon, 53–54.

11. Cole suggests that its theme is mobility itself.

12. In describing what the story does, I do not by any means aim to ascribe any particular intent to the anonymous author. Rather, I am relatively flatly describing what the story does and then interpreting what it does in relation to then current Afro-American literary and political positions, particularly those circulating in the venue in which it was published and those explicitly articulated by the Boyer administration. In short, I draw on historical materialist and Foucauldian methodologies that allow us to conceive texts not simply as authorial products but as historically and materially affected products of discourses, some of which we may try interpretatively to identify.

13. This particular trope yokes together an agential natural world (extremely common in Afro-American cultures of the diaspora and intensely present in later Caribbean writing) and a historical event—namely, the revolutionary war. These lines indicate that even if the protagonists (like readers) might interpret the proximity of natural forces and warfare as indicative of the fact that the natural world points to and is implicated in the revolutionary war (this is certainly one possible interpretation given that St. Domingue's slave army did carefully coordinate their movements with climatological and epidemiological events), in fact this agential natural world, properly understood, does *not* point back to the war that serves as its context. After all, there are no French troops in the zephyrs and there are no French bodies in

tree trunks. Instead, this trope reveals only the beauty and fullness of the island's lush environment. There are two ways to interpret this trope's odd arrangement of what are generally called the "figurative" register (by which is usually meant imaginative and entirely linguistic effects) and the "literal" register (by which is usually meant real events). On the one hand, this particular figure's sublimation of the war that we might take to be the obvious literal event that the story documents might be interpreted as an inadvertent commentary on (or an accidental revelation of) the story's effort to put rhetoric in the place of the historical event. Where we might expect war, there are only figures. On the other hand, we might use this and other bizarre figures in "Theresa" to push forward the theory of materialist figuration offered earlier. Here it is as though the division between figurative and literal meanings that was central to both New Critical and deconstructive accounts of figure is superseded by an account of figure by which figurative and literal interpretations cannot be held in counterpoint. That is, this trope, in eliminating what might be its proper literal referent, allows us to further develop a theory of figure not based on the antipodal status of the figurative and the literal but instead based on their proximity and coordination.

14. A fuller consideration of the role of colonialism and neocolonialism in "Theresa" should take into account that *Freedom's Journal*, which originally rejected African colonization schemes (even though it did report on pro-colonization positions), eventually shifts to a pro-colonization position as Russworm, then the sole editor, advocates the colonization of Afro-Americans outside the United States on the grounds that no genuine liberty was possible for African Americans in the United States, given Anglo-American racism.

15. *Freedom's Journal* ran a six-part series on articles on Haiti in 1827 and a three-part biography of Louverture in 1827.

16. Theresa's proclamation does not only proleptically name Haiti; it also recognizes that it has not yet arrived since she names herself as the sacrifice through which Haiti is not simply announced but manifested. Theresa is not, in fact, sacrificed at the end of the story, which closes in something like happy reconstitution of female family; perhaps this is because the story's implicit logic is that Theresa's apostrophe to the state, not her sacrifice at the hands of divine power, is the medium through which the state is achieved. Thus, in a fashion similar to other revolutionary states, it is rhetoric and rhetoric about God that makes nation-states.

17. This is an odd catachresis as there is a proper name for the terrain—St. Domingue; however, the story presumes that the more proper name would be the postcolonial name Haiti, which doesn't, in fact, exist between 1792 and 1802, but which the story makes exist then as though to cover its "proper name."

18. Susan Buck Morss, *Hegel, Haiti, and Universal History* (Pittsburgh: University of Pittsburgh Press, 2009).

19. As Benedict Anderson argued long ago, this presentation of immemorial existence is a key strategy of young nationalisms; see Anderson, *Imagined Communities*, new ed. (New York: Verso, 2006).

20. Indeed, as Lee notes, another story that circulated in some of the issues of *Freedom's Journal* in which "Theresa" appeared concentrated on Portuguese village life.

21. The first Haitian novel, *Stella*, also names a specific past since it gives Haiti a classical, Roman past in keeping with the classicism of these other revolutionary states.

22. Michel-Rolph Trouillot, *Silencing the Past: Power and the Production of History* (Boston: Beacon, 1997); Sibylle Fischer, *Modernity Disavowed: Haiti and the Cultures of Slavery in the Age of Revolution* (Durham, N.C.: Duke University Press, 2004).

23. See Karen N. Salt's Ph.D. dissertation, "The Haitian Question," Purdue University, 2011. *Freedom's Journal* 1, 9 (May 11, 1827): 3.

24. To be sure, *Freedom's Journal's* audience was not primarily "Western powers" but free black readers with disposable income. Presumably Boyer, the paper's 1828 editor Russworm, and the author of "Theresa" imagined that this free black audience Boyer hoped to attract to Haiti was deeply interested in the normalization of trade relations between Haiti and metropolitan powers. Without this normalization, the bright and prosperous future Boyer predicted could not emerge. This is why a strategy of scrubbing the past that might seem to be aimed primarily at readers and policy-makers in European metropoles could be aimed at free blacks in the Americas. The gamble of *Freedom's Journal* and "Theresa" is that free black readers would be interested to see Haiti presenting itself to an international audience.

25. On the production of specificity in postcolonial and global literatures, see Nirvana Tanoukhi, "The Movement of Specificity," *PMLA* 128, 3 (June 2013): 668–74.

26. Although Britain did not experience a revolution of its political system in the Age of Revolution as did the thirteen American colonies, France, and St. Domingue, the transformations of its political and economic system that resulted from the Glorious Revolution and the Industrial Revolution have led a number of scholars to treat it as a modern revolutionary nationalism. The most famous example is no doubt Eric Hobsbawm's *The Age of Revolution* (New York: Vintage, 1996).

27. James Fenimore Cooper, *The Last of the Mohicans* (New York: Dover Thrift, 2003).

28. Elizabeth Maddock Dillon, "Slaves in Algiers: Race, Republican Genealogies, and the Global Stage," *American Literary History* 6, 3 (Fall 2004). Here Dillon argues that a focus on the global relations in the 1790s, particularly the Tripolitan War, offers evidence that early American nationalism depended on inserting itself

within a global frame. The U.S. refusal to pay what amounted to shipping taxes to Barbary states amounted to a statement about how global trade should work that inserted the United States into global trade. The aim of the Barbary wars was not simply nationalism, Dillon argues, but the production of the United States as a "core" power that could dictate the actions of peripheral powers (like the Barbary states).

29. *Freedom's Journal* also notes that French sanctions against Haiti were not lifted as entirely as the French had promised. See for instance the inaugural issue of the paper.

30. Karl Marx, *The 18th Brumaire of Louis Bonaparte* (New York: International, 1994).

31. My work in this line, in *Ariel's Ecology* (Minneapolis: University of Minnesota Press, 2013), attempted to track how small-scale yet repeated events in colonial peripheries, in particular Afro-American experiences of the body in the plantation zone, gave rise to modes of personhood and affiliation that cannot be integrated to the model of the citizen-subject on which both older national and newer Wallersteinian and cosmopolitan models of inquiry rely.

32. Gilles Deleuze, *The Logic of Sense*, trans. Mark Lester with Charles Stivale (New York: Columbia University Press, 1990), 169–76.

CHAPTER 7. THE CARIBBEAN TURN IN C19
AMERICAN LITERARY STUDIES

1. Amy Kaplan, "Black and Blue on San Juan Hill," in *Cultures of United States Imperialism*, ed. Amy Kaplan and Donald E. Pease (Durham, N.C.: Duke University Press, 1993), 234.

2. Michel Rolph-Trouillot, "From Planters' Journals to Academia: The Haitian Revolution as Unthinkable History," *Journal of Caribbean History* 25, 1 (1991): 81–101.

3. Paul Gilroy, *The Black Atlantic: Modernity and Double Consciousness* (Cambridge, Mass.: Harvard University Press, 1993), 223.

4. Gilroy, *Black Atlantic*, xi.

5. Derek Walcott, "A Far Cry from Africa," in *Derek Walcott: Collected Poems, 1948–1984* (London: Faber and Faber, 1992), 17.

6. Sean X. Goudie, "Towards a Definition of Caribbean American Regionalism: Contesting Anglo-America's Caribbean Designs in Mary Seacole and Sui Sin Far," *American Literature* 80, 2 (2008): 293–322; and "New Regionalisms: U.S.-Caribbean Literary Relations," in *A Companion to American Literary Studies*, ed. Caroline F. Levander and Robert S. Levine (Malden, Mass.: Wiley-Blackwell, 2011), 310–24.

7. Quoted in William Howe Downes, *Life and Works of Winslow Homer* (Boston: Houghton Mifflin, 1911), 149.

8. Peter Wood, *Weathering the Storm: Inside Winslow Homer's Gulf Stream* (Athens: University of Georgia Press, 2004), 87. A series of published lectures, Wood deftly situates the painting's aesthetics in relation to contemporary race concerns, slavery, the War of 1898, and post-Reconstruction, both on its own terms and in the context of many of Homer's other works. Overall Woods provides a systematic, sympathetic treatment of these issues in Homer's works. However, Woods leaves unexamined *The Gulf Stream*'s implicit critique of U.S. corporate expansionism in the Caribbean—causing many laboring Brown and Black Caribbeans to feel imperiled both on land and at sea—a focus of my discussion here.

9. Louis S. Meikle, *Confederation of the British West Indies versus Annexation to the United States of America* (New York: Negro University Press, 1969), 132.

10. Meikle, *Confederation*, 9.

11. Eric Walrond, "The Yellow One," in *Tropic Death* (New York: Macmillan, 1972), 58; hereafter page references in parentheses in the text.

12. Édouard Glissant, *Poetics of Relation* (Ann Arbor: University of Michigan Press, 1997), 6.

13. See esp. Anna Brickhouse, *Transamerican Literary Relations and the Nineteenth-Century Public Sphere* (Cambridge: Cambridge University Press, 2004).

14. Ifeoma Nwankwo, *Black Cosmopolitanism: Racial Consciousness and Transnational Identity in the Nineteenth-Century Americas* (Philadelphia: University of Pennsylvania Press, 2005); Michelle Ann Stephens, *Black Empire: The Masculine Global Imaginary of Caribbean Intellectuals in the United States, 1914–1962* (Durham, N.C.: Duke University Press, 2005); Belinda Edmondson, *Caribbean Middlebrow: Leisure Culture and the Middle Class* (Ithaca, N.Y.: Cornell University Press, 2009).

15. Kirsten Silva Gruesz, *Ambassadors of Culture: The Transamerican Origins of Latino Writing* (Princeton: Princeton University Press, 2002); Rodrigo Lazo, *Writing to Cuba: Filibustering and Cuban Exiles in the United States* (Chapel Hill: University of North Carolina Press, 2005).

16. Sean X. Goudie, *Creole America: The West Indies and the Formation of Literature and Culture in the New Republic* (Philadelphia: University of Pennsylvania Press, 2006); Monique Allewaert, *Ariel's Ecology: Plantations, Personhood, and Colonialism in the American Tropics* (Minneapolis: University of Minnesota Press, 2013); Matthew Pratt Guterl, *American Mediterranean: Southern Slaveholders in the Age of Emancipation* (Cambridge, Mass.: Harvard University Press, 2013).

17. George Lamming, *The Pleasures of Exile* (Ann Arbor: University of Michigan Press, 2002), 153.

18. Lamming, *Pleasures*, 154.

CHAPTER 8. OCEANIC TURNS AND AMERICAN LITERARY HISTORY
IN GLOBAL CONTEXT

1. See Peter Hulme's chapter "Columbus and the Cannibals," in Hulme, *Colonial Encounters: Europe and the Native Caribbean, 1492–1797* (New York: Routledge, 1992), esp. 20–33.

2. Hester Blum, "Introduction: Oceanic Studies," *Atlantic Studies* 10, 2 (2013): 151.

3. Philip Steinberg, "Of Other Seas: Metaphors and Materialities in Maritime Regions," *Atlantic Studies* 10, 2 (2013): 157, 158; Kären Wigen, "Oceans of History," *AHR* 111, 3 (June 2006): 721. See also Alison Games, in the same issue, who remarks that the "land-based" or even "landlocked" character of "Atlantic history that many historians produce is rarely centered around the ocean, and the ocean is rarely relevant to the project"; "Atlantic History: Definitions, Challenges, and Opportunities," 745.

4. For Pacific studies see, for example, Arif Dirlik, *What Is in a Rim? Critical Perspectives on the Pacific Region Idea* (Lanham, Md.: Rowman and Littlefield, 1998) and Yunte Huang, *Transpacific Imaginations: History, Literature, Counterpoetics* (Cambridge, Mass.: Harvard University Press, 2008). For Indian Ocean studies, see Shanti Moorthy and Ashraf Jamal, *Indian Ocean Studies: Cultural, Social, and Political Perspectives* (New York: Routledge, 2009).

5. Felipe Fernández-Armando uses this term to describe those great modern European maritime empires that, as he observes, really occupy the western edges of Europe at the Atlantic's shore, though the term might also be usefully extended to describe the models of study for other oceanic worlds; "Empires in Their Global Context, ca. 1500 to ca. 1800," in *The Atlantic in Global History, 1500–2000*, ed. Jorge Cañizares-Esguerra and Erik R. Seeman (Upper Saddle River, N.J.: Pearson, 2007), 97. For another critique of land-based global perspectives, see Martin W. Lewis and Kären Wigen, *The Myth of Continents: A Critique of Metageography* (Berkeley: University of California Press, 1997). Steinberg refers to the "complex, four-dimensional materiality" of oceanic space (156).

6. Games, 746. Damon Ieremia Salesa accurately notes that "histories of empire and colonialism entwined the Antipodes and the Atlantic from the beginning and ever since." But while "The Antipodes and the Atlantic share some deep histories . . . they have only a shallow shared historiography." "Afterword: Opposite Footers," in *The Atlantic World in the Antipodes: Effects and Transformations Since the Eighteenth Century*, ed. Kate Fullagar (Newcastle upon Tyne: Cambridge Scholars, 2012), 283, 284. Scholars have debated whether the term Pacific, Oceania, or the Antipodes best describes the geographical reach and complexity of the area. While each has its ad-

vantages and limitation, I have chosen to use Pacific, the name of the ocean, to refer to the multiple worlds touched by and drawn into its liquid reach.

7. Ralph Bauer, "Early American Literature and American Literary History at the Hemispheric Turn," *Early American Literature* 45, 2 (2010): 221.

8. Bauer, "Early American," 222.

9. See Michelle Burnham, "Early American Literature and the Revolutionary Pacific," *PMLA* 128, 4 (2013), where I argue that the Revolution's stranglehold on dominant narratives of American literature and history might be resolved by repositioning revolution in transoceanic context.

10. This process is akin to the one identified by A. G. Hopkins in which international features "are often treated as spare parts that have to be bolted on to the national story." "The History of Globalization—and the Globalization of History?" in *Globalization in World History*, ed. Hopkins (New York: Norton, 2002), 16.

11. Sarah Rivett, "Religious Exceptionalism and American Literary History: *The Puritan Origins of the American Self* in 2012," *Early American Literature* 47, 2 (2012): 391.

12. Bartholomew's image represents only the northernmost portion of South America, but it is worth imagining this map in a way that sustains its strange Pacific-Atlantic interchange across both the northern and southern hemispheres. J. G. Bartholomew, *A Literary and Historical Atlas of North and South America* (1911; London: Dent, 1930). This image is also available electronically: http://en.wikipedia.org/wiki/File:Atlantic_Ocean,_Toscanelli,_1474.jpg.

13. Peter Coclanis, "ReOrienting Atlantic History: The Global Dimensions of the 'Western' Rice Trade," in *The Atlantic in Global History*, ed. Cañizares-Esguerra and Seeman, 117; Martine Van Ittersum and Jaap Jacobs, "Are We All Global Historians Now? An Interview with David Armitage," *Itinerario* 36, 2 (August 2012): 25. Jorge Cañizares-Esguerra, *How to Write the History of the New World: Histories, Epistemologies, and Identities in the Eighteenth-Century Atlantic World* (Stanford, Calif.: Stanford University Press, 2001), 219, and Antonio Benítez-Rojo, *The Repeating Island: The Caribbean and the Postmodern Perspective,* trans. James E. Maraniss (Durham, N.C.: Duke University Press, 1992), 7. These latter two texts only begin to gesture toward the possibility of thinking the Atlantic and Pacific literary and cultural histories as intertwined. For work that more directly engages with transoceanic island histories, see Elizabeth M. DeLoughrey, *Routes and Roots: Navigating Caribbean and Pacific Island Literatures* (Honolulu: University of Hawai'i Press, 2007), and Matthew Guterl and Christine Skwiot, "Atlantic and Pacific Crossings: Race, Empire, and the 'Labor Problem' in the Late Nineteenth Century," *Radical History Review* 91 (Winter 2005): 40–61.

14. Robert Marks, *The Origins of the Modern World: A Global and Ecological Narrative* (Lanham, Md.: Rowman and Littlefield, 2002), 43; Enrique Dussel, "Be-

yond Eurocentrism: The World-System and the Limits of Modernity," in *The Cultures of Globalization*, ed. Fredric Jameson and Masao Miyoshi (Durham, N.C.: Duke University Press, 1998), 3–31.

15. Scholars of British literature and history working on the transoceanic connections between the Atlantic and Indian oceans are doing much to enlarge, enrich, and complicate archives, canons, and literary histories. See, for example, David Porter, *The Chinese Taste in Eighteenth-Century England* (Cambridge: Cambridge University Press, 2010) and Saree Makdisi and Felicity Nussbaum, *The Arabian Nights in Historical Context: Between East and West* (New York: Oxford University Press, 2009).

16. These transported persons include such figures as Catarina de San Juan, a young Asian woman who was transported by the Portuguese from the Manila slave market to Mexico, where she became a renowned beata (see Tatiana Seijas, "The Portuguese Slave Trade to Spanish Manila: 1580–1640," *Itinerario* 32, 1 [January 2008]: 19–38), and sailors who escaped the harsh working conditions on Spanish galleons to form a Filipino colony in eighteenth-century Louisiana (see Floro L. Mercene, *Manila Men in the New World: Filipino Migration to Mexico and the Americas from the Sixteenth Century* [Quezon City: University of the Philippines Press, 2007]).

17. Jim Egan, *Oriental Shadows: The Presence of the East in Early American Literature* (Columbus: Ohio State University Press, 2011); Geoffrey Sanborn, *Whipscars and Tattoos: The Last of the Mohicans, Moby-Dick, and the Maori* (New York: Oxford University Press, 2011). Because discussions about the Pacific in relation to American literary history still tend to begin and end with Herman Melville, I have chosen to focus in this essay on such transoceanic connections within a wider, longer, and more unexpected range of texts and authors.

18. Catherine Maria Sedgwick, *Hope Leslie; or, Early Times in the Massachusetts*, ed. Mary Kelley (1824; New Brunswick, N.J.: Rutgers University Press, 1987), 150.

19. Robert W. Cox, "A Perspective on Globalization," in *Globalization: Critical Reflections*, ed. James H. Mittelman (Boulder, Colo.: Lynne Rienner, 1996), 29. Cox suggests that the "space-oriented thinking" of globalization still awaits the articulation of its "time dimension" in which humans might "use the contradictions of globalization to envisage a possible alternative future"; it is in this time dimension that we might find, he suggests, "the remaining medium of freedom" (26). Joyce Chaplin, "Planetary Power? The United States and the History of Around-the-World Travel," *Journal of American Studies* 47, 1 (February 2013): 5.

20. Wai Chee Dimock, *Through Other Continents: American Literature Across Deep Time* (Princeton, N.J.: Princeton University Press, 2006), 5, 79. Because Dimock's archive tends to focus on well-known nineteenth- and twentieth-century texts with unquestionably American identities (such as Emerson, Thoreau, James), it

leaves open the question of how literature from the colonial and revolutionary periods, whose textual productions are far more difficult to categorize within national terms, would register in her literary history.

21. Gretchen Murphy, "Nation, Ocean, Hemisphere, Planet: New Geographies of American Literary Studies." *American Literature* 81, 1 (March 2009): 188; Trish Loughran, "Transcendental Islam: The Worlding of Our America: A Response to Wai Chee Dimock," *American Literary History* 21, 1 (Spring 2009): 56.

22. Meredith L. McGill, *American Literature and the Culture of Reprinting, 1834–1853* (Philadelphia: University of Pennsylvania Press, 2003), 39, 2.

23. James Clifford, *Routes: Travel and Translation in the Late Twentieth Century* (Cambridge, Mass.: Harvard University Press, 1997); Epeli Hauʻofa, *We Are the Ocean: Selected Works* (Honolulu: University of Hawaiʻi Press, 2008), 39, 35, 31.

24. Colleen Glenney Boggs, *Transnationalism and American Literature: Literary Translation, 1773–1892* (New York: Routledge, 2007), 25.

25. See, for example, Philip Gould, "The New Early American Anthology," *Early American Literature* 38, 2 (2003), esp. 309–11.

26. Recent scholarly work makes clear that borders between nations were porous throughout the eighteenth century and that translations of texts poured through and across those channels; see Margaret Cohen and Carolyn Dever, eds., *The Literary Channel: The Inter-National Invention of the Novel* (Princeton, N.J.: Princeton University Press, 2001).

27. DeLoughrey, 11. The naming of Pacific islands after Atlantic sites by such explorers as Fernández de Quirós, Bougainville, and Cook continues what DeLoughrey describes as the "ideological *contraction* of island space and time between the Atlantic and Pacific" that is itself "a product of European *expansion*" (19).

28. Eve Tavor Bannet's *Transatlantic Stories and the History of Reading, 1720–1810: Migrant Fictions* (Cambridge: Cambridge University Press, 2011) locates and examines a number of these eighteenth-century Atlantic stories. Texts that reach out of the Atlantic into other oceans include the serially published Pacific story "A Remarkable Voyage in the South Sea," *Edinburgh Magazine* (March–June 1760): 131–33, 189–92, 231–33, 288–92; and the anonymous *Life and Surprizing Adventures of Don Juliani* (London, 1720) set in the Indian Ocean. See also Srinivas Avaramudan, "East-West Fiction as World Literature: The *Hayy* Problem Reconfigured," *Eighteenth-Century Studies* 47, 2 (Winter 2014), 195–231.

29. Kamau Brathwaite, *ConVERSations with Nathaniel Mackey* (Staten Island, N.Y.: We Press, 1999), 33–34.

30. DeLoughrey, 2, 24.

31. Miles Ogborn, "Atlantic Geographies," *Social and Cultural Geography* 6, 3 (June 2005): 381, 382, 383.

32. Matt Matsuda, "The Pacific," *AHR* 111, 3 (June 2006): 780.

33. Monique Allewaert, "Swamp Sublime: Ecologies of Resistance in the American Plantation Zone," *PMLA* 123 (2008): 341.

34. Philip E. Steinberg, *The Social Construction of the Ocean* (Cambridge: Cambridge University Press, 2001), 207.

35. One possibility is that the increasing number and quality of digital archives and collections ought to take the place of, or at least provide an indispensable supplement to, currently available anthologies—which might themselves take electronic form and/or be integrated with electronic collections. Such access allows and encourages students to explore archives, discover textual connections and material histories, and critically supplement anthology and survey selections with what they discover in those explorations. For one example of a course designed around such a project, see the syllabus for my "Survey of American Literature 1" course, in which students create their own mini-anthology by researching in primary sources: http://web.mnstate.edu/seateaching/syllabi/e31syllabuswithminianthology_MB.pdf.

36. Thomas Bender, "Historians, the Nation, and the Plenitude of Narratives," in *Rethinking American History in a Global Age*, ed. Bender (Berkeley: University of California Press, 2002), 12.

Contributors

༄

Monique Allewaert is Associate Professor of English at the University of Wisconsin-Madison. She is author of *Ariel's Ecology: Plantations, Personhood, and Colonialism in the American Tropics*. She serves on the editorial boards of *American Literature* and *Resilience* and has coedited, with Michael Zizer, a Special Issue of *American Literature* focused on Ecocriticism.

Ralph Bauer is Associate Professor of English and Comparative Literature at the University of Maryland, College Park. His publications include *The Cultural Geography of Colonial American Literatures: Empire, Travel, Modernity*; *An Inca Account of the Conquest of Peru*; *Creole Subjects in the Colonial Americas: Empires, Texts, Identities*, coedited with José Antonio Mazzotti; *The Cultural Politics of Blood, 1500–1900*, coedited with Kim Coles, Carla Peterson, and Zita Zunes; and articles in collections and journals such as *American Literary History, American Literature, Early American Literature, PMLA, Revista Iberoamericana, Colonial Latin American Review, Dieciocho*, and *Latin American Research Review*.

Hester Blum is Associate Professor of English at the Pennsylvania State University and co-founder of C19: The Society of Nineteenth-Century Americanists. She is author of *The View from the Masthead: Maritime Imagination and Antebellum American Sea Narratives*, which received the John Gardner Maritime Research Award, and editor of *Horrors of Slavery*, William Ray's 1808 Barbary captivity narrative. Her work has appeared in *PMLA, American Literature, Early American Studies, J19, Atlantic Studies*, and a number of edited collections.

Martin Brückner is Professor in the English Department and Associate Director of the Center for Material Culture Studies at the University of Delaware. He is author of *The Geographic Revolution in Early America: Maps, Literacy, and National Identity*, which received the 2006–2007 Louis Gottschalk Prize in Eighteenth-Century Studies, and the exhibition catalog *Common Destinations: Maps in the American Experience*. He is editor of two volumes, *Early American Cartographies* and *American Literary Geographies: Spatial Practice and Cultural Production, 1500–1900*. His published essays have appeared in journals such as *American Quarterly, English Literary History, American Literary History, Winterthur Portfolio*, and numerous essay collections.

Michelle Burnham is Professor of English at Santa Clara University, where she teaches early American literature, Native American literature, and popular culture. She is author of *Folded Selves: Colonial New England Writing in the World System* and *Captivity and Sentiment: Cultural Exchange in American Literature, 1682–1861*, and has coedited a second edition of *The Female American*.

Christopher Castiglia is Liberal Arts Research Professor of English at the Pennsylvania State University. He is the author of *Bound and Determined: Captivity, Culture-Crossing, and White Womanhood from Patty Hearst to Mary Rowlandson; Interior States: Institutional Consciousness and the Inner Life of Democracy in Antebellum America*; and, with Christopher Reed, *If Memory Serves: Gay Men, AIDS, and the Promise of the Queer Past*. A co-founder of C19: the Society of Nineteenth-Century Americanists, he is currently coeditor, with Dana D. Nelson, of its journal, *J19: The Journal of Nineteenth-Century Americanists*.

Sean X. Goudie is Associate Professor of English at the Pennsylvania State University and author of *Creole America: the West Indies and the Formation of Literature and Culture in the New Republic* (University of Pennsylvania Press), awarded the 2007 Modern Language Association Prize for a First Book. At Penn State he serves as Director of the Center for American Literary Studies (CALS), which has undertaken initiatives including the founding of C19: the Society of Nineteenth-Century Americanists and the First Book Institute. He has served as Chair of the Lora Romero First Book Prize Committee for the American Studies Association and as Chair of the American Literature to 1800 Division of the MLA, and currently serves on the Editorial Board of *American Literature*.

Meredith L. McGill is Associate Professor of English at Rutgers University. She is author of *American Literature and the Culture of Reprinting, 1834–53* (University of Pennsylvania Press) and editor of two collections of essays: *The Traffic in Poems: Nineteenth-Century Poetry and Transatlantic Exchange* and *Taking Liberties with the Author*. She has published widely on intellectual property, authorship, and the history of the book, most recently "The State of the Discipline: Copyright and Intellectual Property" in *Book History*.

Geoffrey Sanborn is Professor of English at Amherst College. He is author of *The Sign of the Cannibal: Melville and the Making of a Postcolonial Reader; Whipscars and Tattoos: The Last of the Mohicans, Moby-Dick, and the Maori;* and *Plagiarama! William Wells Brown and the Aesthetic of Attractions*. He is also coeditor, with Samuel Otter, of *Melville and Aesthetics*. His essays have appeared in *American Literature, PMLA, ELH, J19, African American Review, Nineteenth-Century Literature, Arizona Quarterly, ESQ,* and elsewhere.

Index

Acknowledgments

⟿

This volume emerges from conversations hosted by the Penn State Center for American Literary Studies, and I am grateful to CALS Director Sean X. Goudie, as well as to the Penn State College of the Liberal Arts and Department of English, for their support of the original "Turn, Turn, Turn" colloquy.

The contributors and I are very grateful to Jerry Singerman at Penn Press for his superlative editorial eye and his guidance of this project. At Penn Press we also thank Hannah Blake for her wonderful assistance, as well as project editor Alison Anderson for shepherding the volume through production so skillfully and smoothly. We are indebted as well to copyeditor Julie d'Angelo for her great work. Dana Nelson and an anonymous reader provided exceptional attention to the manuscript, and *Turns of Event* reflects both their great feedback and their intellectual generosity.